NEWPORT BEACH PUBLIC LIBRARY
1000 AVOCADO AVENUE
NEWPORT BEACH, CA 92660
(949) 717-3800

WITHDRAWN

MAY 0 2 2017

W9-CXW-749

WITHDRAWN

Balancing Life and Education While Being a Part of a Military Family

Balancing Life and Education While Being a Part of a Military Family

A Guide to Navigating Higher Education for the Military Spouse

Jillian Ventrone, Paul Karczewski, and Robert W. Blue Jr.

ROWMAN & LITTLEFIELD
Lanham • Boulder • New York • London

Published by Rowman & Littlefield
A wholly owned subsidiary of The Rowman & Littlefield Publishing Group, Inc.
4501 Forbes Boulevard, Suite 200, Lanham, Maryland 20706
www.rowman.com

Unit A, Whitacre Mews, 26-34 Stannary Street, London SE11 4AB

Copyright © 2017 by Rowman & Littlefield

All rights reserved. No part of this book may be reproduced in any form or by any electronic or mechanical means, including information storage and retrieval systems, without written permission from the publisher, except by a reviewer who may quote passages in a review.

British Library Cataloguing in Publication Information Available

Library of Congress Cataloging-in-Publication Data Available

ISBN 9781442260054 (cloth : alkaline paper)
ISBN 9781442260061 (electronic)

♾ ™ The paper used in this publication meets the minimum requirements of American National Standard for Information Sciences Permanence of Paper for Printed Library Materials, ANSI/NISO Z39.48-1992.

Printed in the United States of America

Contents

Preface

Military spouses are highly motivated to pursue higher education while their partners serve on active duty, but they face numerous challenges, especially considering the sacrifices many have made over the past decade and a half of war. Spouses need to be aware of the resources and options available to them so they can make informed decisions regarding their academic journeys. *Balancing Life and Education While Being a Part of a Military Family: A Guide to Navigating Higher Education for the Military Spouse* fulfills this need by serving as a long-term reference manual that will support spouses throughout their higher education or vocational pursuits and assist with navigating the available funding resources. This book arms readers with the information they need to properly prepare, plan, and perform the tasks necessary for a successful transition into the world of education. If a spouse's goal is to expand his or her credentials through education or training, this is the definitive guidebook.

Introduction

The dependent population is often overlooked when discussing military-based higher education. Spouses require many of the same considerations as service members, such as flexibility in their course work, funding assistance, and convenient school options. These requirements are often hard to find and navigate by oneself. *Balancing Life and Education While Being a Part of a Military Family* assists this population with finding, pursuing, and paying for higher education.

Just like those on active duty, military dependents face many challenges that they must overcome. Each spouse has a unique set of educational needs. Spouses who understand these needs and properly strategize to address these concerns are more likely to be successful. Constant relocation and frequent deployment cycles for the service member can affect the educational pursuits of those who stay behind. Many spouses are far from home, have children but lack affordable child care, and feel that they have very little support available to assist with their educational goals. While their active-duty spouses often have funding options, the lack of available financial assistance for their dependents can be discouraging. As a result, many forego their long-term educational goals for jobs that often pay lower wages even though they are aware of the many advantages that higher education can provide.

The authors of this book counsel military dependents on federal installations daily; in addition, one is a spouse who pursued advanced education during her husband's active-duty service. The knowledge and expertise the authors have combined in this book will assist the dependent population in navigating the maze of possible options and developing a plan of attack for their educational goals. Whether one is interested in traditional higher education, vocational training, or short-term portable certificate training pathways, *Balancing Life and Education While Being a Part of a Military Family* arms spouses with the tools they need to achieve success.

Chapter One

Military Spouse Education Concerns

Military spouses and dependent children who are pursuing higher education often have many of the same needs as their active-duty family members. While counseling this population, we often hear that topics such as flexibility and portability are at the top of the list. Determining what these needs are and learning how to tackle them is the first step in creating goals for your academic pursuits. This chapter addresses many of the special needs that military spouses have regarding their educations, including the following topics: time management, flexible learning, support resources, portability, transferring credit, online versus face-to-face classes, return on investment, and backup plans.

SPOUSAL EDUCATION CONCERNS

Military spouses have unique concerns regarding their educational pursuits, such as numerous permanent change of station (PCS) orders and the deployment cycles of their active-duty spouses. Many families find themselves uprooted every two to three years. A typical military family could be stationed in rural Oklahoma followed by a tour in a major metropolitan area in Florida or even spend a few years at an overseas location. Three major PCS moves in a decade is not an uncommon scenario.

Not every base will have numerous options for training or degrees through classroom attendance. While some bases, such as Naval Air Weapons Station China Lake in California, are located in small communities that do not have four-year colleges in close proximity, many bases do host colleges at the education center office that offer a limited number of associate and bachelor's degree programs that you can pursue in a face-to-face format. The difficulty is in finding the type of learner you are and whether you can start with classroom courses and then transition online, because that will most likely be where you will finish most of your classes.

Even if you are stationed in a major metropolitan area, there may be limitations. For example, while there are several Marine Corps and US Navy bases in the San Diego area, getting into schools offering certain programs, such as physical therapy and nursing, can be difficult. Most state-supported colleges in the San Diego metropolitan area are impacted (not enough seats to accommodate all of the students trying to gain access to the programs) due to the popularity of some of these types of programs. Also, not every school offers the same programs. For example, if you are stationed aboard the Camp Pendleton Marine Corps Base, the nearest school offering a master's degree in physical therapy is more than fifty miles away on traffic-clogged freeways. Plus, the admissions pathways into these schools could close as much as ten months in advance. This means that beyond a long drive, you might also not have enough time on station to gain admissions and finish the degree.

Online Degrees

Sometimes online programs are the most realistic options for busy spouses or for those in isolated areas. Be careful in your search for an online school. Do not simply register with the first school that pops up on an Internet search. Typically, it is possible to find general education classes through a reputable institution in an online format, and many state-supported schools offer this option. This is the best pathway for dependents trying to gain credit prior to their spouse's separation from the service. If you know that you are a solid online learner, check to see whether the community colleges back home (if that is where you and your spouse will return to) offer online class options. This will help you reduce the risk of losing credit upon a transfer from one school to another. If not, the next best option is to stick to the local state schools. These schools offer you the greatest flexibility for transfer credit. Tuition is often lower, and the credits that you earn are academically sound.

Always check an institution's accreditation status (regional accreditation is the most widely transferable) before committing to attending to make sure that you are gaining transferable credit (http://ope.ed.gov/accreditation/). Be aware that there are some institutions in the United States that are very traditional in nature and will not accept any course work that was completed through an online format. Always check with the school that you are interested in completing your bachelor's degree with to determine whether credits earned through online course work will be accepted.

Online degree programs have offered up a new world of possibilities, but not every major institution or training program has options available in this format. For example, fully accredited engineering degrees require heavy classroom time. Depending upon the base, the best option that might be available to a military dependent who is interested in pursuing a degree such as engineering might be to begin pursuing the general education requirements and leave the core courses (the engineering classes) and potentially even the advanced math courses (not often offered online) until later. While not an ideal situation, between waiting for new duty station orders that place you in a location where you will be able to tackle all of the courses versus strictly the core or getting started and making progress while you can, the second option is the better pathway.

If your local base education center offers counseling services to dependent family members, start there. Base education counselors can advise you about on-base programs, off-base programs, and online possibilities. Consider whether online learning is a format that will work for you. Ask yourself if you will you be able to learn independently, without the aid of face-to-face interactions with instructors and fellow students. Writing is often emphasized in online classes. Maybe consider taking your English class first, as it will help you in this regard.

Return on Investment

Return on investment, the cost of a program versus potential salary, should always be considered before choosing a school and a program of study. State-supported institutions are most often the least expensive options for higher education or vocational pursuits. Military dependents qualify for the in-state tuition rate at state schools in the state in which they are stationed with their active-duty spouse. By pursuing academic degrees through these schools, spouses can typically attain a quality education at much lower costs than they would through most private colleges. If a private college charges $20,000 per year in tuition and a state-supported college charges $10,000 per year, is the higher tuition cost worth it even if the private school can offer greater flexibility? Over the course of a four-year bachelor's degree program, that equates to a savings of $40,000 for a student attending the state school.

How long would it take to pay off a student loan debt for a $40,000 degree versus an $80,000 degree?

An education is an investment in a career pathway. The outcome of income and potential job possibilities might be based on factors outside of your degree. For example, some careers have slower-than-average growth rates on a national or state level. When researching a particular career field, it is important to note the growth in the field to try to determine what your job prospects might be like upon achieving the educational attainment necessary to work within the field. The Bureau of Labor Statistics (BLS) maintains the Occupational Outlook Handbook (OOH), which splits these topics into two different areas in order to project this information: the fastest-growing occupations and the occupations adding the most new jobs (http://www.bls.gov/ooh/about/ooh-faqs.htm#growth8). The BLS states that the fastest-growing occupations are the ones that are projected to have the highest percent increase in employment over a decade while the occupations with the largest job growth are the fields that are projected to add the most jobs.[1]

According to the BLS OOH:

> A fast rate of employment growth does not always translate into many new jobs. For example, employment of industrial–organizational psychologists is projected to grow 19 percent through 2024, but because of the occupation's relatively small size, this percent growth accounts for only about 400 new jobs over the 10-year projections decade. In contrast, employment of retail salespersons is projected to grow only 7 percent through 2024, but that employment growth rate corresponds to about 314,200 new jobs over 10 years because of the occupation's large size.[2]

Growth Rates

The BLS OOH shows the national growth rate for the selected career field based upon projections for the decade 2014–2024. If I were considering two different career fields, I might want to check this site to compare the job outlook of the fields. For example, if I want to know the job outlook for high school teachers, I would go to the main site (http://www.bls.gov/ooh/) and click on "Education, Training and Library," then "High School Teachers." At this point I would see that the projected job outlook for this category is 6 percent (average).[3] This means that this particular career field is growing at an average pace. This number will also vary by state. But I'm also considering becoming a diagnostic medical sonographer. I complete the same task by checking under "Healthcare" on the main page then searching for sonographer. I find that the growth rate for this career field is 24 percent (much faster than average).[4] There is a huge difference in the listed rates between the career fields. This might give me some insight into which pathway I will choose.

Occupational growth rates by state are also an important topic to check. If I am moving to Texas upon my spouse's separation from the service, I will want to research the state-based trends as well. This task can be done through the BLS OOH by clicking on the link titled "State & Area Data," then clicking on the "Projections Central" option (http://www.projectionscentral. com/). Once I am on the external site, I click on "Long Term Projections, Through 2022," enter Texas as my state, and "Teachers and Instructors, All Others" as my career search preference. The results show that the teaching profession in the state of Texas will be adding approximately 12,640 new jobs through 2022, which is around a 20 percent positive change in growth. The site also shows that the state expects approximately 2,500 new jobs to be added every year.[5] From these numbers I can determine that the teaching profession in Texas is in an upward growth-rate climb, which means that I have a solid chance at finding a job in this field in this state.

When checking for demonstrations of career viability, always make the effort to check by state as well as nationally. Growth rate by state is a good way to check on whether the particular field you have chosen has job openings in the state you want to work in. Be aware that while growth rates give you the ability to generalize across regions, the size of the state can impact the growth rate. For example, according to the Federal Reserve Bank of Dallas:

> Because of Texas' large population, the state's employment level is one of the highest in the nation. But this fact makes it difficult to compare the number of jobs gained in Texas with the number of jobs gained in smaller states. Such states will have smaller monthly job gains, but employment could be rising at a faster pace than in Texas. In a sense, calculating growth rates levels the playing field between the states. Similarly, economists often compare a state's economy with that of the nation. By calculating growth rates, researchers can make comparisons between the national and regional economies—such as whether state employment is growing faster or slower than the national average.[6]

So, if you are comparing two different states, just because the growth rate of a career field in one state is higher than the other doesn't mean that the state is adding jobs at a faster rate.

For a broader search on the growth rate of different career fields, check the tables on the BLS's Employment Projections' website titled "Fastest growing occupations" and "Occupations with the most job growth" under the category marked "Most Requested EP Tables" located here: http://www.bls. gov/emp/#tables. Broader searches are good for prospective students that have not narrowed down their career pathways. These tables can give you a better idea of the career fields that will offer you the most potential for growth over the time period specified and might help you narrow down your possible choices.

How about the return on investment for a program such as medical assisting? Sixty-five percent of medical assistants hold only a postsecondary certificate or lower.[7] The same O*NET site shows that there is a bright outlook for employment prospects and the median income for 2014 was $30,590 per year. We have counseled numerous spouses that considered applying to medical assistant training programs at for-profit schools that cost $20,000 or more for a twelve-to-sixteen-week training program. Military spouses are often surprised to hear that many state community colleges and technical schools offer quality medical assisting programs at much lower rates, often for under the $4,000 that many spouses are eligible to use through the My Career Advancement Account (MyCAA) program. If you are going to pursue a new career pathway, starting with little or no debt will definitely give you a brighter outlook.

Career Portability

Career portability is an often-discussed topic for military spouses due to the many moves military families make during their active service. If the career you are preparing for involves certifications and state licensing, you must determine how you can meet the standards in a new state. Determine whether it will require more schooling or training and the amount of time it will take to accomplish these requirements. Checking the growth rates in each state through the process listed above will tell you if there is a need for your particular occupation in the state that the military is moving you to. For example, a music teacher may not have as many opportunities to teach in a community with a smaller population, but a math teacher may be more in demand.

Sometimes external circumstances can affect the degree of portability that a career can have within a certain state. For example, I (Jillian) completed a master's degree in education with an attached teaching credential in the state of California in 2009, but the economy was depressed at that time and teaching jobs were scarce. Teachers who had numerous years of teaching experience were getting pink slips and losing their positions, and I was unable to secure a permanent position with a school because of these factors.

In order to become a fully licensed teacher in California, teachers who have completed their degrees and training programs must take part in the Beginning Teacher Support and Assessment (BTSA) Induction (http://www. btsa.ca.gov/) within five years of receiving their preliminary credentials. The BTSA induction program essentially clears teachers to be fully licensed to teach within their specified parameters in the state of California. Since I could not secure a position, I also could not participate with BTSA. I did land my current job, but because I never cleared my credential, I essentially lost it at the five-year mark, in addition to all of the money and time I spent on earning it.

If you earned your teaching credential in another state, California requires you to participate in a CTEL program or pass the CTEL examination. CTEL course work can take many months to complete, plus waiting for the documents from the state can set you back in time as well. To see an example of what a CTEL program would be like and the price of the program, take a look at the following program offered through the University of California at San Diego: http://extension.ucsd.edu/programs/customprogram/clad-ctel. cfm. The program is available online. If you opt for the exam, it will take a significant amount of time to prepare for in order to achieve a passing score, but it is considerably less expensive (http://www.ctcexams.nesinc.com/test_ info_CTEL.asp).

Time Management

The first months at a new duty station can be demanding, especially if you have children in school. Take a good look at your circumstances. The stress involved in a PCS move, adjusting to a new community, and the pressures brought about by a deployment may make you want to temporarily delay your education plans.

Here is a list of questions to ask yourself during the planning phase, before you continue forward:

- Are programs offered during working hours or in the evenings?
- Can you balance school attendance with family demands, working, or while your military spouse is deployed?
- Are you stationed at a base that offers child care, will it be available when you need it (sometimes there are waiting periods to gain a place at the center because they are impacted), and is it affordable? Does the base allow spouses to run daycare centers in their homes? Many do, and spouses might be able to offer you more flexibility with your schedules than a base-run daycare center.
- Will your spouse be deploying soon?

Many military spouses are fortunate to have access to base education support resources. If your base has an education office (or center) offering counseling services to military spouses, take advantage of the service. Base education counselors know about local training and education programs, as well as online programs. Base education counselors are DOD civilian employees, not employees of particular schools. Education and admissions counselors employed by schools want you to enroll in the schools that employ them. If they do not maintain viable enrollment, their schools could be in danger of having to leave the base or their jobs could be in jeopardy. A base education counselor's objective is to find the best option for you rather than enrollment in a particular school. Also, military bases often have employment referral offices and resume writing workshops.

In early 2016, as we compiled this book, the navy announced that it was phasing out its education centers (Navy College Offices) in the continental United States. By October 1, 2017, the navy plans to reduce the operating education centers to strictly the overseas bases and Hawaii and will rely on virtual counseling through phone and email. The virtual counseling program will only be available to active-duty personnel. Navy personnel can still take advantage of the education centers aboard Marine Corps bases, and so can their dependent family members. If you are stationed aboard a Marine Corps base, the education center information can be found on the Marine Corps Community Services website for that particular base. If you are stationed away from a Marine Corps base, you can still use the services of the Marine Corps Education Centers. Locate your closest base and give the center a call. The counselors can set up a time to conduct a phone counseling session with you. The navy is the only branch of the service with plans to eliminate education centers in the United States.

Transfer Credit

Transfer credit is often the goal for spouses and dependent children that know they will only be stationed aboard a base for a short period of time. Typically, the most transferable credit you can earn is through a state community college. Articulation agreements can help with transfer pathways if you find yourself in this situation. Many colleges that work closely with the military have articulation agreements with other, similar types of schools or even with nearby community colleges. The following are two examples:

Central Texas College (CTC) is a state-supported community college that has classroom programs on over twenty-five US Army, Navy, Marine Corps, and Air Force bases in the United States. CTC also has classroom-based programs located overseas on numerous military bases, such as in Guam, Diego Garcia, Mainland Japan, Okinawa, and Korea. CTC has two-plus-two articulation agreements with forty colleges and universities, many of which work closely with the military. If students stay within this cohort of schools when they transfer out of CTC, they are guaranteed that all of the credits they completed will be honored at the next institution. The two-plus-two articulation agreement means that the entirety of the associate's degree is accepted into the bachelor's degree program and there is no loss of credits. Otherwise, the school offering the bachelor's degree you are pursuing might not agree to transfer all of the courses you have completed. This can result in the loss of credits.

Park University serves the military at over forty locations in the United States and has articulation agreements with thirty-six community colleges. This gives you options. Many other schools also have such articulation agreements. Ask the institution you are considering attending whether it has articulated transfer credit with other schools and where can you find this agreement on the website. Articulation agreements are usually shared between a two-year institution and a four-year institution. They state that all of the credits awarded at the two-year institution will count at the four-year institution. This can assist you in maximizing the amount of credit you have earned.

When planning to transfer credits, it pays to choose a school where you intend to finish your degree in advance, if possible, in order to make sure credit will transfer. This allows you to properly manage and strategize your academic career to avoid credit loss and wasted time. Pay attention to the general education or core curriculum courses required by the school you intend to graduate from with your bachelor's degree. For example, a community college on the base where you are stationed may require two natural science courses without labs, entirely lecture oriented in format. However, the four-year college you intend to transfer to may have a requirement for two natural science courses that require labs. Even though the natural science courses without the attached labs meet the requirements for graduation at the community college, they might not meet the requirements outlined at the four-year school.

Backup Plans

Do you have a backup plan? If your first choice for a training program or major is not available, are you willing to enter into a different major? Perhaps you want to train in dental assisting, but there are only medical assisting programs available in your area. You may not have a master's degree in business administration program on your base, but a master's degree in organizational leadership is available. You would need to consider whether this is a good alternative for you. A bit of flexibility can result in more choices for your goals.

Finally, be aware of the different types of grants, scholarships, and financial aid available that can help you with your education. Beware of schools that will not give you a straight answer on the cost of education or training. Be wary of promises of this type:

1. Don't worry about the cost. Our financial aid office will make sure your education is fully covered. (Often such financial aid promised includes expensive loans.)
2. Our graduates make average incomes of _____, so you will be able to repay your loans in no time after you graduate. Request to see this information from several students who graduated from the program and request access to them so that you can ask your questions directly to the source.
3. We have lifetime job placement assistance. (I, Robert, know of a truck-driving program that made this promise. The job placement assistance consisted of the school sending the graduate links to job postings from public listings like http://www.monster.com.)

Any school that makes outright promises regarding its ability to gain you a job is not being honest. Ask to receive all of the information they are promising you over the phone in writing. Also, speak with several people who completed the program through that institution and are now employed. Ask these individuals how difficult it was for them to find a job, if their pay is comparable to people with the same degree of training who attended other schools (state-based institutions), what type of job growth have they experienced, and whether they are considering returning to school to pursue advanced training and why.

Chapter Two

Educational Concerns for Spouses of Active-Duty Personnel, Reservists, and Veterans

Military dependents' educational needs vary depending upon the service status of their active-duty spouse. Identifying an institution that fulfills these specific needs is a high-priority task. If possible, spouses should seek advice through counseling services at an education center on their base first. At minimum, they should consider what types of flexibility they are looking for in an institution and evaluate the possibilities using the resources offered in this book before making a final decision.

ACTIVE-DUTY AND VETERAN MILITARY SPOUSES' EDUCATIONAL NEEDS

In most cases, active-duty military spouses' needs vary greatly from the civilian population. Determining the types of needs you might have prior to settling on an institution will allow you to make a preemptive strike on any service-related issues that might occur upon your family's transition off active duty. Picking an institution that can cater to these needs or is located in an area where your spouse's needs can be met is imperative for creating a positive learning environment. For example, if your active-duty spouse has medical concerns, you might want to choose a school that is located near a VA hospital or medical center when your family makes the transition. If the closest VA center is one hundred miles from where you have decided to attend school, getting help may take more time and money than you initially considered.

If you are pursuing school while your spouse is still on active duty, considering your position, the amount of free time you have, location concerns, learning styles, Internet availability, and your personal needs before you begin searching will help you to make a well-informed choice. While you can transfer schools if your initial choice is not a good fit, you always run the risk of losing credit in the transfer process and having to backtrack. If you are using transferred Post-9/11 GI Bill benefits, you only have a limited amount to use, and this could set you back. The GI Bill may give you the ability to complete a debt-free education if you can plan your academic career accordingly. Use it wisely after educating yourself about higher education or vocational training and learning how your spouse's benefits will work for you.

If your spouse is a reservist, consider whether he or she is looking at activating in the near future. This could impact the amount of time you have to spend attending school, especially if you have children and your spouse's civilian job has regular working hours. If the balance of the time that he or she spent helping with your children's school—for example, transportation to and from and homework help—will now fall to you, will you still have the same amount of time to commit to your own education? If you are already in school and you need to suspend your attendance due to your spouse's activation, will the institution assist you in this process?

Just as not all of our personal needs are the same, not all schools are the same. School offerings will vary by the levels of education, resources, or support systems they can provide. Picking the right institution for you is a personal process and, in most cases, will require quite a bit of research. Understanding what your needs are prior to the planning process will significantly reduce the amount of time you spend conducting your searches by streamlining the process. Active-duty spouses need great flexibility with their learning environment. Often, they require a school that offers a wealth of online courses and degree offerings, shorter or self-paced semesters, military familiarity, understanding professors, and an academic advisor who will always be available. Each of these items is necessary in order for the population to achieve academic success while still maintaining the household and organizing around the service member's military demands.

Be careful in opting for an online-only school if you are a hands-on learner. While this option might offer you more convenience, your grades could suffer, and you might create unneeded and unwanted stress for yourself. Distance learning is not an easier pathway. Online courses require the same amount of work as their face-to-face counterparts. Potential barriers include not having easy access to your professors and minimal class interaction. You need to have solid reading comprehension skills, the motivation to work independently, and the ability to organize on your own in order to process information and keep track of deadlines. If you are unsure of your online-learning capability, take the Self-Evaluation for Students Considering Taking Distance Learning Courses through the Defense Activity for Non-Traditional Education Support (DANTES) website (https://dlrsa.dodmou.com/) to assess your online-learning capability and determine whether you have taken into account all considerations.

Most online courses also have mandatory check-in days and times. If you are considering online courses because your spouse is in and out of the field frequently and you need greater flexibility, make sure to determine how the online classroom environment at your chosen institution works. If the school requires mandatory check-in times and you cannot make them, you run the risk of either failing the class or receiving a reduction in your grades for failure to adhere to school or class policies.

A few schools, such as Coastline Community College (http://military.coastline.edu/msp/page.cfm?LinkID=1332), offer classes that don't require any Internet connectivity (Pocket Ed). The courses are strictly offered in entry-level general education subjects. Currently nine different subjects are available: biology, personal financial planning, geology, US history, Western civilization, cinema, mass communication, psychology, and sociology. Courses begin at the start of each month, and students have three months to complete the work. The classes do require proctors for all exams. This is not a common pathway for schools to take for their course offerings, but sometimes it is possible.

If you need to attend school in a face-to-face setting because it is better for your learning style, check to see whether the school you chose maintains the flexible classroom offerings you need to be successful. Does the institution offer weekend, evening, or hybrid classes? Does it offer classes on your base? Does it offer spouses a military discount? Lastly, what can the school offer in the way of support services?

Check to see if your school offers additional benefits to military spouses, such as tuition discounts or spousal scholarships. For example, Regent University in Virginia Beach offers two scholarships for military spouses and dependents (http://www.regent.edu/military/education_benefits/dependent_ spouse.cfm). One is for face-to-face students, equating to $1,000 annually, and is split equally between semesters. The second scholarship award is for online students and equates to $250 per semester as long as the student enrolls at a minimum of a part-time rate of pursuit. Regent University even offers a 15 percent tuition reduction for spouses pursuing graduate school whose sponsors are on active duty.

Military-based students require high levels of flexibility by both the institution and its professors. Between deployments, PCS moves, and transitions off active service, military spouses need to know that the school they have chosen will assist them at every turn no matter what type of situation arises.

Always try to discuss any concerns with the professor at the start of your class. Most will understand and try to make accommodations, but usually not if you approach them right before an assignment is due or shortly before the class ends. If that pathway does not work, try talking to your academic advisor. This is why it is imperative that schools with significant military populations maintain veterans-only academic advisors/counselors who understand service members' and their spouses' special needs and how to help in situations such as this. Unfortunately, I (Jillian) often hear from military spouses that they cannot locate the academic advisor at their school. Some schools put people in these positions who are not trained, do not understand the special needs of the military population, or do not have the proper level of education. At these schools, these positions tend to turn over frequently, and students might find themselves with a new advisor so often that the individual does not understand their concerns.

Spouses' educational needs can vary greatly depending upon their active-duty spouse's long-term military goals. Spouses of service members who plan on staying in the military for long-term careers are usually aiming for degree completion. Spouses of service members completing only one enlistment are usually aiming for solid transfer credit to take with them and shorten the time they will need to spend in school upon their family's separation from the service.

Degree requirements can be restrictive. Some degrees are difficult or impossible to find in an online format from a reputable institution—for example, the engineering and science fields. If you are pursuing a degree that will limit how much of your education you can complete while your spouse is still on active duty, you might consider completing as much of the degree as possible in an online format, such as all of your general education classes or elective credits. Upon separation from the service, you can tackle the courses that must be completed in a classroom environment.

Credit transferability is a sticky topic. Several concerns should be considered before moving forward if you are pursuing transfer credit. Ultimately, credit acceptance is up to the final institution. Schools usually consider the accreditation of the prior institution and specific program requirements when reviewing credit brought in from other institutions. Some schools have preexisting transfer agreements that will help create a low-stress transfer pathway at a later date.

Some state schools have developed programs to demonstrate to students how credits transfer between the institutions, such as California's Articulation System Stimulating Interinstitutional Student Transfer website (ASSIST). ASSIST (http://www.assist.org) is a cooperative project between the University of California school system, the California State University system, and the state community colleges that allows students to compare class transferability by course of study, department, or general education/ breadth agreements. These are commonly called articulation guides, and checking whether the school is part of a particular system will allow you to choose intelligently when picking classes to transfer.

Classes do not always transfer for the credit they were originally intended to fill. You must also keep an eye on how many credits an institution will accept. For example, Arizona State University (ASU) will transfer a maximum of sixty-four lower-division semester hours (i.e., 100- and 200-level classes) from a regionally accredited community college (https://transfer.asu. edu/credits). If you intend to transfer to ASU to complete a bachelor's degree, taking more than sixty-four lower-division credits from the school you are currently attending would be unproductive. Try your best not to find yourself in a situation where credits will not transfer or might need to be repeated.

Consider a few questions before moving forward in this situation:

• Always check the institution's accreditation. I cannot emphasize this point enough. Chapter 4 in this book reviews the different types of accreditation and concerns to be aware of prior to selecting an institution. If you make the wrong choice, you might have to backtrack later. This could cause you to run out of transferred GI Bill benefits or student aid, requiring you to find alternate funding for your schooling.

- Consider the state you come from or intend to move to before choosing a school to attend. Many schools have satellite locations in other states or at military installations, such as Central Texas College (CTC). CTC is a Texas-state community college that operates aboard many military bases. If you can find one from your state, in most cases it will be better for your needs.
- If you know which institution you would like to attend after separation from the military, check whether the school offers online classes. If feasible, it would be best to start while on active duty at the school where you intend to finish when you and your family separate from the service. Many schools, including state-based two-year and four-year institutions, offer online classes and are approved for Tuition Assistance (TA). Marshall University, Central Michigan University, Penn State, and many other institutions offer strictly online master's degrees. Colorado State University, University of Massachusetts, and University of Maryland are a few of the big four-year universities with fully online bachelor's degrees. Many community colleges offer fully online associate's degrees, such as Coastline Community College, which has representatives on several military installations. Attending a school online that you can continue to attend once separated will make your transition much easier, and you will not run the risk of losing credits during the transfer process.
- If these options are not possible, contact the school you are interested in attending upon separation and ask whether it has transfer agreements with any particular schools. Most big universities are fed by local community colleges, and many community colleges offer online classes. Usually, big state universities have transfer agreements with the local state community colleges.
- Check with the local education center to see which schools have a presence on the base.

The Post-9/11 GI Bill has allowed military families more flexibility than ever before, and schools across the country have had significant increases in their veteran student populations. Unfortunately, military families of the current conflicts face transition issues that pose many difficult challenges. Schools that recognize these challenges and tailor services on the campus to meet the special needs of their veteran-based populations should be recognized for their support.

Be careful when choosing a school that claims it is military friendly. A study conducted by the Center for American Progress determined that the criteria for listing schools as "veteran friendly" on some websites and media outlets are unclear. Schools should offer you a proper academic pathway as well as military family–based support. Be leery of any institution that claims it is "veteran friendly" but cannot back it up with concrete proof.[1]

If possible, always check the available resources to verify information given by the school about external programs not specific to the school. Ask about campus support services for veterans and their families. You should look for veterans-only academic advisors, VA services on the campus, or nearby, nonprofit veteran assistance such as American Veterans (AMVETS) or Disabled American Veterans (DAV), student veteran organizations such as the Student Veterans of America (SVA), financial aid support, unemployment support, contact with off-campus services that specialize in veteran outreach, and a significant student veterans center that is consistently manned. The center should be prepared to handle, or refer to the appropriate agencies, any problem that comes its way.

School location is important for military families for many reasons other than the Monthly Housing Allowance (MHA) attached to Post-9/11. Usually, in a traditional higher-education environment, we live where we go to school. This may not be the case for many military families. Sometimes our active-duty spouse's mission demands dictate where we can live, and driving long distances to get to class may add unneeded stress to an already stressful process. If you are transitioning and have already chosen the place where you would like to live, or are still on active duty, try to find a school within a decent driving distance. Check for veteran services offered around the school, because if your veteran spouse needs help, you may not want to drive one hundred miles to get it.

The setting of the school's location is also important. If you need to be in a city for nightlife or a more fast-paced lifestyle, you should take that into consideration. If you prefer something without many distractions, consider a quieter institution in a small-town location. You can also check to see whether the veterans' center at the school has a designated veterans-only study space allocated for quiet study time as most schools extend the use of the vets centers to family members. Pay attention to the region as well. If you and your spouse are leaving the military without any college credit, you will be spending four years at this institution. If you hate cold weather and snow, you might not want a school in a northern region of the country.

If you are using transferred Post-9/11 benefits, check on whether your school offers early-bird registration to assist students using the GI Bill in achieving the full-time schedule of classes that is required for their degree plans. If a full-time schedule cannot be met, then students will begin to see a reduction in the amount of money they receive. The monthly housing allowance (MHA) and degree plan requirements under Post-9/11 are addressed in the "Cost and Payment Resources" chapter.

Spouses should review the following checklist with a representative/advisor at the school they plan to attend:

- Explain your situation and ask for helpful hints for anything you may need.
- Ask about housing options that might be available. If you and your veteran spouse are attending school together, ask the veterans department if it has any feedback on this subject. Sometimes the schools have special housing for military families.
- Find out what services the school has set in place for its military population. Determine where the closest VA center is located, especially if you and your spouse have separated from the service.
- Ask if the school has any special programs in place for its military population. Some schools do food drives for military families around the holiday season.
- Find out about the institution's military population. How many military spouses attend the school? Does the school/vet center host any spousal activities, such as social gatherings or support groups?
- Ask if military spouses are able to receive priority registration for classes.
- Ask if the institution has a military advisor and whether he or she works with spouses as well.
- Ask whether the institution is a Servicemembers Opportunity College (SOC). Does it participate in the Degree Network System (DNS)? More detailed information regarding the DNS can be found in chapter 8, "Prior Learning Credit."

Many veteran departments at schools actively participate in community events involving veterans and their families or invite agencies such as the Veterans of Foreign Wars or the American Legion to visit their campuses. This is a great way to meet new friends and help your peers. Interaction is not solely for you to create a school support web and make friends. Networking with other veteran spouses and families is a great way to keep in touch with other people who have shared similar experiences. Sharing experiences with those who have "been there, done that" may help you reintegrate faster into civilian life. This network can also be an amazing tool later for job searches and entrepreneurship possibilities.

As my husband (Jillian) is currently in his twenty-third year of service, I have seen many of my military spouse friends go through the transition from active duty to veteran family status. They all make similar comments to me about the transition; while there are many programs available to help the service member's transition, there is limited assistance available to spouses. The new Transition Readiness Program offered on most military bases allows spouses to participate in the programs. Spouses can attend the events alongside their husbands or wives and learn the same information. Attending these programs might give you better insight into your transition. At the very least, the programs will give you useful information to help support your active-duty spouse throughout his or her transition.

If you are still an active-duty family and are interested in career assistance, check out the transition assistance department aboard your base. The advisors can help you with resumes (including the federal resume format), career research, and interview preparation. Most of the information you need, such as points of contact and seminar dates and times, can be found on the base website. Each branch titles the department these services are housed in differently—for example, in the Marine Corps it is the Transition Readiness Department, in the air force it is part of the Airman and Family Readiness Department, and in the navy it is part of the Fleet and Family Support Center. If you have trouble locating this department for your branch of service, ask your spouse to inquire with his or her command.

Most schools will have a Veterans' Services Office (VSO) or a Veterans Resource Center (VRC), which is often where you will find military-specific counselors and find peer groups made up of other veterans and their families. In most cases, military spouses can make use of the school's veterans' services departments. Many of the spouses I (Jillian) have worked with use the veterans' academic advisors/counselors, especially if they are using transferred GI Bill benefits or MyCAA.

Researching the topics mentioned above may help you understand the school's overall culture and attitude toward its military-based population. If the school does not seem to have many military-based services in place, you might want to consider other options. Schools should provide a multitude of support services in case students face unforeseen issues and need help, especially while the military family is still on active duty.

Chapter Three

Academic and Career-Based Research Tools

Before you decide on a specific school to attend or a specific career pathway, you need to complete an in-depth search of your available options. Using the free research tools outlined in this section will enable you to find a school that will meet your academic and career needs, as well as useful career-based information. These sites are not foolproof but are a good start. Each tool offers invaluable information on the different levels involved with planning your future, whether that is a long-term career while your spouse is in the military or a civilian-sector route upon his or her separation from the service. Using all of these sites and cross-referencing the information will benefit the overall organization of your academic career. If possible, always check with an academic counselor on the base where you are stationed for information relevant to your needs—for example, if you are using transferred GI Bill benefits, you will need to determine whether the institution you have selected is approved for the GI Bill, how the benefit works, and how to activate it.

- College Navigator
- O*NET OnLine
- DANTES College & Career Planning Counseling Services, powered by Kuder® Journey
- Military OneSource/My Spouse Education and Career Opportunities
- CareerScope®
- VA Education and Career Counseling Program (Chapter 36) for dependents using transferred GI Bill benefits

- CareerOneStop
- The Department of Labor
- Bureau of Labor Statistics Occupational Outlook Handbook
- California Career Zone
- Base Education Offices and Virtual Counseling
- Base Colleges and Community Colleges

COLLEGE NAVIGATOR

http://nces.ed.gov/collegenavigator/

College Navigator offered by the National Center for Education Statistics is a beneficial tool for both spouses and dependent children. The free site enables users to search schools based upon detailed criteria. Searches may be saved for future reference and dropped into the favorites box for side-by-side comparison. Comparing schools side by side enables users to determine which school better suits their needs. For example, I (Jillian) searched California State University San Marcos (CSUSM) and University of San Diego in California to determine which school would be less expensive. After dropping both schools into my favorites box, I selected the compare option in that section. The side-by-side comparison tool lists CSUSM's tuition rate for a student that lives off campus at $7,269 and USD's rate for the same student at $44,586 (2015–2016 school year). I still need to go directly to both schools' websites for more information, but my initial search is demonstrating the vast difference to me in yearly costs between the two institutions. If I am using transferred GI Bill benefits, I know that the Post-9/11 GI Bill currently only covers up to $21,970.46 (http://www.benefits.va.gov/GIBILL/ resources/benefits_resources/rates/ch33/ch33rates080116.asp) per academic year for a private school, and I know further research would be required to determine whether USD or CSUSM are viable fiscal options for me as a military spouse/dependent student.

If my military spouse is still on active duty, CSUSM might be a better option, because while using the transferred benefits the Post-9/11 GI Bill would fully fund the state school, there would be a gap in tuition costs at USD. If I were a dependent child of a service member who qualified for 100 percent of the Post-9/11 GI Bill, I could also check the Yellow Ribbon option for USD and see if I might be able to fill the gap in tuition charges.

College Navigator allows detailed searches in fields such as distance from zip codes, public and private school options, distance learning possibilities, school costs, percentage of applicants admitted, religious affiliations, specialized missions, and available athletic teams. This way, users can narrow down selections based upon specific needs. For example, if I were interested in attending a school with a Christian background as part of my learning, I could click on the religious affiliations tab at the bottom of the search section and add that criterion to my list.

Beginning each search within a certain number of miles from a zip code will enable users to narrow their search parameters from the start. If the selection is insufficient, try broadening the distance a bit prior to removing all of the other parameters you deem important. Many schools offer some degree of online schooling as part of the learning environment. If you are open to online learning, you may find that you can still attain all of your search parameters comfortably even if the school is a bit farther away.

A generic initial search on College Navigator might resemble this:

1. State—California
2. Zip code—90290, with a maximum distance parameter set at fifteen miles
3. Degree options—business
4. Level of degree awarded—associate
5. School type—public

Results demonstrate that four schools meet my (Jillian's) search criteria: Los Angeles Pierce College, Santa Monica College, Los Angeles Valley College, and West Los Angeles College. Because each of these institutions met my initial search criteria, I might want to narrow the mileage to a selection closer to my home base, or look for other, more particular areas that demonstrate the differences. These areas may include topics such as the student population or programs offered.

Beginning in 2009, schools have been required by the Department of Education to compile three pieces of data to allow students to better analyze the costs and value of attending a particular school. College Navigator provides the information regarding these topics, graduation/retention rates, median borrowing rates, and the cohort loan default rates, on its site. Checking this information can give potential students better insight into an institution's value.

Graduation/retention rates track first-time and full-time students who graduate within 150 percent of the time from beginning their degree. This may only capture a very specific or small population at a particular school. If a student were to transfer in many credits and be classified as a transfer student, this number would not capture him or her. If a school you are considering attending has particularly low graduation/retention rates, it would be wise to contact the institution and inquire about this issue or potentially consider another option. Low rates at state-supported community colleges do not bother me, since many students use these institutions as a transfer pathway and do not stop along the way to attain associate's degrees.

The median borrowing rates are the median amount of debt the student population is taking on to attend that institution. Median is similar to the average, but calculated differently. The cohort loan default rates are the number of students that attended the school and defaulted on their loans after leaving the institution. The assumption often made is that schools with high median borrowing rates and high cohort loan default rates along with low graduation/retention rates do not provide educational value to the student when he or she attempts to attain employment. In other words, students might not be able to afford their loans.

Unfortunately, these numbers are complex and only provide one small piece of the overall puzzle when assessing whether a particular institution is the right choice for a student. Talking to a counselor at the school and investigating the responses offered about these concerns can help a potential student better understand what the statistics may mean.

O*NET ONLINE

http://www.onetonline.org/

O*NET OnLine is a career occupation website that enables users to complete detailed research on any careers they might be interested in pursuing. The career departments on the military bases use O*NET OnLine for resume development. The site details areas such as career fields, needed skills, income possibilities, work contexts, and required education levels.

To research a potential career on O*NET OnLine, enter the name in the upper right-hand corner under the "Occupation Quick Search" tab. For example, I entered "marketing." Upon clicking the link, I was taken to a page that listed marketing managers along with numerous other possibilities that are similar in nature: marketing strategists, market research analysts and marketing specialists, and green marketers. This option enables users to research a broader base of potential career pathways prior to settling on one.

Occupations listed as "Bright Outlook" have growth rates that are faster than average in that field and are projected to have a large number of job openings during the decade from 2014 through 2024. These fields are also considered new and emerging, meaning they will see changes in areas such as technology over the upcoming years. Offering several different occupations under one particular search enables users to broaden their horizons and complete numerous searches that are similar in nature.

Clicking on one particular career pathway will allow you to find the national and state-based median wages for the chosen occupation—for example, the search I conducted under marketing, then marketing strategists, listed the national median wages at $40.10 hourly, $83,410 annually. The projected annual growth rate is between 2 percent and 4 percent, with 37,700 job openings during this time frame. Also listed are the majority of industries where people are finding employment—in this case, professional, scientific, and technical services.

Lastly, schools that offer the proper education pathways can be searched by state. Unfortunately, the school search cannot be narrowed down further by location, type of institution, or other minute detail. For more detailed searches, return to College Navigator.

DANTES COLLEGE AND CAREER PLANNING COUNSELING SERVICES, POWERED BY KUDER® JOURNEY™

http://www.dantes.kuder.com/

DANTES College and Career Planning Counseling Services is available to military service members, veterans, and spouses for free, whether they are still on active duty or already separated from the service. Four main areas of education and career research and planning are available on the site—assessments section, occupations, education and financial aid, and job search.

Spouses can conduct inventory assessments that enable them to see their areas of strength and weakness. This gives test takers insight into career fields that match their personality types, thereby offering a broader base of potential careers to research. Background information on the careers can be researched to determine whether users are interested in pursuing the option further. Under the education section, users can match the requisite type of education to the chosen vocation as well as find schools that offer the desired degrees.

Resume building and job searches can be conducted through the site as well. One interesting tool Kuder offers is the ability for users to build resumes and cover letters, attach other needed or pertinent information, and create a URL that hosts the information to submit to potential employers. This allows multiple pieces of information to be housed in one place in a professional manner for viewing by others.

MY SPOUSE EDUCATION AND
CAREER OPPORTUNITIES (MYSECO)

https://myseco.militaryonesource.mil/portal

MySECO offers military spouses the ability to access career counseling anywhere they are located. So, if you are not located on a base with an education center, you could make use of these services instead, although you can always set up phone-based counseling appointments with an education center. MySECO offers many services, including interest and personality inventories to help you decide on a career, including the Myers-Briggs, Strong Interest Explorer, Kuder Journey, and CareerScope interest inventories. The assessments measure the following essential capabilities:

- Career aptitude assessments
- Interests
- Personality assessments
- Work Values inventories
- Skills assessments

MySECO account holders can use the site for the following career-based tasks:

- Developing a personalized profile
- Exploring new topics
- Importing a Linkedin profile
- Building and managing resumes
- Accessing occupational information and DOL-defined occupations

And if you need help formatting an educational plan to meet your career needs, MySECO counselors can advise you on the following topics:

- Assistance locating funding for education
- Help with locating the right school/program
- Advice on balancing work and family life
- Assistance with resumes, interview skills, and more
- Support in developing an individual career plan for a portable career[1]

CAREERSCOPE® AND MY NEXT MOVE FOR VETERANS

http://www.gibill.va.gov/studenttools/careerscope/index.html
http://www.mynextmove.org/vets/

CareerScope hosts an interest and aptitude assessment tool similar in style to DANTES Kuder. The Veterans Administration hosts CareerScope on the main GI Bill web page. The free site assists service members in finding and planning the best pathways for those transitioning off active duty and into higher education. Spouses can use the site as well. Assessments are conducted directly through the site, and a corresponding report interpretation document demonstrates how to interpret assessment results. The easy-to-understand site is a valuable research tool both for those who have already identified which career pathway they want to take and for those who are still undecided.

VA EDUCATION AND CAREER COUNSELING PROGRAM (CHAPTER 36)

http://www.benefits.va.gov/vocrehab/edu_voc_counseling.asp
http://www.vba.va.gov/pubs/forms/VBA-28-8832-ARE.pdf

Although it is not widely known, the VA offers free education and career counseling advice to veterans. The counseling services are designed to help service members choose careers, detail the required educational pathway, and assist in working through any concerns that arise that might deter success. Dependents using transferred benefits should refer to the website for eligibility, but the main determining factors are the following:

- be eligible for VA education benefits (or dependents using transferred benefits) through one of the following chapters: chapters 30, 31, 32, 33, 35, 1606, or 1607;
- have received an honorable discharge not longer than one year earlier;

- have no more than six months remaining on active duty; or
- be a current VA education beneficiary

Fill out an application that can be found on the website listed above and return it to get the ball rolling. Service members who have already separated from active service and are not located near a military base will find this a solid outlet for assistance.

CAREERONESTOP

http://www.careeronestop.org/

CareerOneStop is one of my (Jillian) go-to sites for career exploration, and it is the first site I visit when I work with students who are interested in apprenticeship programs. The site holds valuable information regarding topics other than apprenticeships as well. It is a comprehensive career exploration site. CareerOneStop has six main sections for exploration:

- Explore careers—learn about career fields, explore different industries, take self-assessments, and research different job skills
- Salary and benefits—information on relocating, wages and salaries, benefits, unemployment insurance, and paying for education or training
- Education and training—information on traditional education and apprenticeship programs, conduct a search for community colleges, find credentials, and research employment trends
- Job search—learn how to network, interview, and negotiate, and find special tips on veterans' reemployment
- Resumes and interviews—samples and formats, create a cover letter and thank-you note, and find out how to get ready for an interview
- People and places to help—workforce services in different locations

If searching for information regarding apprenticeships programs, click on the "Education and Training" tab; then, under the "Find" section, click "Apprenticeship." This page hosts links that cover the following:

- Apprenticeship videos
- A state-based search site
- Information from the Department of Labor (DOL)
- American Job Center information

Academic and Career-Based Research Tools   33

Use the state-based search option to find a program in the state and county of your choosing. For example, Mary Bowen is from Maryland. She would like to participate in an electrician Registered Apprenticeship program. She clicks on the "Find registered apprenticeship programs" tab, then selects her state. At this point, each state will have designed their own websites, so the directions will vary, but you need to find the link to search for apprenticeship programs. For Mary, she clicks on "Find an Apprenticeship" at the top of the page, then "View Links to Program Websites." On this page, she can search for the appropriate link for an electrician program and the contact information.

THE DEPARTMENT OF LABOR

http://www.dol.gov/

The DOL is the one-stop shopping place for many topics, but I use the site for information regarding unemployment, registered apprenticeships, and career exploration. On the main DOL page, under the "Popular Topics" tab, I use the "Training" link for counseling spouses who are interested in an apprenticeship pathway.

The "Training" section has a tab on the right-hand side of the page for information on apprenticeship programs. This page holds information that allows individuals to familiarize themselves with apprenticeships and the process to participating. The DOL is a good place to begin a search for a specific program in a specific location. Read the Fact Sheet before clicking on the "Office of Apprenticeship" tab, which will take users to the main page regarding registered apprenticeships. Anything you need to know about an apprenticeship program can be found here: http://www.doleta.gov/oa/.

BUREAU OF LABOR STATISTICS
OCCUPATIONAL OUTLOOK HANDBOOK

http://www.bls.gov/ooh/

The Bureau of Labor Statistics (BLS) Occupational Outlook Handbook is a resourceful tool to use for career exploration prior to starting down your education journey and is my (Jillian's) go-to site when conducting career research with clients. Conducting career research before starting school will assist you in making a more knowledgeable decision regarding your education. Search career fields by pay levels, educational requirements, training requirements, projected job openings, and projected job-growth rates. You can research various career sectors or find out what are the current fastest-growing job fields. If you want to find out the level of education required to be a petroleum engineer and how much money they make, click on the "Architecture and Engineering" tab and scroll down (the options are in alphabetical order). Here you can view a short job summary, see that the field requires a bachelor's degree, and learn that the median pay in 2014 was $130,050. Clicking on the link takes users to more in-depth information regarding the career field.

CALIFORNIA CAREER ZONE

https://www.cacareerzone.org/

While the California Career Zone is obviously geared for California, it can be a useful tool for research regardless of which state you are looking to settle in. The site hosts four different self-assessment tests that allow users to test based upon their current needs. The assessments are as follows:

- Quick assessment: users match their personality type to potential career fields.
- Interest profiler: users explore occupations based upon their interests.
- Skills profiler: users determine what skills they have already acquired and explore occupations that align to those skills.
- Work interest profiler: users determine which career fields reflect their values.[2]

CA Career Zone hosts a wealth of information regarding different types of job families, including videos for each field. Students can use the site to determine topics such as calculating their college costs, finding schools or training programs, determining the level of education required for the different career fields, creating resumes, building references, and creating budgets.

BASE EDUCATION OFFICES AND VIRTUAL COUNSELING

Some military base education centers can provide counseling services for military spouses. Base education counselors are knowledgeable about the programs available on the base, in the community, and online. If you are assigned to a small military base without an education center, locate the nearest large base to see whether there are education centers on post that can offer counseling to military spouses. Some military branches—the army and navy, for example—offer virtual counseling over the phone or via email. See if the service is also available to military spouses for your branch of the military.

BASE COLLEGES AND COMMUNITY COLLEGES

Advisors working for colleges on military bases can be helpful as well, but remember that an advisor employed by a school is primarily interested in getting you to enroll in the school they represent. For this reason, we always recommend speaking with the base education center counselors first. You can be assured that the colleges on the base have been screened for proper accreditation and policies on treatment of service members, veterans, and family members. For undergraduate course work, tuition is usually set at $250 per semester hour or less (under the quarter system, $166.67 per quarter hour or less). Enrolling in schools on base offers peace of mind regarding academic standards.

State-supported community colleges offer college courses, certificate programs, self-improvement programs, and vocational-technical programs at lower cost. Taking even one or two courses at a community college may allow you to get a better feel for a particular career pathway. Community colleges typically have career centers where you can take personality-based career research tests that the advisors can interpret for you. These tests can help determine what types of careers might be a good fit for you.

There are quite a few reasons to consider state-supported community colleges. State-supported community colleges have the proper accreditation. They are a good place to get back into the world of education, especially for those who need remedial or refresher English writing and math courses. State-supported community colleges are less expensive than four-year colleges.

Classes are usually smaller, allowing for more attention from professors. I (Robert) completed some classes at a major state-supported four-year university with over one hundred enrolled students in each class. Doctoral students were used as teaching aides, and they were assigned the grading duties for papers and exams. Getting an appointment with the actual professor teaching a large class was often difficult.

In many states, community colleges also offer vocational training programs. For example, a medical assistant training program at the community college can be thousands of dollars less than programs offered at private, for-profit schools. At a state-supported community college, the state establishes strict standards for curriculum and instructors, ensuring quality training respected by employers. The quality of instruction for medical assisting programs can vary significantly from school to school, even within the same city.

State-supported community colleges employ admissions counselors or advisors who commonly have master's degrees in education or counseling. The counselors are not expected to be salespeople; they are expected to be guides in assisting the students in achieving the best possible education.

Community colleges are often closer to home. Many states have a network of community colleges designed so that every community will be within reasonable commuting distance from a campus. Scheduling at community colleges is often more flexible. Also, many state-supported community colleges now offer online courses.

Finally, state-supported community colleges tend to have more nontraditional students, including students returning to college after spending years in the workforce (considered adult reentry), working adults seeking career changes, and even military spouses!

Chapter Four

Degree Types and Differences

Understanding the different types of degrees available to pursue and determining how high of a degree is required for your chosen career field will help you plan your education accordingly. This will also help you reduce the risk of choosing a less-than-reputable institution. The following topics will be covered in this chapter:

- Associate's degrees
- Bachelor's degrees
- Master's degrees
- Doctoral degrees
- Professional degrees

DEGREE TYPES AND DIFFERENCES

Associate's Degrees

Associate's degrees are two-year programs of study typically offered by community colleges, trade and vocational colleges, career colleges, and sometimes by four-year universities. Some associate's degrees can be used for transfer into a bachelor's degree program at the junior (third-year) level, but other transfer pathways might require extra course work.

Terminal associate's degrees are commonly referred to as associate's degrees in applied science (also called applied technology) and are not built to transfer into a four-year university in most cases. Associate in applied science degrees are for those who want to earn a two-year degree and enter the workforce without going on to pursue a bachelor's degree. Typically an applied science degree is not intended as a bridge to a bachelor's degree program because far fewer general education courses are required and also due to the vocational/technical nature of the occupation studied.

Many community colleges and career schools offer certificate options or the more extensive applied science/technology associate's degree options. Some examples of career fields include automotive technology, real estate, landscape architecture, culinary arts, and construction trades. Most of these examples offer students the ability to earn a certificate or an associate's degree. Certificate options do not require a full load of general education courses that two-year associate's degree programs demand, and as a result do not take as long to complete. In most cases, students who complete the advanced education, or in this case an associate's degree, tend to earn more when they move into the workforce.

More traditional associate's degrees may be for a particular academic major or in general studies. Students typically opt for an associate's degree in general studies when they have not decided which major they want to pursue at the bachelor's degree level. Associate's degrees require students to complete as many as twenty college courses (in some cases, more) in order to achieve completion. This does not include any remedial or refresher math and English courses that might be required based on placement exam results. Typical academically oriented associate's degree programs require:

English: Composition I and Composition II

Math: College algebra for many degree programs. Engineering and science majors will require higher math courses such as calculus.

Arts and humanities: Three courses which will include literature, music, art, drama, theater, philosophy, and foreign languages.

Social and behavioral sciences: Three courses which include history, government, political science, economics, anthropology, psychology, and sociology.

Natural sciences: Two to three courses in categories that include biology, chemistry, botany, astronomy, physical science, and more. Many schools require lab sciences—for example, a biology lecture course with a lab class that meets separately.

Miscellaneous: Some schools require a speech class, also known as oral communications or public speaking. A few schools still require an introductory computer science course.

If a major is declared, courses related to the major (i.e., criminal justice) will be completed in addition to general education courses. If a major is not declared, the remaining courses may be free electives or courses in just about any subject.

Bachelor's Degrees

Bachelor's degrees typically require four years to achieve and roughly forty courses to complete (twenty if transferring in with an associate's degree). While many schools require the Scholastic Aptitude Test (SAT) or American College Test (ACT) as part of the admissions process, if transferring to a four-year college from a community college, the ACT and SAT entrance exams are usually no longer required. This is because students now have a proven college track record and at this point their grades speak more about their academic abilities than a test score can. Many factors can determine admission if applying directly to a four-year school. Some schools are extremely competitive and review SAT and ACT scores, high school transcripts, and grade point averages for any attempted college work. Some of the more competitive four-year colleges and universities may require an admissions essay as well. Most schools on military bases do not require an SAT or ACT.

Should you start with a community college or apply directly to a four-year institution? Circumstances will vary, but considerations may include cost and convenience. In many states, community colleges have lower tuition and have more locations than state-supported four-year colleges. Community colleges are often more conveniently located to a student's home and are usually better suited to help with past deficiencies in education than four-year institutions.

You may now be ready as an adult to pursue more education as you have gained maturity and discipline compared to your high school days. If you feel that your math and English skills may not be up to par, then a community college might be the best place to start, as they offer many remedial courses in these subjects. Even those students who were serious in high school may need some refresher courses due to a gap in education between graduating from high school and beginning college. If you are deficient in math and science courses required for certain degree programs (i.e., engineering and science degrees), community colleges are a good place to complete the prerequisite classes. For example, many bachelor's degree programs in engineering expect high school students to have completed four years of high school math, including Algebra I, Geometry, Algebra II, and at least one advanced math class that required Algebra II be completed first. If these courses were not completed in high school, or sufficient ACT/SAT scores were not attained, then community college courses are the best option for students to prepare for admissions into an engineering program at a four-year school.

Should you go to a private or state-supported school? One advantage of being a military dependent is receiving the in-state tuition rate at state-supported colleges in whatever state you and your family are stationed. Some private colleges can be expensive, but on-base private colleges offer affordable options because the schools offer special rates to military family members.

Currently, there is a great demand for students to pursue degrees in science, technology, engineering, or math fields (STEM). STEM fields typically offer higher wages and lower levels of unemployment. According to the article "STEM 101: Intro to Tomorrow's Jobs" produced by the Bureau of Labor Statistics's *Occupational Outlook Quarterly*, the "BLS projects overall STEM employment . . . to grow about 13 percent between 2012 and 2022. This is faster than the 11-percent rate of growth projected for all occupations over the decade."[1]

The US Department of Education in the article "Science, Technology, Engineering and Math: Education for Global Leadership" demonstrates growth rates through the year 2020 in the following STEM fields (income levels taken from O*NET OnLine):

- Mathematics: 16 percent, median annual income for a mathematician in 2014 was $103,720
- Computer Systems Analysis: 22 percent, median annual income in 2014 was $82,710
- Systems Software Development: 32 percent, median annual income in 2014 was $102,880
- Medical Scientists: 36 percent, median annual income in 2014 was $79,930
- Biomedical Engineers: 62 percent, median annual income in 2014 was $86,950[2]

Once again, math and science requirements, even general education math and science requirements, are more extensive for highly technical STEM degrees.

If you missed out in high school, work on your math and science skills at a community college to eventually meet the requirements to be admitted to a STEM-based degree program.

Common majors for non-STEM-based degrees or liberal arts degrees include history, literature, foreign language, philosophy, anthropology, communications, education, psychology, sociology, math, and natural sciences. While liberal arts degrees are not getting as much attention as their STEM-based counterparts, they can still net you a viable career pathway. Starting salaries for liberal arts majors may be lower, but income potential increases over the long term, according to the article "Liberal Arts Salaries Are a Marathon, Not a Sprint" from the *Wall Street Journal*.[3] The article "Liberal Arts Degrees Can Net Big Salaries—If You Wait Long Enough," appearing in the business-and-investment-oriented publication *The Motley Fool*, points out that STEM degrees have higher starting pay, but liberal arts majors often have comparable salaries to their STEM counterparts at the midcareer point.[4]

Business degrees are another option for gaining a diverse and multipronged approach to potential career options. Obvious pathways for business majors include fields such as management and marketing. Other, less obvious choices are more diversified and might include sectors such as government, international commerce, health care, and nonprofit organizations. A business degree can also give you the foundations you need to start your own company.

Business degrees can include the following types:

- Business administration and management: Graduates learn to plan and direct business activities. Courses include many in field management, marketing, finance, and accounting.
- International business: Includes many courses found in a business management degree, plus courses in international business and foreign language courses.
- Marketing: Graduates learn how to determine the market for products as well as promote and advertise. Many of the courses that are part of a marketing degree plan are the same as those found in a business administration degree plan, but with more courses specifically dealing with marketing.
- Finance: Finance majors interpret financial data for businesses and nonprofits.

- Human resources management: This is a field related to recruiting, management, training, and administering benefits to employees of an organization. Courses often include legal issues, labor law, employment law, sociology, psychology, and ethics.
- Organizational leadership: Many people who pursue this degree are already in leadership or management positions and need a degree or advanced degree for career advancement. Students complete courses in management, leadership, psychology, sociology, and ethics.

Some schools, such as the University of Houston (http://publications.uh. edu/preview_program.php?catoid=6&poid=1412), have developed bachelor's degrees in business administration with an emphasis on entrepreneurship for those more interested in gaining the fundamentals they need to develop and manage business enterprises. Due to the rapidly changing nature of business environments, students who gain the skills that help them learn to function within these types of structures will be especially valuable to future employers or to the students who intend to create their own small (or large!) businesses.

There are many other types of majors for bachelor's degrees, including agriculture, architecture, social work, criminology, industrial technology, elementary and secondary school education, kinesiology, and forestry. Many of these programs can be completed online, but some are extremely technical in nature, such as all engineering majors, and require more traditional classroom instruction. Check with your base education counselor for advice and recommendations.

Master's Degrees

The next degree level after a bachelor's degree is the master's degree, a program of study to gain a higher level of expertise in a field. Master's degrees can take anywhere from one to four years to complete depending on the subject-matter demands and whether the program has a required thesis or capstone project. Some master's degree programs do not require a thesis or capstone project but may require a comprehensive exam. Length of study will also depend on whether the degree is pursued on a full- or part-time basis. Many master's degree programs require the Graduate Record Exam (GRE) or the Graduate Management Admission Test (GMAT) as part of the admissions process. Schools will also typically require a minimum grade point average (GPA) on undergraduate (bachelor's degree) course work as part of the admissions process. Required GPAs will vary from school to school and program to program.

A liberal arts major may stay in the same field of study. For example, someone with a bachelor of arts degree in English literature could pursue a master's degree in English literature, but he or she could also diversify and consider majors such as fine arts, education, or organizational leadership.

Some master's degree programs are so technical or specialized that the undergraduate degree must be in the same field (for example, a master's degree in civil engineering). Since the civil engineering major is highly specialized, an individual holding a bachelor's degree in civil engineering would be the most qualified. An individual who possesses a bachelor's degree in an unrelated occupation would need to go back to school and complete undergraduate (most likely a bachelor's degree) course work in civil engineering before being considered for a master's degree in the subject.

Sometimes a master's degree is needed to work in a chosen field of study. For example, to become licensed as a marriage and family therapist (MFT), all states require students to go through a licensing program. The programs require completion of a master's degree and two thousand to four thousand hours of supervised clinical experience. MFTs must also pass a state exam and complete a specific amount of continuing education units (annual training) in order to maintain their license.[5] In this case, attaining a bachelor's degree for an individual who wants to work as an MFT is a prerequisite that must be completed to be considered a candidate for an MFT program.

Remember, a base education counselor can advise you on your best options no matter the education level you are pursuing: a certificate, an associate's degree, a bachelor's degree, or a master's degree. A base education counselor will know about the best options on base, in the local community, and online.

Doctoral and Professional Degrees

There are various types of doctoral degrees. Three of the most common are the doctor of philosophy (PhD), the medical doctor (MD), and the doctor of education (EdD). Most of us think of professors teaching at the college level when we hear the term *doctorate*, or our physicians. In most countries, holding a doctorate is a requirement to be part of the world of academia and denotes success in a field of academic research.[6]

The doctor of philosophy is offered in many fields in arts and sciences (not just philosophy), and it is the terminal degree required to teach and hold a teaching professorship or research position at colleges and universities. It is also required for many research positions in government and industry. The program of study is normally three to seven years, involves extensive course work, and requires major research in the form of a dissertation or thesis that contains original research worthy of being published in peer-reviewed publications. Often the dissertation or thesis must be defended before the candidate's dissertation committee, which is appointed by the university. Famous PhD holders include Dr. Albert Einstein (Nobel Prize winner who developed the theory of relativity: "$E = mc^2$"), Dr. Henry Kissinger (secretary of state under President Nixon), Dr. Stephen Hawking (theoretical physicist and author), and Dr. Condoleezza Rice (secretary of state under President George W. Bush).

The Doctor of Medicine degree (MD) is the terminal degree for physicians and surgeons. Usually, it entails a four-year program of study followed by years of internship and residency. Admission to medical school is extremely competitive in the United States and will require several prerequisite classes to be completed with minimum required grades, especially if your undergraduate degree is not in a science-based subject. Schools will also want to see a demonstration of commitment, analytical abilities, and a good grade on the MCAT. If you are interested in this pathway, you can learn more at https://www.petersons.com/graduate-schools/getting-into-medical-school.aspx.

The doctor of education degree prepares a person for academic positions in research, administrative, or leadership positions in schools, colleges, and other organizations both private and public. The program of study is normally three to five years, involves extensive course work, and requires major research in the form of a dissertation or thesis that contains original research worthy of being published in peer-reviewed publications. Famous EdD holders include Dr. Jill Biden (wife of former vice president Joe Biden), Dr. Shaquille O'Neal (former NBA player), and sex therapist Dr. Ruth Westheimer (more commonly known as Dr. Ruth).

What Can I Do with a Major In . . . ?

Have you ever wondered what types of jobs match different majors? There are tools to help you research it. Some schools, such as the University of North Carolina at Wilmington, offer a help site providing examples of professions by major, and some of the possibilities are surprising. Here are just a few examples, but be aware that some of these career fields will require education above and beyond the bachelor's degree level. The information can be found on the following website: http://uncw.edu/career/WhatCanI DoWithaMajorIn.html.

- History: archivist, FBI/CIA agent, government official, park ranger, lawyer, teacher, insurance agent, technical writer
- Sociology: adoption agent, case aid worker, veterans' affairs, social welfare examiner, human resources specialist, child welfare officer, substance abuse counselor
- Philosophy and Religion: pastor, psychologist, counselor, management trainee, professor

Barry University, a private Catholic university in Miami Shores, Florida, also hosts a "What can I do with a major in . . . " website that is located here: https://www.barry.edu/career-development-center/students-alumni/what-can -i-do-with-a-major.html. Barry University takes its website a step beyond UNC's website. In addition to job titles, the information listed by the institution includes some typical employers that hire people in South Florida, related major skills that those within the field should possess, related career titles, professional associations, and jobs and internship search links.

Not every graduate ends up working within the same area of discipline as their college major. The University of California at Berkeley conducts periodic surveys of their graduates pertaining to their employment postgraduation. A sampling of the survey data from 2015 reveals that graduates often work in career fields outside of their chosen major. For example, 60 percent of graduates (respondents) in the letters and sciences division of the school in 2015 were employed in the field of business.[7]

Here are some other colleges and universities offering help sites for finding what you can do with particular majors:

- Kansas State University: http://www.k-state.edu/acic/majorin/
- The University of Washington: http://careers.washington.edu/Students/ What-Can-I-Do-With-a-Major-In
- University of Georgia: http://career.uga.edu/majors_careers/what_can_i_ do_with_a_major_in
- Idaho State University: http://www.isu.edu/career/majors/default.html
- Portland State University: http://www.pdx.edu/careers/what-can-i-do-with-a-degree-in

- University of Wisconsin–Eau Claire: http://www.uwec.edu/Career/students/majors/wcidwamis/index.htm
- Rutgers University: http://careers.rutgers.edu/page.cfm?page_ID=375&section_ID=8
- California State University, Fullerton: http://www.fullerton.edu/aac/Current_Students/Undeclared_Students/can_do.asp

Another way to research majors and occupations is to talk to people already working in the profession that you are considering. For example, if you want to become a registered nurse, you should pursue the advice of nurses at your local clinic or hospital. They can talk about the profession and the education paths that they completed. Also, check out businesses, agencies, and professional societies. If you want to become a Federal Bureau of Investigation (FBI) agent, check the FBI's website: https://www.fbi.gov/. Most agencies have a section on the homepage providing information on jobs, such as the FBI hosts on its website (https://www.fbijobs.gov/), and most list the contact information for the human resources department or recruiting office.

Don't forget to check out businesses, agencies, and professional societies. Do you want to major in political science? Contact the American Political Science Association for advice on education: http://www.apsanet.org/. How about majoring in economics? Visit the website of the American Economic Association (AEA): https://www.aeaweb.org/. For those interested in the counseling profession, much information can be researched on the website of the National Board for Certified Counselors: http://www.nbcc.org/. There are many such resources offered by professional organizations and societies. An Internet search using the term *professional societies* yields hundreds of results, and here are just a few examples:

- American Chemical Society: http://www.acs.org/content/acs/en.html
- American Society for Engineering Education: http://www.asee.org/
- National Council for the Social Studies: http://www.socialstudies.org/
- League of American Communications Professionals: http://www.lacp.com/
- National Healthcareer Association: http://nhanow.com/
- American Physical Therapy Association: https://www.apta.org
- American Occupational Therapy Association: https://www.aota.org
- American Kinesiology Association: http://www.americankinesiology.org/

Use the tactics you have learned in this section to help you in your career and educational planning. The more information you gain before making your decision, the better decision you will be able to make.

The Liberal Arts Degree

The liberal arts bachelor's degree includes majors in many areas, including art, history, literature, music, mathematics, science, and philosophy. It is one of the most common types of bachelor's degrees awarded.[8] In an age when many politicians and leaders in the United States emphasize the importance of the contributions of business on our economy and society, a liberal arts degree is often perceived as not being the most useful degree for jobs in business and industry. Do you want to work on a liberal arts degree? A *Time* magazine article from 2015 talks about ten business chief executive officers who hold liberal arts degrees.[9] The list is fascinating:

- Andrea Jung, former Avon CEO: BA in English Literature
- Carly Fiorina, former Hewlett-Packard CEO: BA in Medieval History and Philosophy
- Howard Schultz, Starbucks CEO: BS in Communications
- Michael Eisner, former Walt Disney Company CEO: BA in English Literature and Theater
- Richard Plepler, HBO CEO: BA in Government
- Jack Mackey, Whole Foods Co-CEO: BA in Philosophy and Religion
- Susan Wojcicki, YouTube CEO: BA in History and Literature
- Steve Ells, Chipotle Co-CEO: BA in Art History
- Alexa Hirschfeld, Paperless Post cofounder: BA in Classics
- Jack Ma, Alibaba Chairman: BA in English

Would you believe a liberal arts degree is even valued in the world of technology? A 2015 article in *Forbes* magazine titled "That Useless Liberal Arts Degree Has Become Tech's Hottest Ticket" reports on technology firms that have found liberal arts majors have creativity and thinking skills that make the firms they work for more robust in their diversity of thinking power. The article states that at many technology hubs throughout the United States, liberal arts thinking is making companies stronger, and liberal arts degree holders are valued for their creativity.[10] So don't rule out the degree you would rather do because another degree may have a higher average salary. There are exceptions to everything.

Chapter Five

Licensing and Certification

Aside from the traditional academic education offered by universities and community colleges, many fields and industries require other, or additional, certifications or credentials that are evaluated by external organizations. These organizations can be private by nature, or administered by the state or federal government. In some cases, the certifications may be required in addition to traditional learning, or they may be stand-alone credentials that are meant to lead directly to employment. While determining the requirements and finding the right institution or training program is your first priority, as a military spouse this can be more difficult than for the average soon-to-be student. Military dependents frequently encounter the same issues as their active-duty spouses, such as difficulty continuing their educations due to frequent PCS moves. One of the appeals of licensure and certification for this population is that the training is often shorter than a traditional degree and can be carried over to find employment in the local community at the next duty station.

The following topics will be covered in this chapter:

- Understanding the difference between certificates, licenses, and certifications/credentials
- Beginning the search and evaluating programs
- What do I need, and how do I obtain it?
- Considerations for military spouses

WHAT'S IN A NAME?

Certification and Credentialing

Credentials can encompass certificates, degrees, and licenses issued by the government.

The term implies that curriculum of some type, whether taught through classes or training, has been learned and competency demonstrated or that a test has been passed. The National Environmental Health Association states:

> A credential is issued by a third party with authoritative power, and is proof of an individual's qualification or competence in a given subject. Possessing a credential not only helps one to prove competency and capability in a given field, but also demonstrates to one's community and employers that the individual is competent, properly trained and equipped to carry out his or her duties.[1]

The main difference between a certificate and a certification/credentialing program is that completing a certificate does not gain you a credential or certification. For example, a student can earn a certificate in college counseling through a university, but the certificate program does not award the school counseling credential that is necessary to have in order to work as an elementary, middle, or high school counselor. The certificate of completion simply demonstrates that the individual has taken some course work and has some knowledge in the field. Earning the credential would require a rigorous academic learning pathway that would potentially include a master's degree as well as a credentialing program.

Certifications and credentials must typically be renewed periodically. For example, CompTIA, an information technology industry trade association certification, produces various IT certification tests that must generally be renewed every three years. This is because the IT knowledge base changes rapidly as technology advances.

Both vocational training institutions and higher education–based institutions offer certificates. They are usually regarded as a resume booster, as the certificate itself does not lead to any type of certification or credential. It simply shows potential employers that you possess knowledge about the subject matter. Vocational certificates typically incorporate the training required to take and pass a certification test. For example, vocational schools might offer an automotive certificate program that prepares you to pass the

Automotive Service Exams (ASEs), which are highly sought after by automotive mechanics. This particular exam does not necessarily require any prerequisite training, especially if you already possess a great deal of knowledge about cars. Therefore, you could earn the automotive certificate and never pass the ASE certifications.

Licensing

Licensing is similar to credentialing in that it requires a specific set of training and passing a test or series of tests. Licensure can be a long, in-depth process that requires extensive education, or it can be fairly short. The big difference between licensing and a certification is that while a certification attests to an individual's knowledge base, a license is granted by a higher authority and gives permission to a trained individual to do something. For example, a medical doctor must pass a standardized national exam that is approved by the state's medical board. The medical board grants authority to the individual to practice medicine in that state upon successful completion of the exam. This is no easy accomplishment, as it requires around eight years of course work (undergraduate and graduate), significant clinical practice (usually during the second two years of medical school), and around three to eight years of residency (paid) to become a doctor.

Nursing is another example of a career field that requires licensing. Licensed Practical Nurses (LPNs) and Licensed Vocational Nurses (LVNs) are nurses that work under the supervision of a registered nurse (RN) or doctor. Training is typically six months to one year in length and requires passing a test to become licensed. The state's board of nursing maintains this test and grants authority to LPNs to practice nursing. Similar to many certifications, licenses must be periodically renewed usually through a process of continuing education units and a fee.

In some cases, even vocationally based course work may count toward a degree from a more traditional institution. Oklahoma maintains a series of twenty-nine technology centers that focus primarily on vocational training. These technology centers do not hold either regional or national accreditation but instead are accredited by the Oklahoma Board of Career and Technology Education. Western Oklahoma State College will grant advanced credit toward their RN program for those that have obtained an LPN at one of their own technology centers, as well as for out-of-state LPN licenses. Western Oklahoma may apply the credit to the following classes: NURS 1119, Nursing I–Foundations of Nursing and Functional Health Patterns, and NURS

1129, or Nursing II–Functional Health Patterns for Maternal/Infant and Child Care. While receiving credit for these classes may not equal the time and effort required to obtain a six-month-to-one-year program for an LPN, it still helps. It could lead to employment faster, particularly if you are changing duty stations soon and want to be ready for employment upon arrival at the next assignment.

Many colleges offer programs that expedite the pathway for LPNs and LVNs to complete RN programs. Here are a few examples:

Northern Virginia Community College LPN to RN: https://www.nvcc. edu/medical/divisions/nursing/lpn-rn-program.html

Mercy School of Nursing in North Carolina: http://www. carolinashealthcare.org/cmc-mercy-school-of-nursing-curriculum-description

California State University San Marcos LVN to BSN: https://www. csusm.edu/nursing/prospective/programs/pro_lvnbsn/

LaGuardia Community College LPN to RN: https://www.laguardia.edu/ LPNtoRNPathway/

Prairie View A&M University (Texas) LVN to BSN: https://www. pvamu.edu/nursing/academics/undergraduate-degree-programs/lvn-bsn-program/

There are many such programs at state-supported colleges, private colleges, and even in the for-profit sector.

If you are a spouse who also happens to be a former navy hospital corpsman, an army or air force medic, or a Coast Guard health services technician, the state of California will allow you to challenge the state LVN exam (http:// www.bvnpt.ca.gov/pdf/method4.pdf). The Texas Board of Nursing has programs to assist former enlisted medical personnel to receive credit toward nursing programs (see https://www.bon.texas.gov/military.asp). The state of Illinois has programs to assist former enlisted medical personnel become Licensed Practical Nurses: https://www.illinois.gov/veterans/programs/ Pages/StateLicensesMilitaryTraining.aspx. Check with your state board of licensing for nurses to find out policies that may help enlisted medical veterans.

BEGINNING THE SEARCH AND EVALUATING PROGRAMS

The process of obtaining a license or certification varies greatly based upon the subject. It can even vary greatly based upon the state in which you are pursuing the program. Speaking to an education counselor at the local education center may be the best way to assist you in your search, although it's possible that even the counselor may not know the exact process for your field of interest. There are literally hundreds of certifications and licenses across the United States, but once you begin your research it's typically not too difficult to find the information you need.

Speaking with someone already in the field will save you a significant amount of time and effort. They have already completed the pathway and should have a solid grasp of the type of training that needs to be completed, which programs are accredited, and the names of any tests you need to take. Also, speak to the academic advisors at the institutions you find that offer the required training. They tend to keep their ears to the ground concerning the industry they are targeting to ensure the integrity of their program, but it would be wise to verify any information they provide you with solid research to make sure that the school is reputable.

Try to find either the body or organization that accredits the programs that help you prepare for the exam or the organization that administers the exam. For example, searching "social work accreditation" on the Internet will bring up the Council on Social Work Education (CSWE) as one of the first links. At this point you need to determine whether this is the premier accreditor, then verify the information you found by finding corroborating sources from other websites. Also, all of the states found at www.socialworklicensure.org maintain that attending a CSWE-accredited school is a must, and that this is the determining feature in an individual's pursuit of taking the state board of social work licensing exam. The organization that administers the tests that are required to become licensed or certified in that state can produce the same results. Using Wisconsin as an example, a Google search of "social worker certification Wisconsin" brings you to the Wisconsin Department of Safety and Professional Services, which outlines the requirements to become a social worker in that state. The very last step lists the certification exams that must be taken in order to earn the license.

In some cases, specific training is not always required, and seeking the certification may be optional, but it might also make you more marketable. For example, to become a certified welder, you can choose to take the exam from the American Welding Society (AWS). If you pass, you can become certified without any prerequisite training. It's common for many private organizations or community colleges to offer training that assists potential applicants in passing the exam. The programs can be as extensive as a two-year welding associate's degree at a community college or a set of study material offered for a cost by a private business that specializes in selling training material for different industries. Having an associate's degree in welding might give your resume a boost as the starting pay with potential employers might be higher, or it might offer you more rapid career advancement. Deciding on what to pursue for your particular career goal is key, since, as a spouse, there may be a multitude of other factors impacting your decision.

Conducting research on the career field that you are interested in might even demonstrate to you that there is a particular need for the occupation in your area. Communities with large elderly populations may have a greater need for LPNs or caregivers. An area with a large industrial complex may require different certifications, such as a mechanized robotics certification, of which Fuji Automatic Numerical Controls (FANUC) has created training titled CERT, or Certified Education in Robot Training.

Requirements for robotics certification, or training with automated machines in the factory or warehouse setting, vary widely because there are a large variety of machines operated by different companies. Robotics technicians require many different skills in order to maintain viability. The National Robotics Training Center (NRTC) offers its own certification titled the Certified Robotics Production Technician (CRPT), and the Robotics Industries Associations (RIA) offers the RIA Certified Robot Integrator certification.

Areas with large populations of children, such as military bases, may need daycare, so an early childhood education certification may lead to better employment. Think about the child-care centers on many military bases. If you are interested in this type of work, then pursuing an early childhood credential might help you find employment at one of these centers.

Career fields such as caregiving tend to have optional certifications, but seeking training and becoming nationally certified through the American Caregiver Association (ACA) might give you a leg up on your resume. This field is not regulated at the national level, and states may have their own caregiver requirements. For example, the Professional Association of Caregivers (PAC) offers training specifically suited to becoming certified in Illinois and California but can still assist with other states. Many states require no training at all. Reaching out to people you may know that are already working in that career field, or contacting various organizations that you are interested in working for, can be informative in a situation such as this. Ask the people you contact whether obtaining this certification would be a benefit for your resume as you apply for positions.

Some certifications require prior knowledge in order to be successful on the test, and others might require you to hold a bachelor's degree in order to be eligible to take the test. Many advanced certifications require both: experience in the field and a degree. The Chartered Financial Analyst (CFA) credential requires a bachelor's degree and four years of professional work experience in the field in order for applicants to be eligible to sit for the exam. While the credential is not required, much like the certified welders certification, it can be a boost to your professional career. The pass rates for the three exams for the CFA (which can be viewed at https://www.cfainstitute.org/programs/cfaprogram/Documents/1963_current_candidate_exam_results.pdf) are fairly low: 42 percent for the first exam, 46 percent for the second, and 54 percent for the third. To earn the CFA, charter applicants must pass all three exams.

If the credential is not mandatory to work in that career field, you will need to decide whether such a certification is useful for you. While your ability to excel in a particular career field is important, if you have the opportunity to enhance your resume through credentialing, you should take advantage of it. For example, the Project Management Professional (PMP) certification is similar to the CFA, but eligibility for the PMP only requires a high school diploma, not a four-year degree. Although not a requirement for a job, it is still a huge selling feature on a resume for those who have obtained it. Many people that attempt the PMP have a bachelor's or master's degree. While the degree is not a prerequisite, having the educational background can assist you on the exam.

Some states are split on how to accredit their programs. For example, licensed professional counselor (LPC) credentials can vary greatly by state. Some states use the National Counselor Exam (NCE) to attest to licensing, and other states use the National Certified Mental Health Counseling Examination (NCMHCE). The mix of licensing and certification terms confuses the topic. In most cases, an internship or practicum is required, which means you must work in a particular field and be monitored by a supervisor for a specified period of time. The qualifications of your supervisor will dictate whether your internship or practicum is sufficient to meet the needs of the state. In this case, check with your state to determine the best course of action.

Other programs, such as nursing, tend to be more streamlined across the states. The Commission of Collegiate Nursing Education (CCNE) and the Accrediting Commission for Education in Nursing (ACEN) are the primary bodies that accredit nursing programs. These two organizations accredit nurses for all of the states and are recognized by the US Secretary of Education. Typically, students begin in a school as non-nursing degree students, complete a set of prerequisite classes, and then apply to gain admissions into the nursing program. Prerequisite classes can include psychology, lifespan development, anatomy and physiology, microbiology, and statistics. In addition to the prerequisite courses, a competitive GPA will be required. Some programs are impacted, meaning that there are more students trying to gain admission into the program than there are available seats. This is typical in California, where it is very difficult to gain admission into most nursing programs, especially those offered at the state-supported institutions. These programs might have a waiting list or offer admission on a point-based system. This may affect your ability to be accepted into the program.

The National Registry of Emergency Medical Technicians (NREMT) certification is required for almost all emergency responders. A college-level course of four to five SHs with a one-credit-hour lab that allows for practical application of the material is required for the Emergency Medical Technology (EMT) certification, and then you must take and pass the test for the national registry. The lab might also require that students spend time working in a hospital under the supervision of a nurse or a doctor. Unlike many academic courses, such as English or psychology, you cannot miss class very often. Your ability to attend class will directly impact your ability to take the test, because if you do not complete a certain number of semester hours, you will not be allowed to sit for the National Registry test.

A teacher's certification is one of the most highly sought-after certifications for spouses due to its portability, because all states require teachers. While a teaching credential can offer spouses the mobility to work in different states, the requirements can vary by state. Some sites, such as www.teach.com, can get you started, but you should contact the state government to inquire about the details. For example, if one wants to become a teacher in California, they should look up the requirements on the California Commission on Teacher Credentialing website (http://www.ctc.ca.gov/).

A typical pathway to earning a teacher credential requires the following:

- Complete a successful program of education such as a bachelor's or master's degree in education or a specific subject matter. Bachelor's degrees typically require a separate teacher-credentialing program that amounts to more than the typical four years necessary for a bachelor's degree.
- Pass the state exam. Which exam you take depends on the state in which you are trying to earn the credential.
- Complete the student teaching portion. Student teaching can require a length of time in the classroom that might be anywhere between six weeks and four months.

While the pathway to becoming a teacher is similar in each state, states differ in that they may require that new teachers enter into monitored programs upon receiving employment in order to gain a cleared credential, such as in California. New teachers in California must enter the Beginning Teacher Support and Assessment (BTSA) Induction program (program takes two years to complete) and clear their preliminary credentials within five years of receiving the preliminary credential or they lose it.

During most bachelor's degree programs for teaching, the student teaching portion takes place during the fourth year of the program. It requires hands-on instruction time under the supervision of a master teacher. This is when you apply the information and knowledge you gained in the degree program to practical use as well as gain valuable classroom management skills. Other bachelor's degree programs require that the credentialing and student teaching portion be completed after the bachelor's degree is earned.

The last option is to enter into a master's degree in education or teaching upon completion of a bachelor's degree. The master's degree must have an attached teacher-credentialing program. If your undergraduate degree is not in a related field, you might have to complete a few prerequisite classes in order to be considered for the program.

The National Certification Board (NCB) offers an optional test that might assist you in demonstrating your ability to teach a certain subject or area. Like many certifications, it can give you a leg up in the area. The tests range from English language arts, to music, and science. Achieving this certification might make you more competitive for employment or gain you more pay.

Teaching children does not necessarily require a degree. The early child-hood education (ECE) field requirements can vary across states, but one of the mostly widely held certificates is the CDA, or Child Development Associate. It is not an associate's degree but implies that the holder is an associate of a teacher for the age group of infant to age five. It requires a high school diploma, work with children up to the age of five in the last five years, and an assessment of your skills, typically by the teacher you are assisting. There is no formal test for qualification since no formal certification or license is required. This field is referred to as a credential, which, as mentioned before, is a general way of saying that something has been earned. The CDA is good for three years, and every five years after that.

Becoming associated with and active in the associations that are important to your field will assist you in finding employment and making the maximum amount of pay possible.

In some cases, joining an association that supports the certification will net you better options. The National Association of the Education of Young Children (NAEYC) supports the CDA, administered by the Council of Professional Development (http://www.naeyc.org/content/cda-candidates). Joining this organization can give your resume a boost when applying to become an ECE caregiver.

Some fields, such as nursing and project management, may require taking professional development units (PDUs) or continuing education units (CEUs), which are additional training courses that help to keep the participant current in that topic. While not always required, CEUs and PDUs allow professionals to take additional education that shows potential employers that they are staying updated in their fields.

WHAT DO I NEED, AND HOW DO I OBTAIN IT?

The process to obtaining your educational goal can be diverse, may have a national requirement, or might vary by state. Knowing where you will be living when you begin looking for employment is important. Since titles of positions can change based on the state you live in, projecting ahead to determine the requirements for your program based upon your location is important. For example, the pathway to become a counselor seems complicated at first look. Titles for counselors can include all of the following: licensed professional counselor (LPC), licensed mental health counselor (LMHC), licensed clinical professional counselor (LCPC), or licensed professional clinical counselor (LPCC). Once you begin searching the field within the state where you want to practice, you will find that one title is more prevalent than another.

Although the titles are different, the educational pathways for the above-mentioned titles are similar: a master's degree in the field and many documented contact hours working with patients under the supervision of a licensed counselor. Sometimes the school you attend will have an avenue for you to obtain the contact hours through a partnership with a local mental health facility. Other times, finding a position to work in to fulfill the contact hour requirement will fall on you. Establishing whether you or the school will be in charge of this will allow you to plan more effectively for your licensing progression.

There are two different tests available for state licensing as a counselor, the National Counselor Examination for Licensure and Certification (NCE) and the National Clinical Mental Health Counseling Examination (NCMHCE). To determine which test your state demands, check the National Board for Certified Counselors (NBCC) directory of state licensure board information (http://www.nbcc.org/Exam/StateLicensureExamRegistration). Also, joining the NBCC and participating in the training the organization offers is another way in which you can demonstrate to potential employers that you are staying current in your field.

Determining the correct course of action requires knowing what your education and career goals are and learning how to obtain them. In some cases, it may be as easy as a three-week course, in others it may be a lengthier process, and it may change drastically per state. Military spouses must pay special attention to program lengths, since many programs are not transferable. This means that you must consider the total amount of time you will spend completing any prerequisite classes, the degree or certificate, and preparing for and taking a state exam if necessary. Compare this against the amount of time your active-duty sponsor has left at that duty station or before separation from the service and decide whether it is enough to complete the program. If not, you may wish to consider an online program that might offer you the flexibility to begin the program in one state and finish it in another.

Spouses often pursue and complete different credentials over the span of their time spent within the military population. Conducting career research on each field before beginning the corresponding educational program will give you a better idea of the longevity of the career field and the payoff of the training. Use the tools outlined in chapter 3, such as Kuder® Journey, for help. Be aware that even with meticulous planning there simply might not be any options available in the area. Installations that are located in more remote areas may offer less, such as Fort Irwin, Fort Drum, or Twentynine Palms, MCAGCC. In these cases, spouses tend to take advantage of local opportunities regardless of what they may be simply to bring in more household income.

If you find yourself in this situation, look to see what options are available for employment aboard the base or nearby. Consider where you might be stationed next and look to see what certifications you can complete online—for example, a real estate licensing program or personal training certifications. Two programs to consider for these pathways are the real estate program through Saddleback College (http://www.saddleback.edu/edbs/real-estate), if you are in California, or the International Sports Science Association's personal training certificate, available online (https://www.issaonline.edu/certification/personal-trainer-certification/).

Forming realistic goals is the first place to start in order to begin planning what you need to do. You may be a registered nurse with a bachelor's of science degree in nursing (BSN), but if the nearby institution does not offer an Advanced Practice Registered Nurse (APRN) or a postgraduate credential in nursing, then you may be stuck with your limited career progression for the time being. At some point, the service member will leave the service, so planning ahead and being able to take advantage of the service member's time on contract will allow you to be ready to hit the ground running later. This way you can formulate a plan for your education and training at your post-transition destination.

Try to find training opportunities that might be available online to help you stay current in the field. This may give your resume a boost if you are applying for admission to a postgraduate program located in your final destination.

Most degree programs require a full load of general education subject classes—think math, English, social and behavioral sciences, natural sciences, and others. This includes two-year and four-year degree programs. This means that a significant amount of your time will be spent on general education classes. Since these topics rarely require hands-on work, many schools offer them through an online format. Sometimes even courses such as speech communication and natural science labs can be completed online. While some schools have successfully transitioned these courses to an online format, you should first check on whether any future programs you may enroll in accept credit completed online. Getting these courses out of the way first allows you to be ready to start the program you are ultimately seeking more quickly if your circumstances change in the future.

CONSIDERATIONS AS A MILITARY SPOUSE

The biggest game killer I run into during counseling is time. Many programs, particularly a teacher's certification, will usually require time spent in the program during the day. This means you must not have a job during the day that conflicts with the time required during classroom instruction. The following are a few of the considerations you might want to think about before settling on a program:

- What are your career goals, and how long will it take to achieve the corresponding educational pathway?
- Do your goals require certification or licensure?
- Does this certification or licensure change by state?
- How long will you be at your spouse's current duty location?
- Are there schools located within the local community that can help you reach this goal?
- If not, what can you do during this time?
- How can you afford this education or training?

In some cases, credits or course work may not transfer. This would result in you repeating the course work. Even if you have the time to complete the program, you then have to determine whether the program can assist you at your next location or once your service member separates from the military.

If you have children, finding local options is usually the easiest factor in determining the program's viability, followed by any current employment demands held by the spouse. Money is typically tight for families of service members holding junior ranks, so some spouses choose to begin working right away. You should also consider what the long-term outcome of the program might have on your income versus the short-term benefit of maintaining employment but not attending school.

Other important factors for military spouses pursuing training options can include the availability of daycare. The waiting list for reduced-cost daycare on some installations can be long, sometimes over a year. It can also still be expensive. This is why many spouses pursue early childhood education

(ECE) and run daycares out of their homes if they live on base. Nonexistent daycare options on base may also lead to more ECE opportunities for spouses who live off base in the local communities.

Spouses with older children may have more time to attend daytime training, which as previously mentioned, is a requirement for some fields. In most cases, this also allows the spouse to hold a job during the day while the children are at school. For example, if the spouse wishes to be a dental assistant, it would be rare to find work at night. Dental assistants work during the day when dentist offices are open.

Take advantage of any changes in service or new orders your active-duty sponsor might have coming in—for example, PCS orders, length of contract changes, reenlistments, or reclassification of the service member's occupation—and plan your time accordingly. As an example, if you are in the last year of a teacher certification program and have PCS orders in the middle of the year, you may have difficulty switching schools, since residency hours must be established at a particular school. Moving to a new location could disrupt the process. In some of these cases, military families may decide that the service member will PCS before the family and move as a geo-bachelor in order to allow the spouse or child to complete their programs. This can lead to significant added costs, such as paying rent in two different locations.

Deployments, TDYs, or time aboard a ship can put more pressure on a spouse. In these cases the spouse is maintaining the household while the service member is away. The extra demands of being the only parent available to take care of the children, the house, and other concerns combined with job demands are hard to manage, and attending a training program may just be too much to add to the mixture at this point. If the program has an online portion and a face-to-face portion, attending the online portion might be possible while your active-duty sponsor is away and might allow you to get moving on the program while saving the face-to-face portion for after the service member's return. Whether this is an option will most likely depend on the type of training you are trying to accomplish. Hands-on vocational training tends to have a more strict and rigid schedule, whereas white collar in nature programs might offer more online possibilities. Keep in mind that service member's pay may be tax free during a deployment, and expenses are sometimes reduced as well, so this means that the employment demands placed upon a spouse during this time might be lessened, giving him or her more time to participate in a program.

Spouses should be sure to use the local resources for support during these times. Many installations have family support groups or other agencies such as the Navy and Marine Corps Relief Society that can provide assistance. Sometimes there are also nonprofit organizations located in communities surrounding the base that are geared to supporting military families. Consider connecting with other spouses who might be able to lend a hand to help out. As an example, some spouses trade babysitting times to help each other facilitate their educations or training programs. Take advantage of the youth services offered by most installations. After-school care programs help if your training program ends after the normal school-day hours. While these services are not typically free, they do not tend to be too expensive on military bases.

With careful planning, licensing and certification programs can be completed while the service member is still on active duty. Scheduling may require patience and persistence on your part, but don't forget that you can take advantage of the education center services to help you create a plan. Comprehensive planning will save you the stress of finding yourself in danger of receiving bad grades, moving in the midst of a nontransferable pathway, or wasting valuable financial resources such as your own funds, MyCAA, transferred GI Bill benefits, or financial aid. Maintain realistic goals, and do not force your life to fit into the requirements of a program; fit the requirements of the program into your life.

Many military spouses successfully complete licensing or certification programs and go on to lead fulfilling careers. The boost in income can be a benefit and makes most programs financially worthwhile. With the right planning and research, many credentials are possible to attain. While it requires hard work, if you are determined to earn your credential, take into account the requirements of the program, and do not overload yourself in the process, anything is possible.

Chapter Six

What Should I Look for in a School?

Choosing a school requires students to consider their personal needs first. Schools are not all the same, and neither are military spouses' educational needs. Your best possible choice for an institution might be the worst possible choice for another spouse. This chapter outlines important institutional factors that will assist you in making an educated decision. The following topics are discussed:

• Types of schools
• Accreditation
• Admission requirements
• Admission process (including essays)
• Standardized admissions tests

TYPES OF SCHOOLS

You have learned about the tools available to help assist in your research, now you need to know what to look for during the search. Different types of schools serve different purposes. Understanding the differences will help you make a more educated and empowered decision.

In most cases, career choices determine the type of institution you should attend. For example, are you taking a vocational or traditional pathway? Do you need a two-year degree or a four-year degree? If two years are sufficient, then you can eliminate most four-year universities from your search. Narrowing your search by a few key factors will help in the selection process.

Technical schools, community colleges, universities, public and private, not-for-profit and for-profit schools have different guiding factors and structures. This section offers brief explanations of the types of schools and how to choose the one that best suits your needs.

Two-Year Schools

Two-year schools are community colleges (CCs) or technical schools. Most are state based, but not always. CCs offer the following:

- Associate's degrees
- Transfer pathways to universities and colleges
- Certificate programs
- Vocational programs that might include apprenticeship opportunities
- Open enrollment, which is especially good if you had trouble with your high school GPA
- No SAT, ACT, or essay required, but may be used to potentially bypass taking the math and English placement exams
- Significantly cheaper tuition and fees than universities and colleges
- More available locations

Two-year community colleges can help students save money and lessen the financial burden college can place on a military family. Students can spend up to two years at the full-time rate of pursuit at a community college before a transfer to a more expensive four-year institution becomes necessary. Many CCs offer specific transfer pathways into the four-year schools located in the state and sometimes for institutions located across the country as well.

Because community colleges are usually found in numerous locations throughout each state, they are easy to find and often convenient to your home, which is helpful because most do not offer on-campus housing. The open-enrollment policy makes for a stress-free transition from being an active-duty family to a veteran family and is the fastest way to start school. Most of the service members and spouses I (Jillian) assist opt for a community college while they are on active duty because of the lower cost and flexible learning options. Sometimes it is the only pathway, especially if university admission deadlines have passed.

Most CCs offer vocational programs that require an associate's degree or a certification process. Many of the vocational pathways also offer significant hands-on learning options, such as apprenticeship programs or on-the-job training options. Attending a vocational program at a state CC gives you a safe, regionally accredited option to transfer credits if you decide later to pursue a bachelor's degree at another regionally accredited school.

Always check with the specific school about the program you would like to attend. Some programs, such as nursing and radiologic technologist, are impacted. This means there are more students than spots available, so acceptance may be delayed. A nearby for-profit school may offer more than enough seats for their students in these types of programs, but you are usually paying a higher premium in tuition for this option. Therefore, knowing the differences between the types of schools available to attend allows you to make the best decision possible.

Community colleges frequently offer internships and apprenticeships within the surrounding community. These programs may help you gain employment at a faster rate, generate work experience for a resume, or credential you for a specific career. Often these pathways are attached to an associate of applied science (AAS) degree. AAS degrees do not require students to take a full course of general education subjects. Typically, they will only require basic freshman-level math and English courses. This can mean faster program completion and a quicker route into the workforce. AAS degrees are not designed as transfer pathways to four-year institutions in most cases. The two main purposes of the AAS degree are skills development for entry-level employment or advancement in an existing position. Some classes, though, may still be transferable.

Four-Year Schools

Colleges and universities are four-year schools. Each state has a state university system, but not all colleges and universities are state based, as you will read about in the next few paragraphs. Four-year schools can offer the following:

- Bachelor's degrees
- Research institutions, centers, and programs
- May specialize in different fields—for example, liberal arts or technology
- Financial aid (four-year colleges can be very expensive)
- On- and off-campus enrichment opportunities, such as study abroad and guest lecture series
- Various fields of study that offer a wide range of job opportunities

- Broader range of course selection than community colleges
- Large, diverse campuses and populations at some of the bigger universities and state schools; smaller campuses and smaller, more familiar class sizes at smaller liberal arts colleges
- Competitive admission process
- On-campus housing possibilities

Many universities also have graduate schools, where students can continue their studies to obtain advanced degrees such as an MA, PhD, MD, or JD. Before going to graduate school, however, students must finish their undergraduate course work, and typically another admission process is necessary for acceptance.

Some schools have developed combined bachelor's and master's degree programs. These programs usually have two pathways toward completion and awarding of the degrees, concurrent or one at a time. If the program runs concurrently, then students complete the requirements for both the bachelor's and the master's degree at the same time. Otherwise, the student would complete the bachelor's degree first, then move on to their graduate-level studies.

Sometimes these dual-degree programs can assist in expediting the overall time a student spends in school by consolidating a pathway that usually takes six years into just five. They often do not require a graduate admission test if the student maintains a minimum GPA. This helps the students get into the workforce faster, cuts down on overall tuition and testing expenses, and eliminates the need for a student to spend long hours preparing for the graduate entrance exam.

Attending a university can sometimes be overwhelming. Classes can be so large that you never have a one-on-one conversation with your professor, which sometimes makes students feel anonymous. Finding your niche might take some time in a large population, but it will afford you more opportunities to interact. Large institutions usually offer numerous degrees and classes to choose from; smaller liberal arts colleges may be a bit more specialized.

If you feel that a four-year institution might be too much, too soon, or you simply do not have the time to organize all of the required admission documents, starting at the local community college might be the best option. Many civilian students take this path for the same reason. Community colleges are also beneficial for students who might need more one-on-one attention during their studies, or simply have not been to school in a long time and feel safer in a smaller, less competitive environment. Whatever the case, arm yourself with information before making a decision. Sometimes a visit to the campus will settle the issue. The school should be a comfortable fit because you will be spending a significant amount of time there.

Some of you might be foreign nationals and met your military spouses while they were stationed abroad. You might also be considering returning to your country to attend college after your spouse's service commitment is up. Veterans can often use their Post-9/11 GI Bill benefits to study abroad, though they must attend a GI Bill–approved foreign institution. You can check to see whether the school he or she is interested in attending is approved on the GI Bill Comparison Tool website (https://www.vets.gov/gi-bill-comparison-tool).

Study abroad can be a fun option. Students may diversify their resumes by demonstrating global understanding of their subject of study. Learning new cultural perspectives through interactions in a foreign environment enhances your education and broadens your community reach. Some students who opt for study abroad are also able to become proficient in a foreign language.

Preparing correctly for study abroad takes some time. Participating in a study abroad program offered through your institution in the United States is a safe option. Attending a foreign institution for your entire degree will require a bit of research first. Most foreign schools do not abide by the regional accreditation that is preferred for traditional education in the United States. This can cause future problems. Make sure to find out whether the degree can be translated in the United States prior to committing.

Information on foreign degree or credit evaluation can be found on the National Association of Credential Evaluation Services (NACES) website (http://www.naces.org/). If the degree from the foreign institution you are considering attending cannot be evaluated by US standards, you may have difficulty later. You run the risk that a potential employer may not value your degree or that an advanced degree program may not recognize the level of education you have achieved.

Public Schools (Universities and Community Colleges)

Public schools, often referred to as "state schools," are typically funded by state and local governments. In-state residents pay lower tuition charges than out-of-state students. Some schools' out-of-state tuition charges can total an extra $10,000 or more per academic year. Sometimes state schools have reciprocal agreements with schools in other states that allow for reduced out-of-state tuition charges—for example, the Midwest Student Exchange Program (MSEP; http://msep.mhec.org/). MSEP has nine participating states with public schools that charge undergraduate students a maximum of 150 percent of the in-state tuition charges and private schools that offer a 10 percent reduction in tuition. More information on other reciprocal agreements made by states within the different regions of the United States can be found in chapter 7, "Cost and Payment Resources."

State schools offer a wide range of classes, degree options, and degree levels, and often state residents get priority admission. Class sizes at state schools can be a concern. Sometimes more than 250 students may be enrolled in a lecture class. This can make it difficult to interact with professors or staff.

Most states have a flagship university with smaller locations available throughout the state for easier access. In some instances, students attending state universities cannot graduate in the standard four-year time frame because mandatory classes are often full. If you are considered a military student by the registrar's office—for example, you are using transferred GI Bill benefits or potentially through the MyCAA program—many institutions now offer priority registration to this population. This might enable you to maintain full-time status while using transferred GI Bill benefits so that you would qualify for full-time benefits, or simply gain you admission into classes that might otherwise be full.

Also keep in mind that public schools are not specifically profit driven and can therefore fall prey to many of the ills that affect any state-administered institution, such as a large amount of bureaucracy and poor customer service. This, of course, does not mean you should avoid public institutions. Just be prepared to research as much as possible and be your own best advocate when seeking assistance and help. If you sent an email or called an advisor at the school and have not received a response, ask to speak to a supervisor and let it be known that you are not receiving the assistance you require.

Private Schools

Private schools do not receive funding from state or local government. They are financially supported by tuition costs, donations, and endowments. They may be nonprofit or for-profit in nature, traditional or nontraditional. Private schools usually charge students the same price whether they are in-state or out-of-state residents. The cost of private school tuition is often more than resident tuition at a state school, but not always. Many private schools offer scholarships and grants to greatly reduce the tuition costs. Usually, private schools have smaller class sizes than public schools, which can mean greater access to your professor. Private school acceptance may be less competitive than state acceptance, but not in top-tier or Ivy League institutions. Some private schools have religious affiliations, are historically black or Hispanic-serving institutions, or are single-sex institutions.

Think about the tuition costs of a private university similarly to the sticker price when buying a car. Unlike public schools, which are required by the state government to charge a specific price, high prices at private schools can sometimes be overcome. If the institution really wants to have you as a student, it may reduce the amount of tuition by offering scholarships. Typically, these are not traditional scholarships; instead, they allow private schools to reduce the amount of tuition at a school through in-house benefits. The amount of tuition paid by a student can vary greatly.

Be upfront with the institution if you are not able to cover all of the tuition and fees. You might still be able to attend depending upon the interest level of the school and the type of student they are looking to add to their classrooms. The cost of college is exploding, so talk to the counselors and the financial aid department during the process; it may save you thousands of dollars in the long run.

Be informed when choosing your school. The College Board reported average costs of published state-school tuition and fees for the 2015–2016 school year at $9,400, and average private-school tuition and fees at $32,405.[1] That is a significant difference in cost to make up.

For-Profit Institutions

The difference between for-profit and not-for-profit basically is in the title. For-profit schools are operated by businesses, are revenue based, and have to account for profits and losses. According to a recent government report on for-profit schools, the "financial performance of these companies is closely tracked by analysts and by investors"; this means that the bottom line is always revenue.[2] For-profit schools typically have open enrollment. Open enrollment can be helpful when you are transitioning from the military and have many other urgent needs at the same time. Open enrollment means that everyone gains entry to the school. That may prove disastrous for an individual who is not ready for the demands of higher education, but if the student is well prepared, it might provide a good pathway.

If you are looking for ease in the transition process and flexible class start dates, for-profit schools can offer you that benefit. Usually, they have classes starting every eight weeks, or the first Monday of every month, with rolling start dates.

For-profit institutions are inherently private, so cost concerns are similar to those described in the private institutions section. They have come under fire recently by Congress for several reasons, including their intake of Federal Student Aid (FSA) and GI Bill money. If you would like more information, see http://www.help.senate.gov/imo/media/for_profit_report/PartI.pdf or http://www.sandiego.edu/veterans-clinic/.

Not-for-Profit Institutions

According to the National Association of Independent Colleges and Universities, "private, not-for-profit higher education institutions' purposes are to offer diverse, affordable, personal, involved, flexible, and successful educations to their students."[3]

Not-for-profit private schools sometimes offer flexible admissions that many state institutions cannot. Offering flexible admissions is a school-specific benefit, and you should address that option with the institutions you are considering attending.

Some private, not-for-profit schools like Harvard and Yale can have tremendous name recognition. On a smaller scale, many private, not-for-profit colleges and universities are well known within local communities. For example, in my (Jillian's) hometown of Chicago, three well-known private, not-for-profit schools are DePaul University, Loyola University, and Columbia College. Each of these schools enjoys an excellent reputation, has a comprehensive veterans' department (needed if you are using transferred GI Bill benefits), and is well known throughout the Midwest.

Attending this type of school is typically a safe pathway, especially when listing your school on a resume. Be aware that private schools can be very expensive, and the cost can sometimes be prohibitive. For example, DePaul is roughly $34,500 per academic year.

Vocational-Technical and Career Colleges

Vocational-technical (votech) schools and career colleges prepare students for skill-based careers in technical fields. Many technical schools are state run, subsidized, and regionally accredited. Credits from these schools are generally accepted elsewhere. Career colleges are private, usually for-profit institutions, and they mostly hold national accreditation. Credits from these schools may not be widely transferable.

Programs at these schools can run anywhere from ten months to four years, depending on the skills required to finish training. Many have rolling admissions. Programs often run year-round, including the summer, in order to get students into the workforce faster.

Typically, in a votech-based program, general education classes such as English and math are not necessary. Program completion results in a certificate of completion or an associate's degree in applied science. The associate in applied science will require entry-level math and English classes. Votech schools focus directly on the task at hand, meaning training for an industry that is skill based and preparing students for a career.

If you have decided to take a votech pathway, research the school's cost, credentials, faculty, program requirements, and student body prior to committing to a specific institution. Cost is important. Spouses or children using transferred GI Bill benefits must be aware that the GI Bill has a set maximum amount it will pay for private school. Find out whether you will also be eligible to apply for Federal Student Aid (FSA), but remember that you are mainly interested in the Pell Grant. You can find more information regarding student aid in chapter 7.

Determine whether the school is licensed by the state and which accreditation it holds. If the program requires licensing by the state but the school does not have the proper licensing agreement, you might not be able to sit for the state exam. Why go through a program that does not allow you full completion and credentialing? That could translate to a lower-paying job or the inability to get hired in your field.

Ask about the professors' backgrounds and qualifications. Find out whether you will be able to apply for prior learning credit toward the program and if the program includes on-the-job training or internship possibilities. Visit the campus to determine what type of equipment you will be trained on and review the faculty setting. Check the school's completion rates (meaning how many students graduate and whether they graduate on time). Last, verify that the school offers job placement services. Find out the following:

- What is its rate of placement?
- Where are students being placed?
- What positions are they getting right out of school?
- How much money are they earning?

Usually, a phone call and follow-up school visit are required to fully understand the program benefits. Remember that vocational fields prepare students for specific career pathways, so transitioning later to a different pathway will require retraining.

Votech schools usually hold national accreditation. Make sure to review the accreditation section later in this chapter, which explains the difference between regional and national accreditation. Nationally accredited programs' credits frequently cannot transfer into a regionally accredited school, although some exceptions exist at schools that hold dual accreditation. For this reason, always check the local community college for similar programs. Many community colleges offer vocational programs that can be converted later to transferable college credit.

ACCREDITATION

Accreditation is an often-overlooked topic that all students need to consider prior to making a final selection on an institution of higher learning. Most students I counsel are not aware of the different types of accreditation that schools may hold but should take the time to research the topic. Selecting a school with the wrong type may cause you significant backtracking at a later date.

The United States does not have a formal federal authority that oversees higher education. Each individual state exercises some level of regulation, but generally speaking, colleges and universities have the ability to self-govern. Accrediting organizations were born to supervise and guide institutions of higher learning to assure students that they were receiving valuable educations. The organizations develop and maintain specific standards for participating schools that hold the institutions accountable for the quality of education they are delivering. The standards "address key areas such as faculty, student support services, finance and facilities, curricula and student learning outcomes."[4]

Accredited schools adhere to the accrediting bodies' standards. Having accreditation is like having quality control for higher education, and when searching for schools, it should be an important factor to consider. Students who attend accredited universities and colleges have a greater chance of receiving a quality education and benefiting from their degrees.

Ultimately, attending an accredited institution means that "a student can have confidence that a degree or credential has value."[5] If a school does not hold accreditation, you will most likely not be able to apply for federal or state-based financial aid. Credit hours earned from nonaccredited schools will not usually transfer into accredited institutions and will not be recognized for entrance into most master's degree programs.

Typically, students need to look for institutional accreditation and possibly programmatic accreditation. Institutional accreditation means that the college or university as a whole is accredited. This enables the entire school to maintain credibility as a higher-learning institution. Only regional or national accrediting agencies can give institutional accreditation.

The degree you choose will dictate the type of accreditation you will need. Traditional degrees such as education, engineering, business, anthropology, and criminal justice require regional accreditation. Nontraditional degrees might (or might not) require national accreditation. In addition, nontraditional education encompasses subjects that are more vocational in nature, such as welding and electrical work.

Every single state school (state community colleges, state colleges, and state universities) in this country holds regional accreditation. Regional accreditation is the most widely recognized and transferable (credit hours) accreditation in this country. There are six regional accrediting bodies in the United States. The accrediting bodies are based on the region of the country:

- Middle States Association of Colleges and Schools: http://www.msche. org/
- New England Association of Schools and Colleges: http://cihe.neasc.org/
- Higher Learning Commission: https://www.hlcommission.org/
- Northwest Commission on Colleges and Universities: http://www.nwccu. org/
- Southern Association of Colleges and Schools: http://www.sacscoc.org/

- Western Association of Schools and Colleges (two organizations: one for four-year schools and one for two-year schools): http://www.wascweb. org/, http://www.accjc.org/

Regional accrediting organizations review schools in their entirety. Both public and private and two- and four-year schools can be reviewed. Holding regional accreditation should allow credits to transfer smoothly between different member schools depending upon the established transfer criteria at the receiving institution. Remember: ultimately, the college or university to which you are trying to transfer has final say on credit transferability.

Schools that hold national accreditation generally offer educational pathways that are more vocational (nontraditional) in nature. This type of education might lead to a completed apprenticeship program or certification. Vocational education is a means of training future workers with skills more directly relevant to the evolving needs of the workforce. These types of career fields are more hands on and technical in nature. Many nationally accredited schools can offer students successful pathways to promising careers. The programs are designed to get students into the workforce as soon as possible, and they can usually be completed in two years or less, significantly faster than a four-year bachelor's degree.

Students do not need to attend a nationally accredited institution to receive vocational training. Many local state community colleges offer nontraditional education and often have apprenticeship or on-the-job training programs offered in addition to the educational classes. This might be a better pathway if you are unsure of your future career demands. Credits from a state community college are more widely transferable than credits from a nationally accredited institution because they hold regional accreditation. Attending a state community college for a vocational program will most likely give you more flexibility at a later date if you decide to pursue further education, such as a bachelor's degree.

Sometimes institutional accreditation is insufficient and programmatic accreditation is also necessary. Programmatic accreditation is specific to a department within an institution and is often needed for certain degrees above and beyond the institutional accreditation, such as nursing, business, and engineering. Programmatic accrediting organizations focus on specific courses of study offered at a college or university. Attending a program that maintains programmatic accreditation can help your degree be more effective (as in getting you a job!) or make earned credit hours more transferable. If you are not sure whether your degree requires programmatic accreditation, search CHEA's website (http://www.chea.org/Directories/special.asp) for further information.

Choosing a school with the right type of accreditation is important. Credits from a regionally accredited institution usually transfer into a nationally accredited institution, but credits from a nationally accredited institution almost never transfer into a regionally accredited institution. The exception would be if a student was transferring into an institution with dual accreditation, but there are very few in the country. This means that a rigorous search for qualifying information must be made in order to determine the proper academic pathway for an individual's selected career.

In these cases, looking at programmatic or specialized accreditation may be more important than institutional accreditation—in other words, regional or national accreditation. For example, Platt College is nationally accredited but holds the diagnostic sonography accreditation from the Commission on Accreditation of Allied Health Education Programs (CAAHEP). This is the premier accreditation for sonography programs. Therefore, these credits may not transfer to a regional institution, but since the program holds the proper accreditation for sonography, you are generally safe in your ability to find a job in sonography after finishing the degree. You should always do the research to see whether your particular industry requires specialized accreditation, and sometimes this will outweigh its institutional accreditation (regional versus national) in an academic sense. Be aware that if you choose this option, your credits will most likely not transfer at a later date.

To search for a specific school's accreditation or a particular program of interest, go online (at http://www.chea.org/search/default.asp) and agree to the search terms. You can also complete a search of the national accrediting agencies that the US Department of Education considers reliable (http://www2.ed.gov/admins/finaid/accred/accreditation_pg6.html) or on College Navigator (http://nces.ed.gov/collegenavigator/).

ADMISSION REQUIREMENTS

Admission requirements at each school will vary depending upon the type of school, specific degree requirements, and the school's ability to offer flexibility to service members. Some, such as community colleges and many vocational schools, maintain open admission. Others, mainly four-year institutions of higher learning (universities), have a predetermined set of admission qualifications that can be quite rigorous. This section will discuss the possible requirements for admission into colleges and vocational schools.

State-Based Community and Technical Schools

Entrance into a local community or technical college is typically much less stressful than entrance into a four-year university. Attending community college is a great way to get started with school for those who have little or no time to prepare the required documents or manage application deadlines. This is a beneficial option for spouses who often have little time between their active-duty spouse's return from deployment and transitioning off active-duty status. Community colleges also do not have the same rigorous admission requirements that universities demand from potential students. This allows students who lost their time to prepare due to mission demands to still get going on their educations without a delay.

State-based community and technical colleges may offer or require the following:

- Open admission
- Acceptance, in most cases with or without a high school diploma or GED
- Early registration (double check with each institution) for those using transferred GI Bill benefits or MyCAA
- An application fee
- Registration deadlines
- Special entrance criteria (prerequisite classes), and a waiting list for start times in specific, high-demand programs (too many applicants and not enough available open spots)
- English and math placement tests, typically, to determine proper level placement
- Admission application, typically online, that only takes a few minutes
- Supporting documents—for example, high school transcripts and residency proof
- Proof of immunizations

Four-Year Colleges and Universities

Four-year institutions of higher learning usually have selective admissions with application requirements and deadlines. Some may offer flexible admissions, but, in most cases, spouses and dependent children will follow the same pathway as civilians. A written timetable of deadlines for all materials can be obtained by contacting the school and checking the admission section of the website. Be prepared to spend a fair amount of time preparing.

College and university admissions may require the following:

- An application (in most cases, this can be done online)
- Application fees
- ACT and SAT test scores (see the "SAT and ACT Study Help" section)
- Essays
- Letters of recommendation
- A college pathway in high school, meeting minimum subject requirements
- High school and college transcripts
- Minimum high school GPA
- Minimum high school class rank
- Demonstration of community service (there are often many great short-term volunteer opportunities aboard a military base)
- Proof of immunizations

Vocational-Technical and Career Colleges

Depending upon the program to which a student is applying within the school, admission requirements may vary. In certain fields, such as nursing, entrance exams may be mandatory. Exams can include physical fitness tests, basic skills exams, and Health Education Systems, Inc. (HESI) entrance exams.

Always research carefully the career you are choosing to determine whether your certification or license from a career college is valid. Often states have mandatory requirements pertaining to the fields of education taught at a technical school, and students need to verify that the school meets these standards. Always check the state government website; many list the state-approved programs.

Typically, admissions are open with a few minimum requirements, such as the following:

- High school transcript and diploma or GED
- Completed admission forms
- An interview
- Statement of general health
- Any mandatory subject-specific exams

THE ADMISSION PROCESS (INCLUDING ESSAYS)

Most schools generally follow the same admission process, even though the requirements can differ drastically from school to school. Whether a student is an incoming freshman, a transfer student, or an applicant to a vocational school, the pathway to gain admittance will follow the same route, but it may vary in difficulty. Prospective students at schools with an open-enrollment policy will normally have a less intensive pathway to admittance. Students pursuing schools with selective admissions will spend more time preparing.

On a typical pathway, you:

1. pick a school or schools, call the veterans' representatives, discuss admission requirements, and decide on an institution;
2. apply (usually online);
3. receive acceptance; and
4. apply for funding and register for classes (choose classes based on a degree plan).

Pick a School

Contacting a counselor at the education center aboard the base where you are stationed, or were previously stationed if your spouse has already separated, is a great way to find out about the local schools. Many military bases have schools located right on the base, where students can attend face-to-face classes if they wish, or representatives from schools that offer online learning options. Speaking with a counselor should initially give you a good understanding of the schools located in the area. If you are the spouse of a veteran, contact the vet reps at the school you are interested in attending. The vet reps have been there and done that already. If there are any special programs available to military spouses, they will know. This also enables you to identify yourself as a military spouse. Your pathway, cost, and required documents may be different from those for the civilian population, and the vet reps will be able to guide you in your quest for the appropriate resources.

Do the appropriate amount of research and request pertinent information, whether it's on paper or online. You will need to know all relevant information, including application and registration deadlines, financial aid timelines, class start dates, dorm-based information (if applicable) or in-town housing options, and, if you are using transferred GI Bill benefits, who will be your point of contact for GI Bill concerns and the Certificate of Eligibility (COE). This topic is covered in depth in chapter 7, "Cost and Payment Resources."

Apply

You have finished your research and settled on a particular school or schools. Now it is time to apply. Make sure you verify with the vet reps whether you need to pay the application fee; some schools waive the fee for military spouses.

Check the school's website prior to applying. In most cases, schools have an application checklist on their admission page. This should help you prepare all relevant documents such as your personal statement, SAT scores, and immunization records in advance.

Often the application checklist for a four-year college or university does not list a personal statement, but after you begin, the process will surprise you by requiring it. Personal statement length requirements range from 350 to 3,000 words. Some institutions list very specific essay prompts they want you to follow instead of writing a generic personal statement.

Writing a personal statement should not be nerve racking, although many students feel tremendous stress during the experience, most just trying to find a starting point. Once you get going, you will find the experience to be a good precursor to your new college life. College does require a fair amount of writing.

Here are a few steps to guide you through your personal essay. Remember that you have unique experiences the typical applicant will not have. Try to impress on the school how these unique experiences have changed you and will help you to make the school a better place if you attend. Most schools would be lucky to have you as a student with real working knowledge of what it is like to be an adult who has lived past the age of eighteen and endured the demands placed upon military families.

Step 1

If you are having trouble starting, try brainstorming. I recommend sticking to topics related to your experiences within the military community, culture, or your own family. Think about the time you have spent within the military community, the accomplishments you achieved, or the hardships you have overcome. Consider the following topics:

- Did your life change when you married your military spouse?
- What is it like having your loved one in the military?
- What type of experiences have you had?
- Did you volunteer with the military community? If so, did it give you a new, more diverse perspective on the community?
- Did you get any training on how to be a spouse to an active-duty service member? As a military spouse, I (Jillian) get a kick out of this one. If I had gotten some type of training, it might have prepared me to function better during deployments!
- Was your spouse assigned to any special duty stations, maybe overseas, that you accompanied him or her to and that helped to better shape your perspectives pertaining to your academic pursuits and future career goals?
- If you lived overseas, how did you feel living in a foreign culture? Did it change your perspectives?
- Did you ever get to visit your spouse during one of his or her deployments?
- Did your spouse deploy to a war zone? Did he or she experience combat? How did it make you feel? Did it affect your family as a whole?

Keep in mind that you are talking to a board of civilians who may not share the same experiences as a military family. Ask yourself what it means or meant to be part of this lifestyle and why most students will not have had the same types of experiences. Consider this: How many other people your age have had to kiss their husbands or wives goodbye for a deployment that might last a year in which your spouse is dodging bullets or running convoys while you try to maintain as normal a household as possible for your children and not succumb to the stress? Do not underestimate your accomplishments. I (Jillian) became a military spouse in my thirties and am constantly surprised by the day-to-day achievements of many of the very young spouses whom I counsel.

Step 2

Next, typically you can pick a subject and narrow the talking points. Sometimes it helps to brainstorm topics that interest you on paper to see whether subjects overlap. Many spouses think life as a military spouse is not that exciting, but try to keep in mind all of the types of events or gatherings that you have to attend that civilians might find different or interesting—for example, navy ombudsman sponsored events, Jane Wayne Days, or the Marine Corps ball. Where else can you participate in these types of activities? Maybe it is all in a day's work for you, but civilians find it fascinating.

Step 3

Once you settle on a topic, write it down on a piece of paper. Think about the topic, and write brief statements about everything that comes to your mind surrounding it. I like to use a brainstorming cluster, which is simply a bunch of bubbles that help to organize your thoughts (see figure 6.1).

For example: When I (Jillian) became a military spouse I realized that part of my life now belonged to the Marine Corps.

Once you have drawn up a list, you need to add more layers to discuss in your writing. Here is an example:

- Patriotism: American flags, command events, promotion ceremonies, deployments, new military vocabulary, sense of communal pride
- Work: work schedule revolves around my spouse's command/mission demands, must have set hours due to available child-care time frames, work opportunities must be within same geographic location as the base where we are stationed
- Military family: new friends, separation from friends during PCS moves or through retirements, common bonds for spouse and children, strength, consistency in its inconsistency
- Security: military bases, spouse's job security, pay, and promotional opportunities
- The war: participate in command send-offs and welcome-home events, fear of the unknown, test of resiliency, face the unknown, perseverance, offer my deployed spouse emotional support, separation and loss, long-lasting concerns

Step 4

Think about the notes you have written. Narrow your subject or topic by eliminating areas that don't seem to fit. For example, I (Jillian) don't think the section on security follows the theme of the other topics. When I review each section, it seems that my life after my husband joined the military changed mostly within the other categories: work, patriotism, wars, and military family. My experiences due to my husband's military service were vastly different from what they would have been had he not joined. I was not able to continue with the same career pathway due to the many changes in duty

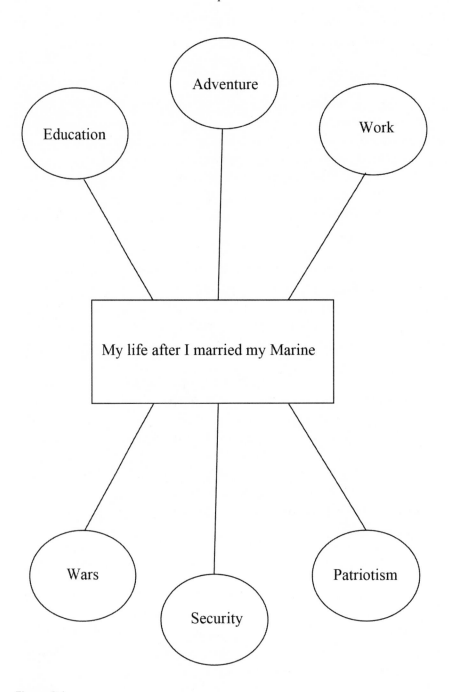

Figure 6.1.

stations that my husband received. I gained a newfound respect for my country and those who choose to serve. My husband's participation in the wars strengthened the bonds of my marriage, and I gained many amazing military friends who supported me during these difficult times.

Step 5

Organize your thoughts in a good writing order, and start to think about expanding the topics into a paper format.

1. Work: work schedule revolves around my spouse's command/mission demands, must have set hours due to available child-care time frames, work opportunities must be within same geographic location as the base where we are stationed
2. Patriotism: American flags, command events, promotion ceremonies, deployments, new military vocabulary, sense of communal pride
3. The wars: participate in command send-offs and welcome-home events, fear of the unknown, test of resiliency, face the unknown, perseverance, offer my deployed spouse emotional support, separation and loss, long-lasting concerns
4. Military family: new friends, separation from friends during PCS moves or through retirements, common bonds for spouse and children, strength, consistency in its inconsistency

Before you begin to write your essay, you need to consider your audience. Here are a few questions to consider while writing:

- Who will read this essay?
- What does the reader already know about this subject, and why is the topic important?
- What do I want the reader to know about this subject?
- What part of my topic is the most interesting?

Your reader could be a dean at the school, an academic counselor, or a professor. Most likely, this individual will have no knowledge of your topic if you write about a particular military experience, but do not discount the fact that she or he could also be a veteran or a military spouse. You need to explain why this experience shaped your decisions moving forward. You want her to see you in a different light than other applicants. You want your essay to stand apart and be more memorable than all of the others. Make sure to pick a topic that you can write about easily and that will attract interest.

I was once told by an admission counselor that the institution she worked for received approximately eighty thousand applicants per year from students seeking admission. This particular school required a personal statement essay. Each admission counselor was required to read at least eighty essays per day during the time period in which the students were selected. The reading went on for a few weeks. Can you imagine how the subject matter covered in the essays could begin to run together? Your job in writing the essay is to produce something that is unique and interesting enough that the admission counselor reading it perks up and pays more attention. In most cases, the other students seeking admission will not have the same military-based experiences to utilize as subject matter that you are able to use for examples.

Essay Example
Married to the Marine Corps

I often joke with my husband that I didn't just marry him; I married him and the entire Marine Corps. I had no idea how much my life would change based on my husband's service. When I consider the areas that changed the most I can point to four topics: career, military lifestyle, military family, and a post-war marriage.

When I decided that it was time to pursue advanced education leading to a new career pathway that would better fit my needs as a military spouse, I pondered these four topics. I realized that separately they didn't seem like much, but combined they had a powerful impact on me and helped lead me to a new career pathway: marriage and family therapist.

My career had taken a back seat to my husband's, as it was difficult to maintain between the multiple permanent change-of-station (PCS) orders. Looking for a career field that would allow me to maintain steady work even through the PCS moves led me to consider an option where I could find a position on any base that we might find ourselves stationed. All of the major bases for my husband's branch of service host counseling services departments that employ marriage and family therapists.

I had new experiences regarding the military lifestyle that would give me insight into the lives of those I might counsel: active-duty personnel, spouses, and dependents. Having this knowledge gives me a better understanding of the demands placed on military personnel and their family members by their service. I also understand many of the family stressors they might be feeling during deployment cycles as my family has faced them as well.

I found a new family of friends through my experiences as a military spouse. Many of us bonded over our shared experiences. Having this network of friends to support me through my spouse's combat deployments enhanced my barrier to the daily stresses I experienced. The little overtures of help the other spouses offered went a long way in helping me survive the seven-month deployments on my own and helped me realize the positive impact a supportive and inclusive environment can make on those involved.

The final factor was my postwar relationship with my husband. He, like many others, underwent a transformation during and after his combat deployments. He came back a slightly different person, so our marriage had to adapt. Having experiences like those our service members faced can have great impacts on a couple—some were good and some were bad. Either way, we find ways to overcome the bad and embrace the good.

Considering my experiences and these four areas of focus, I found that the best option for me was to return to school and pursue advanced education in a career field in which I felt I could make an impact. Choosing a school that offered me the flexibility that I needed along with the proper support was a difficult task. I spent many long hours gathering information on each program. But after reviewing the information, I realized that ABC University was the obvious choice. ABC University's reputation is first rate, and no other institution can offer me the same degree of flexible learning, spousal support, and field placement options that ABC can.

I hope to bring my diverse experience with me into the classroom and to help others gain a more complex understanding of the stressors many military families struggle with. In this way, I will not only learn how to properly assist military families who are seeking assistance or self-betterment but also be able to assist in diversifying the learning environment by shedding light on a much-misunderstood population.

Receive Acceptance

Most open-enrollment schools quickly offer official acceptance. Schools with selective admissions often send official acceptance after many months. Check the school's website for reporting dates, or ask the admission department.

In most cases, your acceptance letter or your student account website will tell you the next steps you must take. These steps may include payment of fees to hold your spot in the school or for on-campus housing. This is typical for face-to-face schooling. If you are pursuing school aboard a military base as an active-duty spouse or dependent child, most likely these extra fees will not be applicable to you. Determine the final date for reimbursement of these fees in case you decide to attend another school at the last minute. That way you will not lose that money!

You have received your school acceptance letters and decided upon an institution. Now it is time to apply for funding assistance. If your spouse is still on active duty, contact the education center closest to you and request assistance in finding funding resources or assistance in learning how or if your spouse might be able to transfer GI Bill benefits to you, and, once the transfer is complete, ask how to apply for and use the benefit. Ask about any military spouse scholarships that might be available. The Camp Pendleton Marine Corps Base Education Center keeps a financial aid resource booklet on their website that might offer a good glimpse into available scholarships (www.mccscp.com/jec).

If you have a state-based benefit that pertains to your situation (typically based on your spouse's level of disability), you may need a bit more one-on-one help to determine your best pathway. Carefully review the state-based benefits section to learn about what might be available to you. Now is also the time to apply for your FSA to try to get some Pell Grant money (for undergraduate degrees) to help toward your academic expenses (see chapter 7, "Cost and Payment Resources"). If you are applying to multiple schools, you can list up to ten on the federal aid application. This might lead to federal money for education expenses that does not need to be paid back! Apply for MyCAA (for associate's degrees, licenses, and certification programs only) if you are eligible based on your spouse's rank.

Register for Classes

You will need to meet with an academic counselor/advisor in order to choose the appropriate classes for your degree pathway. If attending school online, often your academic counselor will email you a degree plan. The degree plan lists every class you need to take to attain your declared degree or certification. The degree plan is your guide that helps you pick your classes every semester.

If you need help registering for classes, you may want to visit the registrar's office of your school; if you are attending school aboard a base and the school has a permanent presence there, give that office a call and request help. In most cases, face-to-face registration will still be possible.

Always be aware of the registration deadlines. Check with your school to see whether the institution offers early registration for military spouses. While this is common for military personnel, it is not as common for military spouses, although some schools give it to spouses using MyCAA. Getting early access to classes that might otherwise be full will help you progress down your degree path at a faster pace.

Active-duty spouses and dependent children may need a copy of the orders that dictate that the active-duty family member is stationed in that state. Often the local community college will want to see a copy of these orders in order to grant the service member's family dependents in-state tuition. Spouses and dependents might also need their dependent identification card in order to receive the in-state tuition rate for some states. Make sure your spouse gives you access to a copy of his or her orders just in case of a deployment. Spouses using transferred Post-9/11 benefits should keep a copy of their service member's DD214 if he or she has already separated.

If you previously attended other schools, you will need to have those transcripts sent to the new institution for evaluation. In most cases, the transcripts will need to go from the old school directly to the new one in order to remain official. It is usually a smart idea to have a couple of spare sets of transcripts on hand. Once a transcript is opened, it is no longer considered official, so order an extra one for yourself. You should take a copy of the transcript with you to meet with your academic counselor to help guide your class selections prior to evaluation of your official transcripts. No point in taking a class you have already taken!

At a community college, you will need to take the math and English placement tests to determine your starting point for these two classes. If you test below college freshman level, the school will place you in remedial classes. This is not a big deal, but it can slow your progress. These classes will help boost your baseline skill level and make you more successful in your future classes. If you would like to boost your math and English skills prior to taking the placement test, go to http://www.petersons.com/DOD and click on the "Online Academic Skills Course (OASC)" link. The same Peterson's website also hosts the College Placement Skills Testing (CPST) program, which was designed to help students score better on college placement tests. Testing into freshman-level math and English helps you avoid remedial course work. Matriculation usually requires an orientation session.

Some schools offer the orientation in an online format; others require you physically to attend. Your academic counselor should inform you when your paperwork has been processed and your official degree plan is on file. Then you have matriculated!

All of the initial hard work to start school is done at this point. Now you need to prepare for everything else.

Start checking out all of the services offered on the school campus or in the surrounding areas. Knowing where the services are located might save you heartache and time later on. Some of the services offer outreach to military families; some might be strictly for socialization or networking. Take advantage of both options.

STANDARDIZED ADMISSIONS TESTS

SAT and ACT

Depending upon the school you select to attend, an ACT (http://www.act.org) or SAT (http://www.collegeboard.org) score may be necessary for acceptance. Many schools aboard the different military bases offer flexible admissions by by-passing these exams, although they might require writing samples and/or placement tests in place of the exams. To determine individual requirements, call the school's representatives aboard the base or contact the local education center for advice. Typically, a quick call can help you learn about all of the required application materials.

If the school requires an ACT or SAT score, you need to develop a plan of attack. You will need to research application deadline dates and test dates and locate study resources. To find the required application dates, check the school's website and contact the vet reps.

Test dates can be tricky. ACT and SAT tests are only offered on specific dates on military bases. Spouses and dependents need to book appointments through their education centers. Make sure to leave plenty of time to prepare appropriately. If possible, SAT and ACT exams should not be taken at a moment's notice.

Always check with a school to determine which test the institution accepts, then focus on that particular test for preparation. Some schools will take either; in that case, students may want to take both and submit their best score.

When testing at a base, you can list your school's name or leave it blank. If you decide to take both the SAT and the ACT and submit your top score, do not list the school's name on the test application. If you list the school's name, your scores will go directly to the institution. If you do not list the school's name, later you can request that your scores be sent from either organization. Scores are always kept by the individual organization that administered that test, such as the College Board for the SAT scores.

If you opt to send your scores to a school or schools during test registration either on the base or off base, you will receive four free score reports for the ACT and SAT. If you decide to wait and send your scores after determining the results, each SAT request will cost $11.25 (http://sat.collegeboard.org/register/us-services-fees), and each ACT request will cost $12 (http://www.actstudent.org/scores/send/costs.html). To put your best foot forward, I recommend that you take both tests, wait until your scores are posted, and then pay to send whichever test produces the most competitive results.

If you are not satisfied with your score, you may retake the ACT and SAT off base during the next test date with no waiting period. On base, the waiting period to retake the ACT is sixty days. To retake the SAT on base, a new form must be requested, and the time this takes will vary. Currently, the SAT runs $54.50 and the ACT $39.50 (with writing $56.50) at the education centers on most military installations.

SAT and ACT scores are not returned immediately. Typically, when testing on a base, test scores take approximately ten weeks to be delivered. However, scores can be viewed earlier on the SAT and ACT websites. ACT multiple-choice scores are typically reported within eight weeks (http://www.actstudent.org/scores/viewing-scores.html); essay scores come roughly two weeks later. SAT scores (http://sat.collegeboard.org/scores/availability) take approximately three weeks to be posted online.

The SAT and ACT are completely different tests. The chart below demonstrates some of the differences. For more detailed explanations of the tests, visit the SAT and ACT websites. The biggest difference is that the SAT tests your ability to apply knowledge while the ACT tests your current level of knowledge on subjects.

You will notice when looking at table 6.2 that the SAT does not test science but the ACT does. You will not need to know incredibly specific science information for the ACT; rather, it tests your reading and reasoning skills. The SAT has a stronger emphasis on vocabulary, and the ACT tests higher-level math concepts than the SAT (trigonometry).

The optional essay on the ACT is not factored into your composite score. If you take it, the essay is scored separately. The SAT essay is required and factored into the writing score.

The ACT keeps each subject area separate, whereas the SAT subject areas move back and forth. This may be difficult for some test takers. Free test preparation for military and dependents for both the SAT and the ACT can be found at http://www.eknowledge.com/Affiliate_Welcome.asp?coupon=

Table 6.1.   SAT/ACT

SAT	ACT
Test covers: reading, vocabulary, grammar and usage, writing, and math (includes essay)	Test covers: grammar and usage, math, reading, science reasoning, and an optional writing section (check with school)
3 main components: critical reasoning, mathematics, an essay	5 main components: English, math, reading, science, and an optional essay (check if school demands essay)
Test time frame: 3 hours, 45 minutes	Test time frame: 3 hours, 30 minutes (4 hours with essay)
Format: multiple choice and grid-in	Format: all multiple choice
Guessing penalty of a quarter-point	No guessing penalty
Measures student's ability to draw inferences, synthesize information, understand the difference between main and supporting ideas, vocabulary in context, apply mathematical concepts, problem solve, interpret charts, communicate ideas, revise and edit, understand grammatical structure	Measures student's written and rhetorical English, mathematical skills, reading comprehension, interpretation, analysis, reasoning, problem solving, writing skills stressed in high school and entry-level college classes
Scoring: Penalty for guessing. Maximum score 2400, each section is worth 800. Average score in 2012 was 1498, critical reading 496, mathematics 514, writing 488.	Scoring: ACT assessment only counts correct answers. Composite scores range from 1 to 36, subscores from 1 to 18. The composite score is an average of the four subscores. National average in 2012 was 21.1.

3A8E9CEFCE (there is a delivery charge). Khan Academy (http://www. khanacademy.org) has free test preparation help for the SAT math section. Both the SAT and the ACT websites have free test questions available for you to use for test preparation as well. Check YouTube for SAT and ACT videos, but always consider the source of the videos before deciding whether to use the information.

Numerous test preparation companies offer classes, but no reimbursement is available for these options. These programs offer structured classroom environments and curriculum that may help some dependents, but classes do not emphasize an individual's strengths and weaknesses as a self-paced program would. Just remember that "self-paced" means "self-motivated." You have to organize your time and effort on your own.

Graduate Record Examination (GRE)/
Graduate Management Admission Test (GMAT)

If you are planning to attend graduate school, you may find that your institution of choice requires a GRE or GMAT score. Always check with the school to determine which standardized admissions test is required for your graduate school program. Traditionally, the GRE is taken for most graduate degrees outside of business, and the GMAT is taken for business school. Only the university and college can tell you exactly which test the institution will demand, but taking the GRE might open more options. Currently, the GRE costs $195 and the GMAT is $250.

In the past few years, the GRE has become more widely accepted for admission to business schools, and many top-tier universities, including Yale, Harvard, and Georgetown, have jumped on board. Princeton Review has a link that lists more than seven hundred schools currently accepting the GRE for business school (http://www.princetonreview.com/uploadedFiles/Sitemap/Home_Page/Business_Hub/Opinions_and_Advice/MBAAccepting GRE.pdf). Try an initial search, and then cross-reference with the institutions that interest you. If your institution of choice accepts either, try taking a practice exam for each test first (check both websites). You might find that you have an aptitude for one more than the other.

Free GRE/GMAT Test Preparation

- GRE: http://www.ets.org/s/gre/pdf/practice_book_GRE_pb_revised_general_test.pdf
- GMAT: http://www.mba.com/us/the-gmat-exam/prepare-for-the-gmat-exam/test-prep-materials/free-gmat-prep-software.aspx
- Georgetown University: http://www.youtube.com/watch?v=xFyqJSucqSo
- Khan Academy: http://www.khanacademy.org/ (GMAT math)

Chapter Seven

Cost and Payment Resources

Cost is a major factor for students to consider prior to making a final choice on an institution to attend to pursue their educational goals. There are several options for potential funding resources; many of the options most military spouses are not aware exist. Funding resources typically come from federally based organizations, state-based, school-based, and community-based organizations.

While not always easy to accomplish, planning in advance can save military spouses a tremendous amount of money throughout their pursuit of higher education. For example, if you are pursuing school while your spouse is still on active duty, always check out the local community colleges first. Often, these are the least expensive options, and they all hold regional accreditation, which is the most widely transferable credit a student can earn. Typically, students can stay at community colleges for the first two years of their pursuit of a bachelor's degree, then switch to a four-year institution. Most four-year colleges are significantly more expensive than the two-year community colleges. Taking this pathway allows students to refrain from paying the bigger bills until absolutely necessary.

The following topics will be covered in this section:

- Financial goals
- MyCAA
- Transferability of Post-9/11 GI Bill benefits to dependents
- Post-9/11
- GI Bill activation and conversion process

- Yellow Ribbon Program
- Feedback system
- Department of Veterans Affairs survivors and dependents assistance
- Federal Student Aid
- State-based veterans education benefits that work for dependents
- State-based opportunities (non-military)
- Scholarships (civilian, school, and branch specific)
- Textbook buying options (buying new or used books and rental options)

FINANCIAL GOALS

Pursuing higher education as a military spouse is no easy task. I (Jillian) often hear from the community that frequent deployments, family commitments, and training cycles get in the way. I can account for this myself, as I am also the spouse of an active-duty service member. When you add college costs to that mix, many of us begin to feel overwhelmed. Unlike our active-duty spouses, we do not have military tuition assistance to tap into for payment of tuition. However, there are many types of aid available that assist spouses more than other students attending school.

Transitioning from the service is a difficult process for spouses as well. Military families that prepare for it in advance will find the experience to be less stressful, enabling them to focus on their studies more effectively. Forming a plan in advance will help to minimize potential distractions. Military families that minimize their risk of distraction during the school year will achieve a higher degree of academic success. Successfully educated or trained veterans and military spouses will be more productive in their future endeavors and be able to enrich their surrounding civilian communities.

Military spouses have three main sources of funding to potentially tap into, not including any potential scholarships that they might apply for and receive. These sources include:

- Federal Student Aid (Pell Grant)
- MyCAA
- State-based options (such as the California-based BOG Waiver)

If a spouse is able to maximize benefits under each of these three options, he or she will have a good starting base and hopefully not have to worry about daily stressors, such as making rent, gas, and food.

Federal Student Aid Pell Grant money can be a great benefit for spouses attending school. Think about having up to an extra $5,815 (as of the 2016–2017 academic year) per academic year to help with education-related expenses. How much better off would you be for spending thirty minutes to fill out the Free Application for Federal Student Aid (FAFSA)? The time will be well spent, especially if you are awarded assistance.

Your previous year's tax information (IRS 1040) is required to fill out the FAFSA, so you need to pay attention to your marital status from that year. If you work as well, then you will need both of your W2s. If you are under the age of twenty-four, you must fill out the FAFSA using your parents' tax return document (IRS 1040), unless you have been emancipated. The Federal Student Aid website (see https://studentaid.ed.gov/sa/fafsa/filling-out/dependency) clearly defines what constitutes an independent student. Typically, for the younger spouses I work with, it is through the second category on marital status that they qualify as independent from their parents. Those of us over the age of twenty-four no longer need to worry about this section.

If your active-duty spouse has recently separated from the military, your tax information may not reflect your current financial situation. For example, if Corporal Kirk separates in July 2017 and plans to begin college in August 2017, he will submit his 2016 taxes on the FAFSA that reflect his military pay, and so will his spouse. The main problem is that he will no longer be working and receiving this level of pay, and oftentimes his spouse might have left a job due to the transition as well. In most cases, a veteran's pay is drastically reduced upon separation. If Corporal Kirk or his spouse do not receive an award or do not receive the full amount, they will need to visit the financial aid counselor at the school, explain that they now have a special circumstance (after passing over the service member's date of separation as terminal leave does not count), and request that their listed income level be readjusted. Hopefully, upon readjustment of the income, they will be eligible for the maximum amount of Pell Grant award.

Be aware that Pell Grant money is based on your tax information, so it will fluctuate from person to person depending upon household finances. I often see both parties in a military family receive the full Pell Grant award. That means, as of the 2016–2017 school year, both the service member and his/her spouse each would receive $5,815 to use toward their academic expenses.

For your transitioning spouse (the service member), the Unemployment Compensation for Ex-Servicemembers (UCX) program may help eligible separating service members rate some level of unemployment. Unemployment will vary state by state because the law of the state determines how much money an individual can receive, the length of time to remain eligible, and any other eligibility conditions. Veterans must have been honorably separated in order to be eligible. Information on unemployment can be located on the Department of Labor's website (http://workforcesecurity.doleta. gov/unemploy/uifactsheet.asp).

Eligible veterans and their spouses may be able to pull unemployment after transitioning from the service, before starting school. Both of you should contact your local State Workforce Agency (http://www. servicelocator.org/OWSLinks.asp) upon separation to determine eligibility and apply. Make sure your veteran spouse has a copy of his or her DD214.

Also, some military members may receive a service-connected disability percentage; others may not. When your spouse separates from the military, the VA will screen him or her to determine whether any injuries or diseases were sustained while on active duty, or if any previous health-related issues were exacerbated by active military service. If a service member receives a minimum rating of 10 percent or higher, he or she may be eligible to receive a tax-free stipend from the VA every month. Zero percent ratings do not have a monetary stipend attached; however, in the "State-Based Benefit" section of this book, you will see that many states offer benefits that are tied to these disability ratings. For example, in California a 0 percent rating equals free schooling for your children at state-supported institutions. This means that if you stay in the state of California and your spouse receives a service-connected disability rating, your children can attend all California state community colleges, as well as any of the California state universities and the University of California, tuition free. Be aware that for most states the service member must have enlisted in that state to be eligible for the benefit. California is one state that does not base eligibility on that factor. In other words, California does not care which state your spouse enlisted in.

If your spouse receives a service-connected disability rating, this may help with your family expenses. Be aware that ratings can take as long as twelve months to be determined, and there is such a thing as no rating. Also, if your spouse receives a 100 percent disability rating (must be permanently and totally disabled), you might be entitled to obtain DEA (Dependent's Education Assistance), Chapter 35, and receive $1,021 dollars a month as a full-time student. While it may not equal the benefits of Post-9/11, it is still a generous stipend to assist with your educational pursuits.

Make sure your military spouse gets screened prior to exiting the military. If you are not sure where to find your local VA office, it might even be on the base where you live. The Disabled American Veterans (DAV) and the Veterans of Foreign Wars (VFW) maintain offices on several military bases and may assist you as well. Many academic institutions have visiting representatives from these organizations. They can help your military spouse with his initial claim if he did not make it while still on active duty. They can also help veterans submit for a claims adjustment should their medical situation change.

Also remember to save for your child's future education as well. 529's are a common tool that many parents use to save for their child's higher education pursuits. Operating much like a retirement account, if the money is withdrawn for purposes not associated with school, you will pay taxes on this amount. These education-based savings accounts can be used for children or any designated beneficiary for the purposes of the school. Speak with your local education counselor or your financial advisor for more advice.

MILITARY SPOUSE CAREER ADVANCEMENT ACCOUNTS (MYCAA)

https://aiportal.acc.af.mil/mycaa

Military OneSource facilitates the MyCAA program. The program offers $4,000 to eligible spouses of active-duty military members to be used for education, either traditional or nontraditional. MyCAA is good for an associate's degree, a certification, or a license. The program cannot be used toward a bachelor's degree, but it can be used for programs after a spouse receives a bachelor's degree. For example, I (Jillian) used the program for a supplementary teaching credential offered through the University of California, San Diego, after completing a master's degree in education when I qualified through my husband's rank. The program saved me close to $3,000 on the training costs.

MyCAA aims to increase the portable career skills of active-duty service members' spouses by developing their professional credentials to help them find and maintain work. Military OneSource counselors can help eligible spouses find specific programs or schools that participate in the program. Counselors can also help spouses identify local sources of assistance, such as state and local financial assistance, transportation, and child care. They can also help with employment referrals.

Eligible spouses must be married to active-duty service members in the following ranks:

- E1–E5
- O1–O2
- WO1–CWO2

MyCAA will *not* cover the following:

- Prior courses
- Books, supplies, student activities, and the like
- Prepayment deposits
- Audited courses or internships
- Nonacademic or ungraded courses
- Courses taken more than one time
- College-Level Examination Program (CLEP) or DSST exams
- Associate of arts degrees in general studies or liberal arts
- Personal enrichment courses
- Transportation, lodging, and child care
- Course extensions
- Study abroad

To apply, visit https://aiportal.acc.af.mil/mycaa or call (800) 342-9647 to speak with a Military OneSource Counselor.

POST-9/11 GI BILL TRANSFERABILITY TO DEPENDENTS

Active-duty service members may be eligible to transfer their Post-9/11 GI Bill benefits to dependents. The transfer process requires a four-year commitment to stay in the military. If benefits are successfully transferred, certain rules apply while the service member remains on active duty. Also, whatever benefits that your military spouse transfers to you are benefits the service member does not have to pursue his or her own education. Be aware that the service member can pull unused portions of the benefit back at any time. This enables them to regain any benefits that spouses and dependents do not expend. In some cases, depending upon the state he or she enlisted in or potentially their levels of disability, the service member might have access to other benefits to fund their own education.

To be eligible to transfer benefits, service members must be eligible for Post-9/11 and:

- have completed six years of active-duty service to transfer
- have four years remaining on contract (enlisted) or commit four more years (officer) *OR* be precluded by standard policy or statute from serving an additional four years (must agree to serve maximum time allowed by such policy). These exceptions commonly include mandatory retirement dates, retention control points, or a medical separation. Transfer must be approved while the service member is still in the armed forces.

In a nutshell, service members need to have completed the required time in service, depending upon transferring to a spouse or a child, and have four years left on contract. The best time to complete the process is at the same time as a reenlistment or extension package that gives the individual the required amount of payback time.

To transfer benefits, follow these steps:

- Service member verifies his or her time in service.
- Visit the website (at http://www.benefits.va.gov/gibill/post911_gibill.asp).
- Click on the "Transfer of Entitlement" option.
- Follow the directions ("Apply Now").
- You will find yourself on the MilConnect webpage and will need to enter your CAC card or Defense Finance and Accounting Services (DFAS) account information.
- Click on the "Go to Transfer of Eligible Benefits" link on the right-hand side.
- Apply the needed information and submit—but you are not finished.
- Obtain a Statement of Understanding (SOU) from the website or the local education center aboard your base.
- Fill out all required information and talk to your military career counselor to verify time in service.
- The commanding officer signs off on the service member's application, and then the document must be routed through the administrative personnel with the command element.
- Once the transfer is approved, eligibility documents will be found in the Transfer Education Benefits (TEB) website (https://www.dmdc.osd.mil/milconnect/faces/index.jspx?_afrLoop=803456499897019&_afrWindow Mode=0&_adf.ctrl-state=6yaicjmzp_4) for each individual.

Service members may revoke transferred benefits at any given time. Designated months may also be changed or eliminated though the website while on active duty or through a written request to the VA once separated.

Dependents who have received transferred benefits will need to apply to use the benefits through the VONAPP website (http://www.benefits.va.gov/gibill/post911_gibill.asp) in the "Post 9/11, Apply for Benefits" section. Dependents may also print the form (22-1990e) and send it to their nearest VA regional office. The form may be found online (http://www.vba.va.gov/pubs/forms/VBA-22-1990e-ARE.pdf), and regional offices may also be found online (http://www.benefits.va.gov/benefits/offices.asp).

Eligible dependents:

- spouse
- service member's children
- combination of spouse and children

Dependents must be in the Defense Enrollment Eligibility Reporting System (DEERS).

Spouses:

- May use the benefit immediately
- Are not entitled to the MHA while the service member remains on active duty but are entitled once the service member separates
- Are entitled to the book stipend
- May use the benefit for up to fifteen years from the service member's EAS date, just like the service member

Children:

- May use the benefit only after the service member has attained ten years on active duty
- May use the benefit while the parent is on active duty or after separation
- Must have obtained a high school diploma or equivalency certificate, or have turned eighteen
- May receive the MHA while a parent remains on active-duty status
- Are entitled to the book stipend
- Do not fall under the fifteen-year delimiting date; however, benefits must be used prior to turning twenty-six years old

- Must have been given the benefit before the age of twenty-one. An extension can be granted by DEERS to transfer the benefit before the age of twenty-three if you are still on active duty

Service members can commit the required payback time of four years after separating from active duty and dropping into the reserves.

For more details, visit http://www.gibill.va.gov/benefits/post_911_gibill/transfer_of_benefits.html.

The DOD Fact Sheet on Post-9/11 GI Bill Transferability can be found at http://www.benefits.va.gov/gibill/docs/factsheets/Transferability_Factsheet.pdf.

POST-9/11 GI BILL

After determining whether your spouse is eligible to transfer his or her Post-9/11 GI Bill to you, the next step is to learn how to use the benefit to its greatest extent. Using transferred Post-9/11 benefits while your spouse remains on active duty means missing out on the monthly housing allowance (MHA), but dependent children will receive the MHA in this case. You must decide where the benefit is best spent at this point.

The Post-9/11 GI Bill has three financial components built into the program: books and supplies, housing, and tuition.

Books and Supplies

Post-9/11 has a books and supplies stipend. The stipend is prorated at $41.67 per credit hour for a maximum of $1,000 per academic year. A regular full-time student, who enrolls in a minimum of twelve credits per semester, would receive the full $1,000. The stipend is broken into two payments per academic year and paid at the beginning of each semester.

You should take note that $1,000 is not actually a great amount for books. Oftentimes books can run over $200 per class. Many universities list the approximate costs of textbooks for the school year on their website. For example, California State University, Long Beach (CSULB), estimates its books at $1,898 for the 2016–2017 academic year. According to the school's calculations, $1,000 won't cut it for books. You definitely need to check into other options. The "Textbook-Buying Options" section in this chapter is dedicated to helping you find used or rental books.

Housing

The housing stipend gets slightly more complicated. Referred to as the monthly housing allowance (MHA), it is equivalent to the salary for an E-5 with dependents. Remember that spouses using transferred benefits while the service member is still serving on active duty are not entitled to the housing stipend, but children who use transferred benefits are eligible. Spouses who use transferred benefits after the service member separates are entitled to the stipend. You can use the GI Bill Comparison Tool (http://department-of-veterans-affairs.github.io/gi-bill-comparison-tool/) to determine the amount of MHA attached to the institution you would like to attend. That is right; the MHA is based on the zip code of the school, not your abode. So, all veterans or dependents using transferred benefits attending the institution will be set at the same rate for their stipends.

If attending school strictly online, the Post-9/11 housing rate is set at $805.50 as of August 1, 2016. This amount can vary each year. Check the website, http://www.benefits.va.gov/GIBILL/resources/benefits_resources/rates/ch33/ch33rates080116.asp, for current rates.

Tuition

Tuition under the Post-9/11 GI Bill can get complicated to explain. I am going to keep it simple. If you follow the most basic of parameters, you will not pay a dime for your school. Go outside of these parameters and you run into technical billing questions; in this case, you should contact the school you are interested in attending for further information. If you are pursuing an undergraduate or graduate degree, plan on attending a state school and transferred Post-9/11 GI Bill benefits, and finish your degree within the number of months of benefit that you have allotted, your schooling should be covered. The full thirty-six months of benefit is enough for most bachelor's degrees if you stay on track because it equates to nine months of school per year over the course of four years. Traditionally, we do not usually attend school in the summer as an undergraduate degree-seeking student, although you may if you are interested. Every school sets its own summer school schedule. Classes can typically run between four to ten weeks in length. Double check with your school to determine whether you will be considered a full-time student based upon your desired summer schedule—this will tell you if using the GI Bill is an option. If one of these factors changes, your benefit might change as well.

Veterans and dependents using transferred benefits that choose to attend private school will receive a maximum of $21,970.46 for the academic year 2016–2017 (see http://benefits.va.gov/GIBILL/resources/benefits_resources/rates/ch33/ch33rates080116.asp). Anything above that amount, and you run the risk of having to pay out of pocket. I state it this way because many schools participate in the Yellow Ribbon Program (YRP) (http://www.benefits.va.gov/gibill/yellow_ribbon.asp), and it might help cover private school costs that come in above the maximum VA-allotted threshold. You can read more about the YRP and your eligibility later in this chapter.

What about out-of-state tuition, you ask? Out-of-state tuition is what non-residents must pay a public school when enrolled. Tuition can be much higher for nonresidents because they have not contributed to the tax pool of that state, hence they have not earned the resident rate of tuition. The Veterans Access, Choice, and Accountability Act of 2014 (https://veterans.house.gov/the-veterans-access-choice-and-accountability-act-of-2014-highlights) was passed in July 2014, and as of the academic year 2015–2016, schools that take Post-9/11 dollars will need to list veterans and dependents using transferred benefits as in-state residents for tuition purposes. If you attend a public college within three years of your separation date and use a GI Bill for payment, out-of-state tuition charges should not be a problem. If you decide to remain off the GI Bill in the beginning, schools do not have to extend the honorary in-state residency benefit to you, although some states, such as Oklahoma, have state-based benefits in place that extend in-state residency to veterans and their spouses. The rules are different in each state, so verify with the veterans department at your institution.

As stated above, the VA will pay you the full-time housing allowance if you pursue school at the full-time rate as long as your spouse has already separated from the service and you are taking at least one credit hour in the face-to-face format. The VA considers twelve credit hours to be full time. However, if you have no previous college credit and intend on pursuing a bachelor's degree, twelve credits per semester will not suffice. Most bachelor's degrees require students to complete 120 semester credit hours of a specific subject matter in order to have the degree conferred on them. That equates to fifteen credit hours each semester, or five classes, to total thirty credit hours each year.

The college year is similar to the high school year: two semesters each year over the course of four years. So, 120 semester hours breaks down to fifteen semester hours each semester to total thirty credits each year (freshman year: 30; sophomore year: 30; junior year: 30; senior year: 30—total: 120). If you follow the VA's minimum guidelines of twelve credits each semester, or four classes, you will run out of benefits at the end of your senior year but only have earned ninety-six semester credit hours, which will make you twenty-four credits shy of the 120 required. You will be out of benefit but will not have obtained your degree. The academic counselors at the school you attend will help you with your degree plans. If you need to make changes or have questions, contact them for further advice.

The Comparison Tool on the main GI Bill website (http://department-of-veterans-affairs.github.io/gi-bill-comparison-tool/) will allow you to complete a quick comparison between schools that you might be interested in attending. You can determine factors such as what you will receive based upon the federal benefit you elect to use, the amount of money you will receive for the housing stipend under Post-9/11, graduation rates, how many veterans attend the school, and the institution's Yellow Ribbon status.

GI BILL APPLICATION AND CONVERSION PROCESS

Dependents using transferred GI Bill benefits must apply to use the benefit just as the service member would; they just fill out a different form—the VA Form 22-1990E. The application process for the GI Bill is not complicated; however, it does currently take approximately four to six weeks to receive the Certificate of Eligibility (COE) statement. Make sure to allot time for the wait prior to starting school. If you find yourself in a time crunch, check with your school to see whether the institution might take your confirmation number from your submitted application and let you get started. Also, this process can occur before or after your spouse separates from the military.

To activate the GI Bill, you will need to access the Veterans Online Application (VONAPP; see http://vabenefits.vba.va.gov/vonapp/). You can also access it by going to the main GI Bill website (http://www.benefits.va.gov/gibill/): select the "Post-9/11" link on the right-hand side, select "Get Started" on the left-hand side, select "Apply for Benefits," and lastly select "Apply Online." You will need three pieces of information before you proceed:

- Your school's name and address
- A bank account and routing number (VA is direct deposit)
- An address you will be at in the next four to six weeks to receive the COE

The easiest way to prepare for the application process is to be accepted to your intended institution prior to applying to activate your benefit, but you can change the required information at a later date by contacting the VA at 1-888-GIBILL-1.

The VA does not send hard checks anymore. Inputting your bank account and routing numbers enables them to direct deposit your MHA and book stipend money. You may change this information at a later date using the VA's Direct Deposit form if you change your bank.

The address you list will be where your COE is delivered. If you currently live on base but will be moving back to your home of record soon, you might want to list a family member's address instead. Just make sure that the individuals located at the listed address keep an eye out for the document and inform you when it arrives. You will need to take that document to the veterans' representative at your school as soon as you receive it because it is the school's ticket to receive payment from the VA. This is part of the process for you to receive the housing allowance if you are eligible.

Process of Applying

Upon entering the VONAPP website (http://vabenefits.vba.va.gov/vonapp/), you will be asked whether you are a first-time VONAAP user; answer accordingly. Next, you will be asked if you possess an eBenefits Account. Only service members will have access to an eBenefits account; spouses and dependent children will need to create a VONAPP account. Once settled, select the "22-1990E" form to proceed.

If you are concerned about the questions on the 22-1990E or whether you are making the correct choices, contact the VA at 1-888-GIBILL-1. The veterans' representatives at your intended school are usually good sources of information as well. Check with your base's education center to see whether they keep paper copies of the 22-1990Es if you would like to view the required information in advance.

Once you receive the COE, you need to take it (a copy!) to the veterans' representatives at your school. You will also need to send a copy of your spouse's DD214 to your local VA processing center if he or she has separated from the service. When you finish filling out and submitting the 22-1990E, the main page on the VONAPP will maintain two links (side by side) with required printable information; one is your submitted application (this link has been disabled for quite some time), and the other is your local processing center, which is oftentimes not in the same state. Most institutions will also want a copy of your spouse's DD214 for verification purposes.

If you have used the VA benefit before and are transferring to a new school, you will need to fill out the 22-1995 form. The 22-1995 form can be found on the VONAPP website.

YELLOW RIBBON PROGRAM (YRP)

http://www.benefits.va.gov/gibill/yellow_ribbon.asp

YRP is designed to cover tuition above and beyond the maximum allowable rate for a private school or foreign school. While it will not work for spouses who have had Post-9/11 benefits transferred to them, it will for dependent children.

YRP is not automatic, and there are many stipulations to watch out for prior to determining whether the benefit will work for your particular purpose. YRP does not pay the student any money.

Eligibility

- Must rate 100 percent of the Post-9/11 GI Bill (the service member)
- Active-duty members of the military are not eligible, nor are their spouses; however, children of active-duty service members may qualify (if the active-duty parent is eligible for 100 percent of 9/11). The service member must have separated from the service to use YRP, and the same rule applies to spouses.

YRP potentially enables veterans to cover costs above and beyond the Post-9/11 GI Bill parameters. Not all schools participate, and a school's participation one year does not guarantee participation in subsequent years. You do not need to maintain full-time status in order to be eligible for YRP. Summer terms may be eligible as well, but check with your particular institution.

Schools must reestablish their YRP program with the VA every year. This means, and I have seen it happen, that a school may participate one year but not the next. You could get left hanging. For example, a corporal attended a well-known private school in Georgia. The school participated during her first year, but not the following years. She was out of pocket roughly $22,000 per year for her school at that point—ouch!

Schools may participate on different levels by limiting the amount of YRP spots available and the amount of money they offer. This can restrict veterans and dependent children using transferred benefits from considering certain institutions based on financial constraints. The following is a hypothetical breakdown:

- School A participates in YRP with unlimited spots and unlimited money. Therefore, you shouldn't pay out of pocket. But you still run the risk of the school choosing not to participate in upcoming years.
- School B participates with twenty spots and $4,000 per student. Therefore, you may or may not get one of those twenty spots (remember that it is first come, first served!), and the VA will match the $4,000, effectively giving you an extra $8,000 toward tuition (this is a rough explanation of how it actually works).

You must also check to see how the program at your school is participating. Consider the following hypothetical situation:

- School C: The graduate-level school of business participates with seventeen spots and $11,000 per student.
- School C: The graduate-level school of education participates with four spots and $6,000 per student.

Notice that different programs within the same level of education and the same school may participate with different amounts of money and available spots.

Last, a school may participate differently at the graduate level than it does at the undergraduate level. See the following example:

- School E participates at the undergraduate level with five spots and $8,000 per student.
- School E participates at the graduate level with three spots and $1,000 per student.

You can search YRP participating schools by state (at http://www.benefits.va.gov/gibill/yellow_ribbon.asp). However, I (Jillian) always recommend contacting the VA directly for solid confirmation that the school you are applying for does participate and to what degree.

Remember that both you and the school must apply to participate in the YRP. You must apply each year for the YRP. The school must also agree to participate. If you are in the position of applying to an expensive private school that the $21,970.46 under Post-9/11 does not cover per year, ask the school how to apply for the YRP. Additionally, you should do your own homework. What if the school drops the YRP program the next year? The only option for many spouses and dependent children is loans. Do research into how long the school has been a YRP recipient and if they plan to continue to do so in the future; otherwise, you may find yourself in the position of taking on loans to cover the difference (if you decide to stay with that current school).

The YRP can be instrumental in your ability to attend the school of your choice, so do not make the mistake of thinking that a small, off-the-beaten-path school might not fill their YRP seats. I spoke with a small college in Washington State that participates in the YRP, wondering if they often fill their openings. Prior to speaking to the veterans' representative, I thought to myself that it was nice they had allotted so many spots even though they probably did not need them. I mean, how many veterans or dependents using transferred benefits were relocating to this rural area? I was so wrong! The school had a waiting list for its YRP spots that was in the double digits. Apparently, even though the school was located in a rural area, it was the closest school to one of the state's main snowboarding mountains and maintained a fairly large veteran population. On the flipside, I was happy to hear that our veterans and their families were getting some much-needed R&R after their military service along with a good education.

If you intend to transfer, you must speak with your new school regarding YRP eligibility at their institution. Eligibility at one institution does not guarantee eligibility at another. If you take a hiatus from your school and were enrolled in YRP, you may get dropped for subsequent semesters. Before you make any decisions, talk with your academic advisor and/or veterans' department. The more informed you are, the better you can plan.

VA GI BILL FEEDBACK SYSTEM

http://www.benefits.va.gov/GIBILL/Feedback.asp

The VA has recently implemented a new system to handle complaints pertaining to issues involving the Principles of Excellence. Educational institutions that have agreed to abide by the specific guidelines of the program are agreeing to do the following:

- Inform students in writing of the costs associated with education at that institution.
- Produce educational plans for military and veteran beneficiaries.
- Cease all misleading recruiting techniques.
- Accommodate those who are absent due to military requirements.
- Appoint a point of contact (POC) that offers education-related and financial advice.
- Confirm that all new programs are accredited before enrolling students.
- Align refund policies with Title IV policies (Federal Student Aid).

Schools that participate in the Principles of Excellence program can be found on the VA website (see http://www.benefits.va.gov/gibill/principles_of_ excellence.asp).

Complaints should be submitted when institutions participating in the program fall below the above-listed set of standards. Complaints are filed on subjects such as recruiting practices, education quality, accreditation issues, grade policies, failure to release transcripts, credit transfer, financial topics, student loan concerns, refund problems, job opportunities after degree completion, and degree plan changes and subsequent requirements. To file a complaint, visit the website and follow the directions.

DEPARTMENT OF VETERANS' AFFAIRS SURVIVORS' AND DEPENDENTS' ASSISTANCE

While not an easy topic to discuss or one that is well known, survivors of service members who died in the wars and dependent spouses of service members who are permanently and totally disabled have options available for funding their education. To clarify eligibility and benefit usage, contact the closest VA center for advice and check with the local VA processing center to determine whether the program you are interested in attending is approved for benefits. Dependents eligible for VA benefits can also apply for free counseling through the VA to help determine an appropriate educational or vocational pathway for their career desires.

"Survivors' and Dependents' Assistance" is the broadly used term for two of the VA's premier programs for dependents of service members who are permanently or totally disabled or who were killed in action. The first, and least generous of the two, is the Survivors' and Dependents' Educational Assistance (DEA) program, also titled Chapter 35. The second is the Marine Gunnery Sergeant John David Fry Scholarship, often referred to as the Fry Scholarship. It is important to note that using transferred benefits under Post-9/11 as a dependent is actually not a VA program, but instead a separate DoD program, even though Post-9/11 is used by the dependent. The VA strictly administers the two programs described here.

For either benefit, you must complete the VA Form 22-5490, which can be found here: http://www.vba.va.gov/pubs/forms/VBA-22-5490-ARE.pdf, and send it to the Regional Processing Center for your state, which can be found here: http://www.benefits.va.gov/benefits/offices.asp. This form must be submitted to both the VA and the school that the dependent wishes to attend. To find a list of eligible schools and types of training that accept the GI Bill, use the Comparison Tool found here: http://www.benefits.va.gov/gibill/comparison.

Survivors' and Dependents' Educational Assistance (DEA)

Both spouses and children may be eligible for this benefit if the service member was permanently or totally disabled (usually meaning a 100 percent disability rating from the VA), died while in the line of duty, or, in many cases, is currently being imprisoned by a hostile force or missing in action. Children tend to be eligible between the ages of eighteen and twenty-six, though exceptions may be granted. Spouses may use the benefit up to twenty years from the date of the effective disability rating or up to ten years from the date that the VA finds you eligible or from the date of death of the service member in the line of duty. This benefit can be used for a total of forty-five months.

It is important to note that spouses and children may be eligible to receive Dependency and Indemnity Compensation (DIC) for service members killed in action. Children often receive these benefits if they are not included in the spouse's DIC, are unmarried, and are under eighteen or between eighteen and twenty-three while attending school. Children will not continue to receive these benefits if they apply for the DEA. However, spouses can continue to receive both DIC and DEA. If the spouse remarries before the age of fifty-seven, they will lose DEA eligibility. It is imperative that the spouse, and potentially the child, speak to the VA concerning both DIC and DEA eligibility due to the complexity of how they interact.

It is not uncommon for permanently or totally disabled service members transitioning from the service to be told by transition personnel that their children and spouses will receive "fully paid education benefits," and it is usually in reference to the DEA. However, under DEA the dependent will receive $1,021 a month as a full-time student. This is not particularly generous in comparison to what most service members think of as "fully paid education benefits" due to the now-famous generosity of transferred Post-9/11 benefits. Over the span of a typical four-month semester, this only amounts to $4,072, which will not cover the cost of tuition at most public schools.

Many service members going through a medical board evaluation, which undoubtedly all permanently and totally disabled service members will, may still have a means of recourse to transfer the Post-9/11 under a number of possible exceptions. Using the DEA benefit does help alleviate the financial cost for a spouse or child for a veteran that still wishes to retain and use his or her own benefit. Those interested in this option should pursue all possibilities and not simply rely on the often general description of the DEA as a "fully paid education benefit." In many cases, this may require talking to a military career counselor before separating and/or being fully approved for a medical separation.

The $1,021 is paid directly to the student if they are full time, and all school costs must be covered from this amount. This amount is prorated at a three-quarter, half-time, or less-than-half-time rate depending upon the class load the student takes. Since this amount will come to the student on a monthly basis, it may require that the student request a delayed payment plan from the school, use another benefit, or apply for financial aid to cover the cost of school and then pocketing the DEA amount. The good news is that this amount will not prohibit applying for additional scholarships that may cover tuition, thereby allowing the student to keep the maximum amount possible of the $1,021 every month.

Most VA programs tend to be very flexible in where they can be used and for what types of programs. DEA will pay for colleges, technical and vocational programs, certification tests, apprenticeships and on-the-job training, tutorial assistance, and work-study programs. Here is the VA's published brochure for the DEA program: http://www.benefits.va.gov/gibill/docs/pamphlets/ch35_pamphlet_2.pdf. Do not let it serve as your only guide. You should have a thorough and in-depth conversation with a VA counselor to determine eligibility.

Marine Gunnery Sergeant John David Fry Scholarship

Spouses and children of service members who died in the line of duty after September 10, 2011, should apply for the Fry Scholarship. This program operates identically to benefits that have been transferred from the Post-9/11 GI Bill and can also be used for a total of thirty-six months at the full-time rate. It will pay up to the cost of in-state tuition at public schools and up to $21,970.46 a year toward a private or foreign school as of the 2016–2017 school year.

The Fry Scholarship can also pay the spouse or child an MHA rate equal to an E5 with dependents based on the zip code of the school and up to $1,000 a year as a book stipend. This benefit will pay for all of the same types of programs as DEA, but it also includes vocational flight training. The biggest difference between this benefit and transferred Post-9/11 benefits is that the Yellow Ribbon Program cannot be used with the Fry Scholarship, which means it cannot be used to cover the difference of the cost of tuition for private, foreign, or out-of-state schools.

If a spouse is eligible for DEA and the Fry Scholarship, they must make an irrevocable decision to use one or the other. The child of a service member who died while on active duty after September 10, 2001, but before August 1, 2011, may use both the forty-five months of DEA and the thirty-six months of the Fry Scholarship, for a total of eighty-one months based on the same service member's death; however, they cannot be used concurrently. Similar to spouses, if the death occurred after August 1, 2011, the child must also make an irrevocable decision to choose one or the other. In the majority of cases it is highly likely the Fry Scholarship will exceed the monthly benefit of the DEA, but this should be verified by calculating the cost of attending a particular school using the GI Bill Comparison Tool. Additionally, the interaction between the DIC benefit and Fry Scholarship is identical to the DEA, in that it may be lost for children but spouses may be able to continue to receive both.

Spouses have fifteen years after the service member's death to use the Fry Scholarship, but if the spouse remarries, they will lose eligibility. This may make for some difficult life decisions, so plan accordingly. Children can begin using the benefit at the age of eighteen, upon graduating high school, or perhaps earlier if they graduated at an earlier date. They have until their thirty-third birthday to use the benefit, even if they get married. If either the spouse or the child has their own VA education benefits, they must relinquish previously held benefits to use the Fry Scholarship (e.g., Montgomery GI

Bill–Active Duty, or the Montgomery GI Bill–Selected Reserve). If the spouse or child is currently on active duty, they will receive benefits at the active-duty rate. This typically means they will not receive an additional MHA. They are able to use the Fry Scholarship in addition to any Post-9/11 entitlement earned from their own service, as well as Post-9/11 benefits that may have been transferred to them. The nature of the discharge from service for either the spouse or the child will not impact eligibility for the Fry Scholarship. In other words, if the child or spouse is dishonorably discharged and loses their own GI Bill benefit, whether it is the Post-9/11 GI Bill or any other, they can still apply for the Fry Scholarship based on a parent's or spouse's death in the line of duty.

FEDERAL STUDENT AID (FSA)

Federal Student Aid (FSA) is often the first topic that we discuss with spouses who are looking for information pertaining to funding sources for higher education. Besides MyCAA, it is often the best benefit they can use when attending an educational or training program. Student aid money is a civilian-based benefit offered by the US federal government, states, schools, and nonprofit organizations. FSA money is the most actively sought-after money by students looking for financial assistance and is available through the US Department of Education. Spouses and dependent children using transferred Post-9/11 GI Bill benefits can also apply for Federal Student Aid, and they should be encouraged to do so in order to cover any extra costs they are unable to get funded. For example, under the Post-9/11 GI Bill, if a student attends school full time, he or she will receive $1,000 per academic year toward books and supplies. In most cases, this is not enough to cover book expenses. Federal Student Aid might be a viable option to help in these circumstances if an individual qualifies.

Prior to choosing a school, it is important to consider the costs associated with attending a particular institution. While you might have educational benefits available to use because of your spouse's military status, these benefits do not cover all expenses in most cases. School expenses can vary significantly from institution to institution. Prospective students should consider expenses above and beyond the tuition and fees. Books, travel, and equipment costs can add up and create a substantial financial burden for military families.

The US Department of Education recommends that if attending a particular school is going to require you to pay money above and beyond the amounts covered under your available benefits,

> You'll want to make sure that the cost of your school is reasonable compared to your earning potential in your future career. In other words, you want to make sure that you can earn enough money to cover any student loan payments you may need to make, along with living expenses, after you graduate. [1]

Schools that participate in federal student aid programs are required to provide potential students information pertaining to the cost of attending and to provide a net price calculator on their websites. Students can also access the College Scorecard (https://collegescorecard.ed.gov/), provided by the U.S. Department of Education's College Affordability and Transparency Center, to help in making more informed decisions regarding an institution's value and affordability.

Prior to applying for Federal Student Aid, it is important to understand what it is, how it works, and what you would want to accept. Federal Student Aid, or Title IV Programs as they are categorized, comes in three forms: work-study, loans, and grants. For spouses or dependent children using transferred GI Bill benefits, loans are usually not necessary. In fact, it is best to avoid them at all costs. In many cases, spouses will have access to MyCAA, scholarships, and state/federal grants. Loans have to be repaid with interest, and you should think carefully before accepting them.

The federal Pell Grant money should be the goal for most undergraduate students. Pell Grant money does not need to be repaid and is awarded for first-time bachelor's or associate's degree-seeking students only. In certain instances, students might receive a Pell Grant award if they are attending a postbaccalaureate teacher certification program. The maximum Pell Grant award is currently set at $5,815 for the 2016–2017 academic year. That amount is based upon maximum financial need and a full-time rate of pursuit.

In order to be eligible to apply for Federal Student Aid, students must meet the following parameters:

- Most programs require demonstrating financial need
- Must be a US citizen or eligible noncitizen
- Have a valid social security number (exceptions apply)
- Be registered with the Selective Service (if male)

- Be enrolled or accepted at minimum of half-time as a regular student into an eligible degree or certificate program
- Maintain satisfactory progress

Federal Student Aid applicants will also need to sign statements stating:

- Student is not defaulting on any federal student loans.
- Student does not owe money on any federal grants.
- Student will only use aid money for educational-related expenses.
- Student must demonstrate evidence of eligibility by having a high school diploma, GED, or completed homeschool program approved by state law.

Financial need eligibility is based upon "your Expected Family Contribution, your year in school, your enrollment status, and the cost of attendance at the school you will be attending."[2] The Expected Family Contribution (EFC) is a number that the financial aid department employees use to help determine the amount of financial aid you would potentially need to attend that particular school. The information that you file when completing the Free Application for Federal Student Aid (FAFSA) is used within a special formula that was established by law to determine your EFC. Financial information pertaining to your taxed and untaxed income, benefits, and assets can all be taken into account, as well as your family size. More detailed information on how the EFC is calculated can be found at http://ifap.ed.gov/efcformula guide/attachments/091913EFCFormulaGuide1415.pdf.

Your enrollment status is simply your rate of pursuit. Award amounts are based upon the degree to which you pursue school and are reported by your school to the DoEd. Full-time school is usually difficult for spouses of active-duty military personnel to maintain considering mission demands. Students using transferred GI Bill benefits must attend school at the full-time rate in order to rate full-time Post-9/11 GI Bill benefits.

The cost of attendance (COA) is the actual amount of money needed in order for you to attend an institution. Typically, for traditional educational programs the COA is calculated on a yearly basis. The estimate includes:

- tuition and fees;
- the cost of room and board (or living expenses for students who do not contract with the school for room and board);

- the cost of books, supplies, transportation, loan fees, and miscellaneous expenses (including a reasonable amount for the documented cost of a personal computer);
- an allowance for child care or other dependent care;
- costs related to a disability; and/or
- reasonable costs for eligible study-abroad programs. [3]

After determining the COA, your EFC is subtracted from your COA to determine your financial need.

Spouses need to reapply for FSA every year even if they were not awarded Pell Grant money the previous year. Economic circumstances for military members can change drastically from year to year, thereby changing financial need determination. For example, military members change billets and can have a different level of pay attached to them, or they might have been in a combat zone. Also, you might have just gotten married or divorced, your spouse might have separated from the military recently, or you had a child, all of which can affect your financial situation. I (Jillian) often work with higher-ranking service members who tell me they will not be eligible for a Pell Grant award because they make too much money. I have worked with E-9s who have received the full award and E-2s who have been denied, so let the Department of Education tell you what might be available to assist with your educational expenses.

If a student is awarded Pell Grant money, the amount is sent to the school, and the school pays the student. If any money is owed toward tuition and fees, schools deduct that amount from the award prior to turning the remainder of the money over to the student. Award money is typically turned over to students in check, cash, or bank deposit. Federal Pell Grant money is paid out in at least two disbursements. Most schools pay students at least once per semester.

Pell Grant awards must be used toward costs associated with going to school. This may include books, a new laptop to do your homework, paying for daycare while you are at class, and gas used to go to class. These funds should also be saved to pay for future classes in the event that you run out of whatever current funding is available to you.

If you are considering taking out loans to pay for your education, be sure to research and understand where the student loan is coming from prior to accepting any money. Student loans can be federal or private depending on the source. Federally backed loans and private loans have many differences.

Here are just a few of the reasons that federally backed loans can offer greater flexibility than loans from private sources.

- Federal loans can offer borrowers fixed interest rates that are typically lower than private sources of loans.
- Borrowers are given a six-month grace period upon completion of the degree to begin repayments. Often, private school loans will require payments to be made while the student is still attending school.
- Only federally backed loans are subsidized, meaning the government pays the interest for a period of time.
- Interest may be deductible, not an option for private loans.
- Federal loans can be consolidated into a Direct Consolidation Loan; private loans cannot.
- Private loans may require that the borrower already has an established credit record. Most federal student loans do not require a credit check.
- Federal loans tend to have greater offer forbearance or deferment options.
- Private loans may demand that repayments begin immediately. (Information taken from the following site, http://studentaid.ed.gov/types/loans/federal-vs-private.)

Federal student loans come in three forms: Direct Subsidized Loans or Direct Unsubsidized Loans, Direct PLUS Loans (for advanced education), or Federal Perkins Loans.

According to the Department of Education, Direct Subsidized Loans have slightly better parameters for students with financial need. Direct Subsidized loans are only available for undergraduate students, and the amount awarded cannot exceed the financial need. Interest on this type of loan is covered by the US Department of Education while students remain in school at a minimum of half time and for the first six months after graduation (grace period).

Direct Unsubsidized Loans demand a demonstration of financial need and are available for undergraduate and graduate school. The amount borrowed is regulated by the school and is based upon the school's costs. Interest is the responsibility of the borrower at all times. If the borrower chooses not to pay interest while in school, the amount accrues and is added into the overall loan and will be reflected in payments when they come due.

Federal PLUS loans are available for graduate or professional degree-seeking students and parents of dependent undergraduate students. Schools must participate in the program for students to be eligible. Loans are fixed at a specific rate, and borrowers must not have an adverse credit history. For information on the current rates for loans, visit the DoEd website (https://studentaid.ed.gov/types/loans/interest-rates#what-are-the-interest-rates-of-federal-student-loans).

The National Student Loan Data System (NSLDS), the DOE's central database for student aid, maintains information regarding Title IV loans and grants. If you have already received loans or grants and need information regarding your awards, you can access the information at https://www.nslds.ed.gov/.

If you plan on applying for Federal Student Aid, you will need access to your taxes from the previous year. For example, if you are applying for student aid for the 2016–2017 school year, you will need your 2015 taxes. The FAFSA application typically opens in January of each year and must be reapplied for each year, but starting in 2016 for the 2017–2018 school year the application will open three months earlier, on October 1. You will then use your tax information from two years earlier.

If you are not eligible for any money one year, do not let it deter you from applying in subsequent years. You may be eligible at another time. If you are under the age of twenty-four but have already served on active duty, you will not need to enter your parents' tax information on the FAFSA. You will enter your personal tax information.

If you are interested in applying for Federal Student Aid but are unsure how to proceed, contact your local Education Center or the Financial Aid office of your school for further guidance.

Here is a quick checklist for applying for federal financial aid:

1. Have your tax information from the previous year on hand.
2. Apply on https://fsaid.ed.gov/npas/index.htm for your FSA ID.
3. Apply for Federal Student Aid through FAFSA (http://www.fafsa.ed.gov; you will need to list your school and can list up to ten options).
4. Verify your submission with your school's Financial Aid Office.
5. Keep an eye out for your financial aid award letter, and monitor your student account on your school's website.
6. Hopefully receive a payment!
7. The http://www.fafsa.ed.gov website offers many helpful hints if you get stuck while filling out the FAFSA. The application will take twenty to thirty minutes to complete online.

More information on Federal Student Aid can be found through the following resources:

- The Federal Student Aid Information Center (FSAIC): 1-800-4-FED-AID (1-800-433-3243)
- Federal Student Aid: https://studentaid.ed.gov/
- Free Application for Federal Student Aid: https://fafsa.ed.gov/
- Veterans Total and Permanent Disability (TPD) Discharge: https://www.disabilitydischarge.com/
- YouTube: http://www.youtube.com/user/FederalStudentAid

The army has the Spouse Education Assistance Program (SEAP). SEAP requires that eligibility be determined by the FAFSA process. Income and household size will play a large role in determining eligibility. A spouse must be pursuing school at a minimum rate of part time and have a cumulative GPA of 2.0. This benefit can also apply to widowers of soldiers who died while on active duty and the spouses of retired active-duty members. This is a rare benefit. Contact the local Army Emergency Relief (AER) office on your installation to inquire into the application process. Most of AER's funds come from the donations of other soldiers, and the ebb and flow of these donations can determine the monies available.

The Overseas Educational Assistance Program (OSEAP) is the overseas version of SEAP, and in some cases, the award may be less than the stateside version of SEAP. That is because there are less opportunities for spouses to find a particular program they may be looking to attain. While this benefit is not widely available, if you are looking to obtain a long-term credential such as an associate's or bachelor's degree, it may be worth some attention. Always check on whether your local military community has scholarships available. More on military-based scholarships can be found later in this chapter.

STATE-BASED MILITARY BENEFITS THAT WORK FOR DEPENDENTS

Some states offer veterans and their dependents state-based benefits. Most of these states have prerequisites that determine spouses' eligibility based upon the service member's level of VA-based disability. Some states require the veteran to be completely disabled according to the VA or to have died while serving on active duty. A few state-based university systems across the country may also offer veterans and their dependents in-state tuition without a state-based benefit in place.

Veterans and dependents using transferred benefits beginning school on or after fall of 2015 will receive honorary in-state residency at any state school across the country as long as they are entering the institution under the GI Bill and are within three years of the service member's date of separation from the service. This helps to eliminate the burden of out-of-state tuition and fees that the Post-9/11 GI Bill did not previously cover.

Some institutions of higher learning have also adopted scholarships for disabled veterans and their dependents—for example, the University of Idaho has the Operation Education scholarship that may provide financial assistance for eligible service-connected disabled veterans and their spouses (http://www.uidaho.edu/operationeducation). Check with the institutions you are interested in attending to obtain information regarding policies or programs that may benefit you.

The Higher Education Opportunity Act (HEA) dictates that active-duty service members and dependent family members receive the in-state tuition rate at public institutions of higher learning within the state where they are currently stationed. You can read an excerpt of the law here: https://www.law.cornell.edu/uscode/text/20/1015d. This means that if there are any state-based tuition waivers, such as the Board of Governors (BOG) Tuition Waiver that is available for all of the state community colleges in California, and spouses qualify, they might receive the benefit. Most of these types of benefits are based upon income in some manner. They can alleviate many monetary concerns in some cases. For example, if a spouse is eligible for the BOG Waiver in California, he or she can attend the state community colleges tuition free.

The following are states with state-based education benefits for dependents at this time. Most of the information is taken directly from the state VA websites.

ALABAMA

http://www.va.state.al.us/otherbenefits.aspx
http://www.va.state.al.us/gi_dep_scholarship.aspx

Benefit

State residents with service-connected disability ratings of 20 percent or higher may qualify for his or her:

- Spouse: three standard academic years without payment of tuition, mandatory textbooks, or instructional fees at a state institution of higher learning, or for a prescribed technical course not to exceed twenty-seven months of training at a state institution.
- Dependent children: five standard academic years or part-time equivalent at any Alabama state-supported institution of higher learning or a state-supported technical school without payment of any tuition, mandatory textbooks, or instructional fees. Dependent children must start school prior to age twenty-six.

Eligibility and residency requirements for veteran:

- Veteran must have honorably served at least ninety days of continuous active federal military service during wartime, or been honorably discharged by reason of service-connected disability after serving less than ninety days of continuous active federal military service during wartime.
- Permanent civilian resident of the state of Alabama for at least one year immediately prior to (1) the initial entry into active military service or (2) any subsequent period of military service in which a break (one year or more) in service occurred and the Alabama civilian residency was established.
- Permanently service-connected veterans rated at 100 percent who did not enter service from Alabama may qualify but must first establish at least five years of permanent residency in Alabama prior to application.

CALIFORNIA

https://www.calvet.ca.gov/VetServices/Pages/College-Fee-Waiver.aspx

Benefit

- Dependent children tuition waiver at state-supported schools for service-connected disabled veterans.

The California state benefit has four different pathways for eligibility. They can be confusing. Mainly, they are Medal of Honor recipients and their children, National Guard, children of veterans with service-connected disabilities (the most common category), and spouses (veteran is totally disabled, or whose death was service connected). Let's discuss the most common category: children. California veterans who rate a 0 percent disability rating or higher may qualify for their children to receive waivers of tuition at state community colleges and universities. Please note that a 0 percent disability rating is an actual rating. Fees for books, housing, parking, and so on are not included in the waiver. The state of California does not care where you enlisted. If you separate, have a service-connected disability, and become a California resident, you may be eligible.

This is a great way to have your children's college covered. Many veterans use the benefit to send their children to state schools to pursue higher education and not worry about the bills. The universities in the state are used to children using this benefit, and the veterans' representatives at the institutions know how to facilitate it for dependent children.

To read a more thorough breakdown of eligibility, check at https://www.calvet.ca.gov/VetServices/Pages/College-Fee-Waiver.aspx.

Eligibility and residency requirements for a child for the most common pathway:

- Make less than the annual income limit (changes yearly to reflect cost of living).
- Meet in-state residency requirements determined by school.
- Provide proof of relationship to the veteran.

ILLINOIS

http://www2.illinois.gov/veterans/benefits/Pages/education.aspx

Benefit

- Children of Veterans Scholarship: https://secure.osfa.illinois.edu/scholarship-database/detail.aspx?id=1522

Each county is authorized one scholarship yearly at the University of Illinois for children of veterans of World War I, World War II, the Korean

War, the Vietnam War, Operation Enduring Freedom, or Operation Iraqi Freedom. Children of deceased and disabled veterans are given priority. These children can receive four consecutive years tuition free (undergraduate, graduate, or professional studies) at the University of Illinois (Urbana-Champaign, Chicago Health Sciences Center, or Springfield Campus).

INDIANA

http://www.in.gov/dva/2378.htm

Benefit

Be aware that the law changed in 2011. Here are the differences between the old and new laws:

- Free resident tuition for the children of disabled veterans or Purple Heart recipients.
- Benefit includes 124 semester hours of tuition and mandatory fees at the undergraduate rate.
- Benefit can be used for graduate school, but the difference between the undergraduate and graduate rate is the responsibility of the student.

Eligibility and residency requirements:

- Biological (adopted by age twenty-four) and legally adopted children of eligible disabled Indiana veterans.
- Child must produce a copy of the birth certificate or adoption papers.
- Veteran must have served during a period of wartime.
- Veteran must have been a resident of Indiana for a minimum of three consecutive years at some point in his or her lifetime.
- Must rate a service-connected disability (or have died a service-connected death) or have received the Purple Heart (demonstration of proof is necessary for either).

Under the new law, for a veteran who entered service *on or after* July 1, 2011:

- Free resident tuition for the children of disabled veterans or Purple Heart recipients.

- Benefit includes 124 semester hours of tuition and mandatory fees for undergraduate study only.
- Benefit is based on the level of disability the veteran rates (see below).
- Student must maintain a mandatory minimum GPA (see below).
- The program limits the student to eight years.

Eligibility and residency requirements:

- Biological (adopted by age eighteen) and legally adopted children of eligible disabled Indiana veterans.
- Child must produce a copy of birth certificate or adoption papers.
- Veteran must have served during a period of wartime.
- Must rate a service-connected disability (or have died a service-connected death) or have received the Purple Heart (demonstration of proof is necessary for either).
- Student must apply prior to turning thirty-two years old.

Disability rating prorated schedule for tuition, taken directly from the website:

- Children of veterans rated 80 percent service-connected disabled or higher by the VA or whose veteran parent is/was a recipient of the Purple Heart will receive 100 percent fee remission.
- Children of veterans rated less than 80 percent service-connected disabled will receive 20 percent fee remission plus the disability rating of the veteran.
- If the disability rating of the veteran changes after the beginning of the academic semester, quarter, or other period, the change in the disability rating shall be applied beginning immediately following the academic semester, quarter, or other period.

GPA requirements:

- First-year student must maintain satisfactory academic progress.
- Second-, third-, and fourth-year students must maintain a minimum cumulative GPA of 2.5.

MARYLAND

http://veterans.maryland.gov/education-supports-and-scholarships/

Benefit

• Edward T. Conroy Memorial Scholarship

Aid for qualifying veterans or children of veterans to attend part-time or full-time Maryland state school (community college, university, or private career school). Benefit works for undergraduate and graduate school. Award is not based on economic need. The award is for tuition and fees. Award works for five years at the full-time attendance rate or eight years at part time. More detailed information can be found at http://mhec.maryland.gov/preparing/Pages/FinancialAid/ProgramDescriptions/prog_conroy.aspx.

Eligibility and residency requirements:

• Children of veterans who have died or are 100 percent disabled as a result of military service.
• Veterans who have a 25 percent or greater disability rating with the VA and have exhausted federal veterans' education benefits.
• Be a Maryland resident.

Benefit

• Veterans of the Afghanistan and Iraq Conflicts (VAIC) Scholarship Program

Award is 50 percent of tuition and fees and room and board at the in-state undergraduate rate at a school within the University of Maryland system (UMUC and University of Maryland, Baltimore, are exempt from this award). All undergraduate majors are eligible. Award works for five years at the full-time attendance rate or eight years at part time. Students must maintain a minimum 2.5 GPA.

Eligibility and residency requirements:

• Have served in Afghanistan (minimum sixty days) on or after October 24, 2001, or in Iraq on or after March 19, 2003 (minimum sixty days).

- Be on active duty, or a veteran (honorable discharge), or the son, daughter, or spouse of the aforementioned group.
- Must attend school part or full time and be degree seeking.
- Supporting documentation of relationship to veteran is necessary (birth certificate or marriage certificate).
- Supporting documentation of active-duty status (orders) or DD214 is necessary.
- Applicant must be a resident of Maryland (active-duty military stationed in the state at the time of application qualify).

More detailed information can be found on the website: http://www.mhec.state.md.us/financialAid/ProgramDescriptions/prog_vaic.asp.

NEW YORK

http://www.hesc.ny.gov/pay-for-college/financial-aid/types-of-financial-aid/nys-grants-scholarships-awards/msrs-scholarship.html

Benefit

- Military Enhanced Recognition Incentive and Tribute (MERIT) Scholarship

Financial aid for qualifying veterans and dependents of veterans. Award is a maximum of four years (five for approved five-year programs) of full-time study at the undergraduate level. Award works at SUNY or City University of New York (CUNY) schools for the actual tuition and mandatory fees, plus room and board (on campus) and books and supplies. Those who attend school off campus will receive an allowance. Private school attendees will receive a sum equal to the public school costs.

Eligibility and residency requirements:

- New York residents who died or became severely and permanently disabled (verify degree of disability with the state) while participating in hostilities, or in training for duty in a combat theater.
- Must have occurred on or after August 2, 1990.

NORTH CAROLINA

http://www.wcu.edu/WebFiles/PDFs/NCDVAScholarship.pdf

Benefit

• North Carolina Division of Veterans Affairs Scholarship

Scholarships for dependent children of veterans who rate a minimum of 20 percent disability and served during wartime or received the Purple Heart. Maximum of one hundred awards per year. Award is for eight semesters completed within eight years. It covers tuition, an allowance for room and board, and exemption from certain mandatory fees at public, community, and technical colleges and institutions, or $4,500 per academic year at private schools.

Eligibility and residency requirements:

• Natural and adopted (prior to age fifteen) children of qualifying veterans.
• Be under the age of twenty-five.
• Upon submission of application, student must be a resident of North Carolina.
• Veteran must have entered service in North Carolina, or the applicant must have been born in North Carolina and maintained continuous residency in the state.

SOUTH CAROLINA

http://va.sc.gov/benefits.html, (800) 647-2434

Benefit

• Tuition Assistance for Certain War Veterans' Children

Free tuition for children of veterans who have been awarded the Purple Heart for wounds received in combat. Award can be used at state-supported schools or technical education institutions.

Eligibility and residency requirements:

- Veteran must have been a resident at time of entry into the military and throughout the service period, or has been a resident of South Carolina for a minimum of one year and still resides in the state.
- Veteran was honorably discharged.
- Served during a war period.
- Student must be twenty-six years old or younger.

TEXAS

http://www.tvc.texas.gov/Hazlewood-Act.aspx#Legacy Act

Benefit

- Legacy Program

Children may be eligible to have unused Hazlewood benefits transferred to them. The award can only be used at state-supported institutions. A list of eligible schools can be found at http://www.collegeforalltexans.com/index. cfm?ObjectID=D57D0AC5-AB2D-EFB0-FC201080B528442A under the Public School list. The award covers tuition, dues, fees, and other required charges up to 150 semester hours. The award will not cover room and board, books, student services fees, or deposit fees. For a spouse to qualify for the Legacy Act, the veteran must have died while in the line of duty or as a result of injury or illness directly related to military service, or became totally disabled for purposes of employability.

Eligibility and residency requirements:

- Veteran was a Texas state resident when he or she entered the military, designated Texas as home of record, or entered the service in Texas.
- Child must be the biological child, stepchild, adopted child, or claimed as a dependent in the current or previous tax year.
- Be under the age of twenty-five at the beginning of any term for which the benefit is being claimed (some exemptions may apply).
- Make satisfactory academic progress.
- Provide proof of veteran's honorable discharge.

Benefit

- Combat Tuition Exemption (not currently funded)

Dependent children of service members deployed in combat zones receive tuition waivers (fees not exempted).
Eligibility and residency requirements:

- Child must be a resident of Texas, or entitled to receive the in-state tuition rate (dependents of military personnel stationed in Texas).
- Must be enrolled during the time the service member is deployed in a combat zone.
- If out-of-state resident, child may need to provide copy of parent's orders.

Be aware that state reimbursement for this program is not available. It is up to each institution to decide whether they will grant this award.

WISCONSIN

http://dva.state.wi.us/Pages/benefitsClaims/StateFederalResources.aspx

Benefit

- Wisconsin GI Bill tuition remission benefit program (WI GI Bill)

Remission of tuition and fees at state institutions (University of Wisconsin and Wisconsin Technical Colleges) for eligible veterans and dependents. The award is good for a maximum of eight semesters (or 128 semester credits), undergraduate and graduate education, and professional programs. There are no income restrictions or delimiting periods. Many fees are not covered, such as books, meals, room and board, and online fees. Award cannot be combined with federal benefits.
Eligibility and residency requirements:

- Veteran must have served since September 10, 2001, and entered the service from Wisconsin.
- Must apply for Post-9/11 GI Bill benefits first, if eligible. (*Note*: Talk to an education counselor or the veterans' representatives before you elect which GI Bill you will use!)

- Children and spouses of veterans with a combined rating of 30 percent or greater from the VA may be eligible for the award.
- Child must be the biological child, stepchild, or adopted child, or any other child who is a member of the veteran's household.
- Child must be at least seventeen, but no older than twenty-six, and must be a resident of the state.
- Spouse must be a resident of the state for tuition purposes.
- Spouse has ten years from the date of the veteran's VA rating to use the benefit.

STATE-BASED EDUCATION BENEFITS BASED ON SEVERE LEVELS OF DISABILITY OR DEATH

There are other states besides those listed above that offer education benefits for spouses and/or children. In the case of these states, the veteran must be severely and permanently disabled, or have died while on active-duty service (in many cases, in combat or combat-related situations). I am not going to cover the specific details of these benefits, but below you will find a list of the states that offer this benefit and the links to their websites.

Alabama: http://www.va.state.al.us/gi_dep_scholarship.aspx
Alaska: http://veterans.alaska.gov/education-benefits.html
Arkansas: http://www.veterans.arkansas.gov/benefits
California: https://www.calvet.ca.gov/VetServices/Pages/College-Fee-Waiver.aspx
Delaware: http://veteransaffairs.delaware.gov/veterans_benefits.shtml
Florida: http://floridavets.org/benefits-services/education/
Idaho: https://boardofed.idaho.gov/scholarship/pub_safety.asp
Iowa: http://www.in.gov/dva/2378.htm
Kentucky: http://veterans.ky.gov/Benefits/Documents/KDVAInfoBook letIssueAugust2010.pdf
Louisiana: http://www.vetaffairs.la.gov/
Maine: http://www.maine.gov/dvem/bvs/VDEB_2.pdf
Maryland: http://veterans.maryland.gov/wp-content/uploads/sites/2/2013/10/MDBenefitsGuide.pdf
Massachusetts: http://www.mass.gov/veterans/education/for-family/mslf.html
Michigan: http://www.michigan.gov/documents/mistudentaid/CVTGFact Sheet_271497_7.pdf

Minnesota: http://www.mdva.state.mn.us/education/SurvivingSpouse
   DependentInformationSheet.pdf
Missouri: http://mvc.dps.mo.gov/docs/veterans-benefits-guide.pdf
Montana: http://montanadma.org/state-montana-veterans-benefits
Nebraska: http://www.vets.state.ne.us/waiver.html
New Hampshire: http://www.nh.gov/nhveterans/benefits/education.htm
New Jersey: http://www.state.nj.us/military/veterans/programs.html
New Mexico: http://www.dvs.state.nm.us/benefits.html
New York: http://www.veterans.ny.gov/
North Carolina: http://www.nc4vets.com/education
North Dakota: http://www.nd.gov/veterans/benefits/nd-dependent-tuition
   -waiver
Ohio: https://www.ohiohighered.org/ohio-war-orphans
Oregon: http://www.oregon.gov/ODVA/Pages/index.aspx
Pennsylvania: http://www.pheaa.org/funding-opportunities/other-educa
   tional-aid/postsecondary-educational-gratuity.shtml
South Carolina: http://va.sc.gov/benefits.html
South Dakota: http://vetaffairs.sd.gov/benefits/State/State%20Education
   %20Programs.aspx
Tennessee: https://www.tn.gov/veteran/section/veteran-education
Texas: http://www.tvc.texas.gov/Hazlewood-Act.aspx
Utah: http://veterans.utah.gov/state-benefits/
Virginia: http://www.dvs.virginia.gov/veterans-benefits.shtml
Washington: http://www.dva.wa.gov/benefits/education-and-training
West Virginia: http://www.veterans.wv.gov/programs/Pages/default.aspx
Wisconsin: http://dva.state.wi.us/Ben-education.asp#Tuition
Wyoming: http://wyomilitary.wyo.gov/veterans/

STATE-BASED OPPORTUNITIES (NON-MILITARY)

Remember that whatever state your military spouse is stationed in, you and
the rest of his or her dependents qualify for the in-state tuition rate. That
means that you should not be charged the out-of-state tuition rate, which is
typically much greater. Some states also offer state-based benefits at the state
community colleges or universities to their civilian population. A few states
even set aside aid for students attending private schools. Once you clear
residency at one of these institutions, you should be eligible to apply for the
state-based aid as well. This does not mean that you will automatically be

awarded the benefit. Many of these benefits are based upon levels of income, cost of the school you are attending, and will include consideration for any of the dependents that you might be supporting.

The following is just a sample of what might be available. Always check with the school you are attending for benefits that might be available. Most of these options require submission of the FAFSA to determine eligibility. Since the state community colleges are typically the cheapest route, starting at one if you are not already too far along with your schooling will usually help to keep the cost of tuition down, and they are often the institutions where these types of benefits are available. You can find a current list of your state department of education offices here: http://www2.ed.gov/about/contacts/state/index.html.

ALABAMA

Benefit: Alabama Students Grant Program

Available to eligible undergraduate students attending at either the half-time or the full-time rate of pursuit at an eligible Alabama independent college or university. Check the website for a list of participating schools. Award is up to $1,200 per academic year. Check the financial aid office of your school for an application.

Benefit: Alabama Student Assistance Program

Alabama Student Assistance Program is awarded in amounts ranging from $300 to $5,000 for undergraduate students attending eligible Alabama institutions (around eighty schools possible) and is need based. Eligible students should fill out the FAFSA located at www.fafsa.gov.

ALASKA

Benefit: Alaska Education Grant

http://acpe.alaska.gov/FINANCIAL_AID/Grants_Scholarships/Alaska_
Education_Grant

Students must be admitted into an undergraduate degree–seeking program or a vocational program at an eligible Alaska institution, have a high school diploma or a GED, be an Alaska resident, be enrolled at a minimum of part time, be a first-time bachelor's degree–seeking student, and have at minimum a $500 unmet need. Students should fill out the FAFSA as early as possible for consideration, but the deadline for filing is June 30. Awards range between $500 and $4,000 per academic year. In some cases, students might be eligible for increased award amounts.

Benefit: Alaska Performance Scholarship

http://acpe.alaska.gov/FINANCIAL_AID/Grants_Scholarships/Alaska_ Performance_Scholarship

Award amounts and eligibility criteria vary. Eligible candidates must also be Alaska residents and have graduated from an Alaska high school in 2011 or later. The award must be used within six years of high school graduation. Students must "take a more rigorous curriculum, get good grades, and score well on college placement or work ready exams" to be eligible for this grant.[4]

ARIZONA

Benefit: Arizona Leveraging Educational Assistance Partnership (AzLEAP)

https://azgrants.az.gov/arizona-leveraging-educational-assistance- partnership-azleap

A list of eligible schools can be found on the website. The AzLEAP grant is for low-income, undergraduate students and pays a maximum of $2,500 per academic year. Students must be attending a regionally or nationally accredited Arizona postsecondary school, demonstrate a significant financial need, and be enrolled at minimum at the half-time rate of pursuit. A list of participating schools can be found on the website.

ARKANSAS

Benefit: Governor's Scholarship and Governor's Distinguished Scholarship

http://scholarships.adhe.edu/scholarships/detail/governors-distinguished- scholarship

Number of awards is based upon funding, but three hundred is the overall maximum amount. Based on high performance in high school. For the Governor's Scholarship award, students must have a high school GPA of 3.5 or higher, an ACT composite score of 27, or a combined SAT score of 1220. For the Governor's Distinguished Scholarship, students must have a minimum of a 32 on a single ACT score, or a 1410 combined math and critical reasoning, and either a 3.50 GPA or selection as a National Achievement Finalist or National Merit Finalist.

Benefit: Academic Challenge Scholarship

http://scholarships.adhe.edu/scholarships-and-programs/non-traditional/

Eligible students must have an ACT score of 19, a high school GPA of 2.5 if they graduated from an Arkansas high school, or a minimum GPA of 2.5 at the collegiate level if the applicant has completed at least twelve credit hours. Application deadline is June 1. Award is not based upon academic status, so students currently attending college, entering college for the first time, or graduating high school seniors may apply.

CALIFORNIA

Benefit: The Board of Governors Fee Waiver (BOG Waiver)

http://home.cccapply.org/money/bog-fee-waiver

Eligible state residents attending California state community colleges may qualify to have their tuition costs waived. Students will still have some semester-based fees that will need to be covered if attending face to face. The community colleges will take your information from your FAFSA application to determine eligibility (http://home.cccapply.org/money/bog-fee-waiver).

Benefit: Cal Grant

Cal Grants are awarded by the California Student Aid Commission. Awardees must be California residents (remember the rule about residency for military dependents!). The application process is completed through the FAFSA. The deadline is March 2 each year, and your school must verify your GPA. Awards are based upon items such as academic performance and financial needs.

COLORADO

Benefit: Colorado Student Grant, Colorado Graduate Grant

Both grants are based upon financial need. Students must be attending eligible institutions. Students must be first-time undergraduate degree–seeking students or first-time graduate degree–seeking students and not be in default on any other educational grants or loans.

CONNECTICUT

Benefit: Connecticut Minority Teacher Grant

http://www.ctohe.org/SFA/pdfs/MTIPForm.pdf

The Minority Teacher Grant may provide a maximum of $5,000 per year for the last two years of study for minority undergraduates pursuing and enrolled in a Connecticut teacher preparation program. Eligible awardees may also receive up to $2,500 in yearly stipends for a maximum of four years of teaching in a Connecticut public elementary or secondary school. In order to be eligible, students must be attending school full time, within their junior or senior years, be nominated by an education dean at the school they are attending, and be of African American, Hispanic/Latino, Asian American, or Native American heritage. They receive the $2,500 yearly stipends while teaching, and students must begin teaching at an eligible school within sixteen months of graduation.

Benefit: Governor's Scholarship: Need and Merit-Based Award, Need-Based Award, Academic Incentive Award

http://www.ctohe.org/SFA/sfa.shtml#Governor

Need and Merit-Based Award

Must be a high school senior or graduate and must have been ranked within the top 20 percent of their class for junior year. Eligible students must have scored a minimum of 1800 on the SAT or 27 on the ACT. Awards can only be used at public or private, nonprofit institutions. Maximum award is $5,000 for a four-year program and $3,500 for a two-year course of study. Check website for deadline dates.

Need-Based Award

Eligible students must be attending a public or private, nonprofit institution and have a federal EFC within the allowable range. Award is a maximum of $3,000 for either a two-year or a four-year course of study.

Academic Incentive Award

Student must have completed a minimum of 30 credit hours the previous year and received the need-based Governor's Scholarship. Award amount is a maximum of $1,200 for a two-year or four-year course of study, and students must be attending at the full-time rate of pursuit.

DELAWARE

Benefit: Scholarship Incentive Program

http://dedoe.schoolwires.net/Page/996

To be eligible for the awards, students must file the FAFSA by April 15 every year. Students must have a financial need and a minimum cumulative GPA of 2.5–4.0 and enroll at the full-time rate of pursuit in an undergraduate degree program at a nonprofit, regionally accredited institution in Delaware or Pennsylvania or enroll full time at a nonprofit, regionally accredited college for an undergraduate or graduate degree program that is not offered at the University of Delaware, Delaware State University, or Delaware Technical Community College. Check the website to determine whether there are any restrictions in place and for deadline dates.

DISTRICT OF COLUMBIA

Benefit: DC Tuition Assistance Grant Program (DC TAG)

http://osse.dc.gov/service/dc-tuition-assistance-grant-dc-tag

DC TAG award amounts are up to $10,000 per academic year at a four-year institution and up to $2,500 at a two-year institution. The award is designated for assistance in covering the difference between in-state and out-of-state tuition at four-year public colleges and universities in the United States, Guam, and Puerto Rico. The program can also cover up to $2,500 per academic year for private school tuition within the DC metropolitan area, nationwide at two-year institutions of higher learning, and private historically black colleges and universities (HBCUs). Check website for eligibility rules.

Benefit: DC Mayor's Scholars Undergraduate Program

http://osse.dc.gov/mayorsscholars

Eligible applicants must be earning their first associate's or bachelor's degree through select schools in the area. The award is designed to bridge the gap between a student's financial aid package and the cost of attendance. The award is up to $4,000 per academic year and is funded on a first-come, first-served basis.

FLORIDA

Benefit: First Generation Matching Grant Program (FGMG)

http://www.floridastudentfinancialaid.org/SSFAD/factsheets/FGMG.pdf

Eligible students must not have a parent who has earned a bachelor's degree or higher. Students must have a substantial financial need that will be demonstrated through submission of the FAFSA. Institutions set the applications, award amounts, and deadlines, and the award is only available at Florida state universities and public community colleges.

Benefit: William L. Boyd IV Florida Resident Access Grant Program (FRAG)

http://www.floridastudentfinancialaid.org/SSFAD/factsheets/FRAG.pdf

For eligible Florida resident students attending Florida private, not-for-profit colleges or universities. Eligible schools determine deadlines, applications, and student eligibility. Students must be enrolled in a minimum of twelve credit hours per term and not have already earned a bachelor's degree.

Benefit: Florida Student Assistance Grant Program (FSAG)

http://www.floridastudentfinancialaid.org/SSFAD/factsheets/FSAG.pdf

FSAG has different options available based upon the type of school the student is attending—for example, the Florida Public Student Assistance Grant, the Florida Private Student Assistance Grant, the Florida Postsecondary Student Assistance Grant, and the Florida Public Postsecondary Career Education Student Assistance Grant. The Public Student Assistance Grant is for resident students who are attending Florida state universities and Florida colleges (public community colleges). The Florida Private Student Assistance Grant is for resident students attending eligible private, nonprofit, four-year colleges and universities located in Florida. The Florida Postsecondary Student Assistance Grant is for students attending eligible degree-granting private colleges and universities not eligible under the Florida Private Student Assistance Grant. The Florida Public Postsecondary Career Education Student Assistance Grant is for students attending eligible and participating Florida colleges (public community colleges) or career centers operated by district school boards. Eligibility parameters and award amounts vary. Check with your participating school for more information or review the listed websites.

GEORGIA

https://tcsg.edu/paying_for_college.php

Benefit: Georgia's HOPE Grant Program

https://secure.gacollege411.org/Financial_Aid_Planning/HOPE_
    Program/Georgia_s_HOPE_Grant_Program.aspx

Eligible students must be working toward a certificate or diploma. Students must maintain a minimum of a 2.0 GPA in college, but full-time enrollment is not required. Students that are receiving the HOPE grant and attending an approved program might also be eligible for the Strategic Industries Workforce Development Grant (SIWDG). SIWDG students' awards are a fixed amount each term and are based upon the credit load of the student and his or her program of study. SIWDG eligible course of study can be found here: https://tcsg.edu/freecollege.php.

HAWAII

Benefit: Hawaii State Need-Based Opportunity Grant

http://uhcc.hawaii.edu/financial/grants.php

Students must have a financial need and be attending school at the part-time rate of pursuit at minimum. Award amount may be up to the full cost of tuition.

IDAHO

Benefit: Opportunity Scholarship

https://boardofed.idaho.gov/scholarship/opportunity.asp

Requires students to submit the FAFSA and the State Board of Education scholarship application by March 1. Have a minimum GPA of 3.0, be an Idaho resident, and have graduated from an Idaho high school (GED from Idaho is acceptable). Students must enroll at the full-time undergraduate rate of pursuit seeking their first bachelor's degree. Eligible schools can be found on the website.

Benefit: Governor's Cup

https://boardofed.idaho.gov/scholarship/documents/governor's%20cup%20scholarship%20app16%20v1.pdf
https://boardofed.idaho.gov/scholarship/gov_cup.asp

The Governor's Cup is for high school seniors attending school in Idaho and planning on attending an Idaho college or university for academic or professional-technical education. Approximately twenty-five awards of $3,000 are granted based upon funding for the year and are renewable for up to four years for traditional school and three years for professional-technical education. Students must have a GPA of at least 2.8 or higher and attend college the first semester after graduation from high school. A five-hundred-word essay is required. Volunteer work is given high consideration.

ILLINOIS

Benefit: Monetary Award Program (MAP)

https://www.isac.org/students/during-college/types-of-financial-aid/
grants/monetary-award-program/#Description

Eligible students must not already possess a bachelor's degree, must be enrolled in an approved school (www.isac.org/students/during-college/types-of-financial-aid/grants/monetary-award-program/1617-approved-schools-for-the-map-program.html), and be enrolled in a minimum of three hours per term. The total award amount cannot exceed the cost of attendance at the student's institution.

INDIANA

Benefit: The Frank O'Bannon Grant

http://www.in.gov/che/4506.htm

This need-based grant is designed to provide money toward tuition and regularly assessed fees. Awards can vary greatly from year to year. Students must be pursuing an associate or bachelor's degree for the first time and be pursuing school at the full-time rate. Applications are completed through the FAFSA and must be submitted by March 10 each year for the following school year.

Benefit: Part-Time Grant

http://www.in.gov/che/4509.htm

The Part-Time Grant is for returning adult students who are pursuing either an associate or a bachelor's degree or a certificate program. A link to the application appears at the end of the FAFSA and must be completed by July 1 every year. The Part-Time Grant is designed to assist working adults to switch their rate of pursuit from full time to part time depending upon the semester.

IOWA

Benefit: Tuition Grant

https://www.iowacollegeaid.gov/content/iowa-tuition-grant

The Iowa Tuition Grant is for eligible students pursuing an undergraduate degree through an eligible Iowa-based private college or university. The grant is need based and maxes out at $6,000 per academic year, but can vary depending upon funding. Part-time students may be eligible, and the award can be received for a maximum of four years. Applicants should fill out the FAFSA application prior to July 1 of each year.

Benefit: Iowa Barber and Cosmetology Arts and Sciences Tuition Grant

https://www.iowacollegeaid.gov/content/barber-and-cosmetology-grant

Priority for this award is given to first-year students who have the greatest need for financial assistance, and the maximum award amount is $1,200 per school year. Students must fill out the FAFSA by July 1 of each year.

KANSAS

Benefit: Kansas Career Technical Workforce Grant

Students must be enrolled in eligible career technical education programs that award associate of applied science degrees or certificates. The programs must be determined to be in high demand areas or a critical industry field (http://www.kansasregents.org/resources/PDF/Students/Student_Financial_ Aid/CT_eligible_programs_1516.pdf). The award is need-based, and the priority deadline is May 1 of each year.

Benefit: Kansas Comprehensive Grant

A need-based grant for eligible students pursuing college at the full-time rate at eighteen different private colleges and universities, six state universities, and Washburn University. Award amounts range from $200 to $3,500 for the private schools and from $200 to $1,500 for state schools. The priority deadline for the FAFSA is April 1 of each year.

KENTUCKY

Benefit: Go Higher Grant

https://www.kheaa.com/website/kheaa/gohighergrant?main=1

The Go Higher Grant is need based, awards up to $1,000 per academic year, and is for students age twenty-four or older. Students must be pursuing their first undergraduate degree at a participating school at the half-time rate of pursuit (roughly one or two courses per semester). Students must complete both the FAFSA and the Go Higher Grant application (https://www.kheaa.com/pdf/gohighergrant.pdf).

Benefit: Kentucky Tuition Grant

https://www.kheaa.com/website/kheaa/ktg?main=1

This need-based grant is for eligible students attending a private university or college (https://www.kheaa.com/website/kheaa/kyschools?main=1&type=ktg). Award amount is up to $2,910 and is awarded on a first-come, first-served basis. Students should fill out the FAFSA as early as possible. Eligible students must not have outstanding debt with KHEAA or federal Title IV programs.

Benefit: College Access Program Grant

https://www.kheaa.com/website/kheaa/cap?main=1

Students must demonstrate financial need through submission of the FAFSA, be attending an eligible public or private college or university, proprietary school, or technical college, and be pursuing school at the part-time rate at minimum and in a program of at least two years in length. Award amounts are up to $1,900.

LOUISIANA

Benefit: Louisiana Go Grant Program

http://www.osfa.louisiana.gov/go_grant.htm

Award amounts varied for the 2015–2016 academic year between $300 and $3,000. Students must file the FAFSA, receive a Pell Grant award, still have a remaining need after acceptance of a Pell Grant award, and be pursuing education at an eligible Louisiana state school at a minimum of the half-time rate or higher.

Benefit: Tops Tech Early Start Program

The program is for Louisianan public high school students (eleventh or twelfth grade) who concurrently enroll for up to six credit hours in a semester at an eligible state or private college. Students must maintain a minimum GPA of 2.0 on a 4.0 scale, enroll in an eligible program (http://www.osfa. louisiana.gov/MainSitePDFs/ttes_eligible_programs.pdf), have an approved education and career plan, be in "good standing" at their high school, and score 15 or above on the mathematics AND English portion of the ACT PLAN Assessment, the traditional ACT, or through an equivalent SAT score (http://www.osfa.louisiana.gov/).

MAINE

Benefit: State of Maine Grant Program

> http://www.famemaine.com/maine_grants_loans/state-of-maine-grant-program/

Eligible students must file the FAFSA by May 1 of each year, be an under-graduate student attending school at an eligible institution, and be pursuing school at least at the half-time rate of pursuit.

MARYLAND

Benefit: Part-Time Grant

> http://www.mhec.state.md.us/financialAid/ProgramDescriptions/prog_ptgrant.asp

The Part-Time Grant is for high school students who are also enrolled in a Maryland institution of higher education (two-year or four-year institution) and are seeking an undergraduate degree. Students must be enrolled for six to eleven credits per semester and have a financial need. Need is determined through the FAFSA submission. Awards range from $200 to $2,000. Awards may be renewable.

Benefit: Hard P. Rawlings Educational Assistance Grant (EA)

http://www.mhec.state.md.us/financialAid/ProgramDescriptions/prog_
ea.asp

Eligible students include high school seniors and undergraduate students attending school at the full-time rate of pursuit for their first bachelor's degree. All majors are eligible. Students must enroll at a two-year or four-year Maryland state institution of higher learning and demonstrate financial need through submission of the FAFSA. Award amounts vary depending upon the student and the school (two-year or four-year institution).

MASSACHUSETTS

Benefit: Need-Based Tuition Waiver Program

Eligible students must demonstrate financial need through submission of the FAFSA, be pursuing their first undergraduate degree, and maintain satisfactory academic progression. Students must be attending an eligible institution (see   https://malegislature.gov/Laws/GeneralLaws/PartI/TitleII/Chapter15A/ Section5) and be enrolled in three credit hours at minimum per semester. Awards can be partial or full tuition. Contact the school you plan on attending for application demands and deadlines.

Benefit: Gilbert Matching Student Grant Program

http://www.mass.edu/osfa/programs/gilbert.asp

The Massachusetts Gilbert Matching Student Grant Program (GMSGP) is for first-time degree-seeking undergraduate students or students pursuing their first diploma from a hospital or professional nursing program who are considered dependent upon their parents for support or independent students who have been residents for twelve months prior to the start of the academic year. Students must be pursuing school at the full-time rate of pursuit and not be on default on any federal or state student loans or owe any refunds. Students must demonstrate financial need and attend an eligible school. Awards range between $200 and $2,500 per year.

Benefit: MASSGrant

http://www.mass.edu/osfa/programs/massgrant.asp

The MASSGrant is need based and can be used by awardees attending eligible institutions (see website for institutional parameters) for higher education programs. Students demonstrate need through submission of the FAFSA, must be enrolled at the full-time rate of pursuit, and be pursuing their first bachelor's degree. Award amounts vary depending upon the type of institution and the student's Estimated Family Contribution (EFC).

MICHIGAN

Benefit: Michigan Tuition Grant

http://www.michigan.gov/mistudentaid/0,4636,7-128-60969_61016-274564--,00.html

A need-based grant available to undergraduate students through independent, nonprofit, degree-granting Michigan institutions postsecondary and covers only the cost of tuition and fees (up to $1,830 per academic year). More specific information can be found on the current fact sheet: http://www.michigan.gov/documents/mistudentaid/MTGFactSheet2015-16_495494_7.pdf?20150803082638.

MINNESOTA

Benefit: Minnesota State Grant

http://www.ohe.state.mn.us/mPg.cfm?pageID=138

Students must file the FAFSA in order to determine eligibility, and the award works at public community and technical colleges, schools of nursing and related health professions, private colleges, private career institutions, and the University of Minnesota. Students must be enrolled as undergraduates, pursuing their first undergraduate degree, and be pursuing at least three credits per term, but to receive the full amount a student must be enrolled at a full-time rate of pursuit each semester (fifteen credit hours). Award amounts vary each year, but the average award is approximately $1,735.

MISSISSIPPI

Benefit: Mississippi Eminent Scholars Grant (MESG)

http://riseupms.com/state-aid/mesg/

Students must be accepted and enrolled at an approved (check the website for a list) public or nonprofit two-year or four-year college or university and be pursuing school at the full-time rate of pursuit. High school applicants must have a minimum GPA of 3.5 on a 4.0 scale and have scored a minimum of 1290 on the SAT or 29 on the ACT or be a National Merit or National Achievement Finalist or Semi-Finalist. College applicants meet all of the same eligibility requirements as the high school applicants but need a 3.5 GPA on a 4.0 scale for their college classes. Students must also be pursuing their first certificate, associate's degree, or bachelor's degree. Maximum award amount is $2,500 (amount may not exceed tuition and fees owed). Applications and deadline dates can be found on the website.

Benefit: Mississippi Tuition Assistance Grant (MTAG)

http://riseupms.com/state-aid/mtag/

Students must be accepted and enrolled at an approved (check the website for a list) public or nonprofit two-year or four-year college or university and be pursuing school at the full-time rate of pursuit. Students must have a minimum high school GPA of 2.5 on a 4.0 scale and have scored at least 15 on the ACT. Students must also be pursuing their first certificate, associate's degree, or bachelor's degree. Maximum award amount is $500 per academic year.

MISSOURI

Benefit: Access Missouri Grant

http://dhe.mo.gov/ppc/grants/MissouriStudentFinancialAid.php

The Access Missouri Financial Assistance Program is a needs-based grant that students can apply for through submission of the FAFSA. The FAFSA must be submitted by April 1 of each year in order to be eligible. Award amounts can vary, but the 2015–2016 academic year awards were set at a maximum of $850 for two-year colleges and $1,850 for four-year universities. Students must not have received their first bachelor's degree or be pursuing a certificate or degree in theology or divinity. Eligible schools can be found here: http://dhe.mo.gov/documents/ParticipatingSchools.pdf.

MONTANA

Benefit: Community College 2 + 2 Honors Scholarship

http://www.umt.edu/finaid/types-of-aid/tuition-waivers/default.php

Eligible students receive an associate's degree from a Montana state two-year community college or a two-year Montana University System (MUS) school and must have attended that eligible school for a minimum of two semesters prior to graduation. Students must also be enrolled in an eligible four-year institution and be prepared to use the award immediately following the semester they graduate with the associate's degree.

NEBRASKA

Benefit: Nebraska Opportunity Grant (NOG)

https://ccpe.nebraska.gov/nebraska-opportunity-grant-nog

Students must have a financial need and be attending a Nebraska postsecondary institution. Need is determined through submission of the FAFSA, but some institutions might also require an institutional application. Students must receive the federal Pell Grant and still have a remaining financial need.

NEVADA

Benefit: Silver State Opportunity Grant (SSOG)

https://www.nevada.edu/ir/Page.php?p=ssog

Students must submit the FAFSA in order to determine eligibility amount. Visit the website to see a list of approved schools. Students must demonstrate financial need, be enrolled at the full-time rate of pursuit (15 SHs), be college ready (based on placement or enrollment in college-level math and English courses), be pursuing their first bachelor's degree, and be enrolled in a degree or certificate program.

NEW HAMPSHIRE

Benefit: Leveraged Incentive Grant

http://education.nh.gov/highered/

Eligible students are high school sophomores, juniors, or seniors and amounts range from $250 to $7,500. The award is based on merit and financial need. Speak to your high school counselor for more information.

NEW JERSEY

Benefit: New Jersey Tuition Aid Grant (TAG)

http://www.hesaa.org/Documents/TAG_program.pdf

TAG is a need-based award available to students attending eligible institutions of higher learning within the state (see website) full-time. A Part-Time TAG Program is available for students taking between six and eleven credits through a county college. Awards are not solely based on need, but also take into account the cost of attending a particular institution and available funding. The award is renewable, if the student is eligible, but can only cover up to the cost of tuition. Students must submit the FAFSA and the New Jersey state application, which is made available at the end of the FAFSA through a link. Check the website for deadline dates as they vary based on the semester of attendance and whether the student is renewing an existing grant or applying for the first time.

NEW MEXICO

Benefit: Student Incentive Grant Program

http://www.hed.state.nm.us/students/nmsig.aspx

For undergraduate students who demonstrate financial need and are attending public or private nonprofit institutions within the state. Award amounts range between $200 and $2,500 per academic year and may be renewed. Students must be pursuing school at the undergraduate level at a minimum of part time and submit the FAFSA.

Benefit: College Affordability Grant

http://www.hed.state.nm.us/students/college-affordability-grant.aspx

Students must demonstrate a financial need and be attending a New Mexico state college or university. The maximum award amount is $1,000 per semester and may be renewed. Students must be attending school at the undergraduate level at a minimum of part time and submit the FAFSA.

NEW YORK

Benefit: New York State Tuition Assistance Program (TAP)

https://www.hesc.ny.gov/pay-for-college/apply-for-financial-aid/nys-tap.html

https://www.hesc.ny.gov/pay-for-college/apply-for-financial-aid/nys-tap/part-time-tap.html

Programs are available for both full-time and part-time students. Full-time students must be pursuing at least twelve credits per semester that are applicable to their major and be attending an eligible institution. Students must be making satisfactory academic progress. Part-time students must be taking at least six but less than twelve credits per semester.

NORTH CAROLINA

Benefit: North Carolina Education Lottery Scholarship (ELS)

http://www.cfnc.org/index.jsp

Grant is need based, and students must complete the FAFSA in order to be considered. Students must be pursuing at least six credit hours per semester, maintain satisfactory academic standards (required by the institution), and must be classified as an undergraduate (degree, certificate, and diploma programs are eligible). Award amounts range based upon the academic year.

NORTH DAKOTA

Benefit: North Dakota State Student Incentive Program

https://www.ndus.edu/students/paying-for-college/

Award amount is up to $975 per semester and can be reapplied for every year, but it is limited to eight semesters or completion of a bachelor's degree. Award is for undergraduate students who are pursuing school at least at the quarter-time rate of pursuit. Submission of the FAFSA is required prior to April 1 of each year.

Benefit: North Dakota Scholars Program

https://www.ndus.edu/students/paying-for-college/grants-scholarships/
    #NDSP

The North Dakota Scholars Program is merit based and offers full tuition scholarships for an undergraduate rate of pursuit. Students may receive the award for a maximum of eight semesters or when the student attains a bachelor's degree, whichever occurs first. Stipends cannot exceed $2,000 a year. To be eligible for the award, students must score at or above the 95 percentile of those who took the ACT by July 1 of the year proceeding the student's enrollment in college.

OHIO

Benefit: Ohio College Opportunity Grant (OCOG)

https://www.ohiohighered.org/ocog

The award is need based, and students should fill out the FAFSA to apply. Award works at eligible Ohio and Pennsylvania schools. Students must be pursuing an associate's degree, first bachelor's degree, or a nursing diploma. Students must have a maximum Expected Family Contribution (see website to determine) of $2,190 or less and a maximum household income of $75,000. Those attending Ohio state community colleges are not excluded, but they must be attending an eligible institution year-round.

OKLAHOMA

Benefit: Oklahoma Tuition Aid Grant (OTAG)

https://secure.okcollegestart.org/financial_aid_planning/oklahoma_
grants/oklahoma_tuition_aid_grant.aspx

OTAG strictly uses students' FAFSA applications to determine OTAG awards. This award can be granted for students attending private schools as well as state-supported institutions of higher learning. A list of eligible schools can be found here: https://secure.okcollegestart.org/Financial_Aid_Planning/Oklahoma_Grants/OTAG_Eligible_Schools.aspx. "The maximum annual award is the lesser of 75 percent of enrollment costs or $1,000 for students attending public colleges, universities or career technology centers, and $1,300 for students attending eligible private colleges or universities."[5] The award is broken into two semester payments, one during the first semester and another during the second semester. The award is based upon financial need and is determined by the Expected Family Contribution (EFC), which is calculated on the student's Federal Student Aid application.

OREGON

Benefit: Oregon Opportunity Grant (OOG)

http://www.oregonstudentaid.gov/oregon-opportunity-grant.aspx

Awards are given on a first-come, first-served basis. Amount can vary each year depending upon funding. The 2015–2016 award amount was $2,100 for eligible students to use at any Oregon-based postsecondary institution. Students should fill out the FAFSA as soon as possible after the application opens on January 1, as the awards are often depleted around February 1. Students can use tax returns from the previous year to file initially, then update the information after filing the current year's taxes.

PENNSYLVANIA

Benefit: Pennsylvania State Grant Program

https://www.pheaa.org/funding-opportunities/state-grant-program/index.shtml

Eligible students should have graduated from high school, be attending a postsecondary school that is approved by the Pennsylvania Higher Education Assistance Agency (PHEAA), not have already earned a bachelor's degree, and be taking a minimum of six credit hours but less than twelve credit hours per semester. Programs of study must take at least two academic years to complete, and students must maintain satisfactory academic progress during this time frame. Award amounts can be found here: https://www.pheaa.org/funding-opportunities/state-grant-program/prepare.shtml.

SOUTH CAROLINA

Benefit: South Carolina Need-Based Grant

https://www.che.sc.gov/CHE_Docs/studentservices/needbased/q_and_a_for_nbg.pdf

The South Carolina Need-Based Grant is applied for through submission of the FAFSA. Students who are enrolled at the full-time rate of pursuit may be eligible for up to $2,500 per academic year, and students attending school at the part-time rate of pursuit may be eligible for up to $1,250 per academic year. Any award must go directly toward the cost of attending the institution. Students must be enrolled through an eligible South Carolina state institution (check the website for a list of eligible schools) as degree seeking.

SOUTH DAKOTA

Benefit: South Dakota Opportunity Scholarship

https://sdos.sdbor.edu/

Students must meet five prerequisites in order to be eligible: must have been a resident upon high school graduation, enter college within five years of graduating high school (or within one year of separating from the service), attend an eligible institution, have a high school GPA of 3.0 or higher and not have received any grades lower than a C, and have a minimum ACT composite score of 24 or higher or an SAT (verbal and mathematics) of at least 1090. Award will work for four academic (or equivalent) years, eight consecutive fall and spring terms, or until the student attains a bachelor's degree. Awards are dispersed in two payments, one in the fall semester and one in the spring. See the website for current payment rates.

Benefit: Critical Teaching Needs Scholarship

https://www.sdbor.edu/student-information/Pages/Critical-Teaching-Needs-Scholarship.aspx

Students do not need to have graduated from a South Dakota high school nor be residents of the state, but students must commit in writing to stay in South Dakota and work in a critical-need occupation for five years upon completion of school. If a student opts to leave the state before completion of the five required years, he or she will have the scholarship converted into an interest-bearing loan. Students must attend an eligible institution at the undergraduate rate of pursuit, be within their final two years of college, and already be admitted into a teaching program (in a critical-needs area).

TENNESSEE

Benefit: Tennessee Student Assistance Award (TSAA)

https://www.tn.gov/collegepays/article/tennessee-student-assistance-award

TSAA is a need-based award that does not need to be repaid. Students must be enrolled at a minimum of the part-time rate of pursuit and complete the FAFSA. Students must be attending an eligible institution (www.tn.gov/collegepays/article/tennessee-student-assistance-award-eligible-institutions), make satisfactory academic progress, and be pursuing their first bachelor's degree. See website for award amounts.

Benefit: Wilder-Naifeh Technical Skills Grant

https://www.tn.gov/collegepays/article/wilder-naifeh-technical-skills-grant

Students must submit the FAFSA and be pursuing a certificate or a diploma through a Tennessee College of Applied Technology. Award amount is $2,000 but cannot exceed the cost of attendance. Check the website deadline dates for the different school terms.

TEXAS

Benefit: Texas Public Education Grant (TPEG)

http://www.collegeforalltexans.com/apps/financialaid/tofa.cfm?Kind=GS

TPEG is for students who have a financial need and are attending Texas state public colleges or universities. Deadlines and amounts vary, and awards are given from the schools' own resources. Awards may not be in amounts that are more than the student's financial need. Verify requirements with your institution.

Benefit: Texas Educational Opportunity Grant Program (TEOG)

The Educational Opportunity Grant Program is for eligible students who have a financial need and are attending Texas state community colleges. Students must have a nine-month expected family contribution (EFC) of no more than $4,800, be enrolled at least at the half-time rate of pursuit, and be within the first thirty semester hours of their associate's degree or certificate program.

UTAH

Benefit: Higher Education Success Stipend Program (HESSP)

http://higheredutah.org/pdf/databook/2015/TabF.pdf

Students must have qualified for a Federal Pell Grant and be enrolled at minimum at the part-time rate of pursuit. Award amounts vary. Check with your institution to determine deadline dates and award amounts.

VERMONT

Benefit: Vermont Incentive Grant

http://services.vsac.org/wps/wcm/connect/vsac/vsac/pay+for+college/
funding+sources/grants/vsac+-+pay+-+funding+sources+-+grants

Eligible students are taking at least twelve credits per semester, are pursuing their first bachelor's degree, are attending the University of Vermont College of Medicine, or are enrolled in a doctor of veterinary medicine program. The grant amount varies each year and is need based.

Benefit: Vermont Non-Degree Grant

Students must be enrolled in a program that is not matriculated and that is geared to improve their employability. Award is for up to two enrollment terms per financial aid year and can be used at an approved institution of higher learning in the United States or Canada, a Vermont technical center, or a private organization within the United States that is approved and offers training courses. Award amount is need based and based upon yearly funding.

VIRGINIA

Benefit: Tuition Assistance Grant Program

http://www.cicv.org/Affordability/Tuition-Assistance-Grant.aspx

Students must be attending eligible (check the website for a list) private, nonprofit schools (may not be pursuing religious training or theological education). Students should check with the financial aid offices of their institutions for applications. The application period is July 31 to December 1 of each year. Students must be attending school full time as undergraduate students or a graduate program for a health profession related–professional program. The undergraduate award amount is $3,100, and the graduate award amount is $1,550.

WASHINGTON

Benefit: Washington State Need Grant (SNG)

http://readysetgrad.org/college/state-need-grant

Eligible students must be pursuing a first associate's or bachelor's degree or a certificate in any field except theology and take a minimum of three credits at an eligible institution that can be found here: http://readysetgrad.org/eligible-institutions. Students must have a family income at or below predetermined amounts that can be found here: http://readysetgrad.org/college/state-need-grant. Check the website for all other eligibility requirements. The maximum lifetime award is fifteen quarters and is based upon a funds-available basis. Award amounts are based on different qualifying criteria. Check the website or the FAQ sheet (http://readysetgrad.org/sites/default/files/2014. sng.faq.pdf) for more information.

Benefit: Washington State Opportunity Scholarship

http://www.waopportunityscholarship.org/home

Eligible students must have earned a high school diploma or GED from a Washington State high school, be pursuing an in-demand major (STEM or health care), be working toward a first bachelor's degree, be planning on enrolling at the full-time rate of pursuit, be enrolling in a Washington State college or university or be planning on transferring to one within the first ninety quarter credits that they earn, be a high school senior or a college student who has not completed more than six quarter hours or four semester hours prior to the application due date, and have a minimum GPA of 2.75.

WEST VIRGINIA

Benefit: West Virginia Higher Education Grant

https://www.cfwv.com/Financial_Aid_Planning/Scholarships/
    Scholarships_and_Grants/West_Virginia_Higher_Education_Grant.
    aspx

Award is need based and renewable, and it must be used at an eligible state or private institution in West Virginia or Pennsylvania. Students must be pursuing their first bachelor's degree and submit the FAFSA prior to April 15. Award amount varies (set at a maximum of $2,600 for the 2016–2017 academic year).

WISCONSIN

Benefit: Wisconsin Grant

http://heab.state.wi.us/programs.html

Eligible undergraduate students (Wisconsin residents) attend school within the UW system, Wisconsin technical colleges, or tribal colleges system at a minimum of part time. Students complete the FAFSA in order to determine award. Awards are based upon financial need and range between $250 and $3,000 for eligible students.

Wisconsin Grant-Private Non-Profit

http://heab.state.wi.us/programs.html

Eligible undergraduate students are Wisconsin residents and must demonstrate financial need through filing the FAFSA. Students must be pursuing school at a minimum of half time and be enrolled in degree or certificate programs at nonprofit, independent colleges or universities based in Wisconsin.

Minority Undergraduate Retention Grant

http://heab.state.wi.us/programs.html

Eligible minority students must be attending a Wisconsin technical college, independent college or university, or a tribal college and be pursuing school at a minimum rate of part time.

Wisconsin resident minority undergraduates, excluding first-year students, must be enrolled at least half time in independent, tribal, or Wisconsin technical college institutions. Students must demonstrate a financial need, and award amounts are a maximum of $2,500 per year, for a maximum of eight semesters. See the website for the minority student classification parameters.

WYOMING

Benefit: Wyoming College Access Grant

http://www.wyo4ed.org/paying/grants

Award is need based, and students must have been awarded Pell Grant funds in order to be eligible. Students must be attending college for the first time, and priority is given to graduating high school students. Approximately six hundred awards per academic year will be given at $1,000 per award. Students must complete the FAFSA and be enrolled at the full-time rate of pursuit. Eligible institutions are those that participate in the Federal Pell Grant program in any state within the United States.

STATE-BASED TUITION EXCHANGE PROGRAMS
FOR REDUCED RESIDENCY COSTS

Students who opt to attend college at a state institution that is not within the state where they hold residency are charged out-of-state tuition rates. These charges can often be upward of $10,000 a year or more on top of the regular tuition rates, making it a financially difficult option for many. Some states have addressed this problem on a regional basis and formed higher education tuition exchanges with other states located close by that allow students residing within these locations to receive discounted out-of-state tuition rates. That means that if you live in one state but prefer to attend college within another state, it may become more affordable to you if you are able to participate in the program. Each program's coverage parameters vary, and it is important to pay attention to the eligibility rules.

Benefit: Western Interstate Commission for Higher Education, Western Undergraduate Exchange (WUE)

http://www.wiche.edu/wue

The Western Undergraduate Exchange (WUE) program's member states include Alaska, Arizona, California, Colorado, Hawaii, Idaho, Montana, Nevada, New Mexico, North Dakota, Oregon, South Dakota, Utah, Washington, Wyoming, and the Commonwealth of the Northern Mariana Islands. Students who are from one of these eligible states can ask for a reduced out-of-state tuition rate that would equate to 150 percent of the in-state resident rate. This program works at state two-year and four-year colleges and universities. Some states limit the amount of WUE awards each year, so it is important to apply as early as possible. Some states require that the WUE program be applied to every year, and others will allow eligible students to renew their WUE for two (associate's degree) to four years depending on whether the student is pursuing an associate's or bachelor's degree.

Benefit: Southern Regional Education Board, Academic Common Market

http://www.sreb.org/page/1304/academic_common_market.html

The Academic Common Market program's member states include Alabama, Arkansas, Delaware, Georgia, Kentucky, Louisiana, Maryland, Mississippi,

Oklahoma, South Carolina, Tennessee, Virginia, and West Virginia. Florida and Texas participate at the graduate level. Students interested in pursuing degrees that are not offered at schools within their state can apply to a participating Academic Common Market program school located out of state, submit the state's ACM certification application, and receive the in-state tuition rate. First professional degree programs (law, medicine, dentistry, pharmacy, and optometry) are not eligible.

Benefit: New England Board of Higher Education, Tuition Break, the New England Regional Student Program (RSP)

http://www.nebhe.org/programs-overview/rsp-tuition-break/overview/

RSP participating states include Connecticut, Maine, Massachusetts, New Hampshire, Rhode Island, and Vermont. Students from these states can enroll in out-of-state schools within this cohort and receive tuition discounts as long as they are enrolling in a degree program that is not offered at a state school within their home state. There are more than eight hundred participating programs. The program works at state two-year and four-year institutions of higher learning. To see the list of schools and the discounts offered for the 2015–2016 academic year, visit the following site: http://www.nebhe.org/info/pdf/tuitionbreak/2015-16_RSP_TuitionBreak_TuitionRates.pdf.

Benefit: Midwestern Higher Education Compact (MHEC), Midwest Student Exchange Program (MSEP)

http://msep.mhec.org/

MSEP participating states include Illinois, Indiana, Kansas, Michigan, Minnesota, Missouri, Nebraska, North Dakota, and Wisconsin. Participating MSEP institutions agree to tuition charges for out-of-state residents that do not exceed more than 150 percent of the in-state tuition rate. Rates change from school to school, but students usually receive a discount somewhere between $500 and $5,000 per academic year. To verify school participation and eligibility parameters, check the website.

SCHOLARSHIPS

Although quite a bit of scholarship money is available for military spouses, you must be proactive in your pursuit. No one is going to hand you the money without you making an effort. Applying for scholarships is not as difficult as it seems. Oftentimes, you can reuse information, so keep everything you write. Most education centers have financial aid packets available for you to pick up or are posted on their websites. These packets offer a good place to start conducting your search.

Scholarships come in all shapes and sizes. You will need to determine which scholarships may apply to you. Do not narrow yourself to simply military spouse–based possibilities. You can apply for civilian scholarships as well. Most break down into specific categories, such as pursuit of study, age, gender, race, disability, state-based, or school-based options.

You will also need to inquire into whether the scholarship only pays tuition or perhaps goes into your pocket similar to FSA. If you are using transferred Post-9/11 GI Bill benefits and all of your tuition is already covered, applying for scholarships that pay tuition might not be beneficial.

When you begin your search, remember it will take some time to find and determine eligibility. Start by making a quick search on your school's website. Many schools list scholarships specific to their institution right on their own web pages. Check with your school's veterans' representatives, the financial aid department, and the local education center on your base for possible scholarship opportunities. Libraries are also an underused resource for scholarship opportunities. Check opportunities based on options within the military community, then check the civilian sector–based scholarships.

Most scholarships will require an essay, so prepare the best essay possible, and then see whether someone in the education center is willing to proofread it for you. Always start well in advance. Most scholarships are due during the spring semester in order to pay out for the following fall.

Be very careful of organizations demanding you pay money in order to be eligible for a scholarship. Scholarship information is widely available, and you should not have to pay to find, receive, or complete an application. Most certainly, *never* give any credit card information. If you need help, contact your school's financial aid department.

Applying for scholarships can require a lot of legwork, and many students are not willing to put in the effort. This limits the pool of competitors and increases the chances of you being awarded a scholarship. Additionally, many veterans will not bother to explore other options outside of the GI Bill to increase their sources of funding, so military-related scholarships can have even less potential competitors. Use this to your advantage.

Lastly, remember that once you apply for a scholarship, each subsequent scholarship becomes easier. Many essay requirements are similar and share a common theme of "How will you use your education to make better or change the world?" Essays can be modified slightly and used multiple times. Plus, once you have been through the process of filling out an application, listing information and extracurricular activities, you can just copy and paste the same answers for each subsequent application. If transcripts are required, perhaps to demonstrate a GPA or degree progression, the same copy can usually be used repeatedly. Keeping these tips in mind will give you the psychological edge required to endure the legwork far beyond your potential competitors to hopefully receive a financial reward.

SCHOLARSHIP POSSIBILITIES FOR DEPENDENTS

Below is a list of scholarships available for spouses and dependent children. Always check with the Officer's Spouse's Clubs at the base where you are stationed if your spouse is still on active duty with the military. The clubs usually have scholarship possibilities every year. The National Military Family Association has a list of military bases with officer spousal clubs that offer scholarship opportunities (see http://www.militaryfamily.org/spouses-scholarships/scholarships.html). The following are a few more notable options.

Ladies Auxiliary VFW

Continuing Education Scholarship

> http://usascholarships.com/ladies-auxiliary-vfw-continuing-education-scholarship/

Spouses, sons, and daughters of members may be eligible if they are pursuing a college degree or career pathway at a technical school.

The Veterans of Foreign Wars (VFW)

Patriots Pen

> http://www.vfw.org/PatriotsPen/

Open to students in grades 6–8. Students must be enrolled in a public, private, or parochial high school or home study program within the United

States or its territories. Deadline is November 1. Essay must be between three hundred and four hundred words. Judging is based upon three criteria: knowledge, theme development, and clarity of ideas.

Voice of Democracy

http://www.vfw.org/VOD/

Open to students in grades 9–12. Students must be enrolled in a public, private, or parochial high school or home study program within the United States or its territories. Deadline is November 1. Students write and record a reading of their essay and submit for judging. Judging is based upon three criteria: originality, content, and delivery.

The Camp Pendleton Officer's Spouses Club–Marines

http://www.osccp.org/page-1371830

Amount of award varies. Spouses whose active-duty partners are stationed aboard the Camp Pendleton Marine Corps base, either Marines or sailors or other sister services, are eligible. Sponsors may be enlisted or officers/retirees (navy and Marine Corps). Sponsors and applicants must live within a fifty-mile radius of Camp Pendleton.

The Patriot Spouses' Club

http://www.fortsillpsc.org

Both spouses and children are eligible to apply for this scholarship. The nature and amount of this scholarship varies. In many cases, there are not enough applicants, so amounts per scholarship may be modified each year. If not enough people apply, then those who do and outshine the others will receive more money. This scholarship is awarded based on scholastic merit as well as community involvement. High school seniors, college students no older than twenty-four, and spouses are eligible to apply.

Vice Admiral Robert L. Walters Surface Navy Association (SNA) Scholarship Application–Navy

https://www.navysna.org/sna/Awards/Scholarship/ApplicationIndex.htm

Applications must be postmarked by March 1 of each year. Scholarship is awarded for demonstrations of leadership, academic achievement, and community service. Applicants must be members of the Surface Navy Association or a dependent child, stepchild, ward, or spouse of a current SNA member who must be in their second year of membership with the SNA (must be subsequent years). Members can still be on active duty, be honorably discharged, or retired. Scholarship amount is $2,000 per year for a maximum of four years.

The Anchor Scholarship Foundation–Navy

http://www.anchorscholarship.com/

Scholarships for dependent children and spouses of active-duty, retired, or honorably discharged surface navy personnel. Candidates must demonstrate academic performance, character, extracurricular activities, and financial need. Scholarship is only for tuition and tuition-related expenses. Dependent children must be pursuing a four-year BA or BS degree. Spouses can be pursuing an associate's or bachelor's degree.

Fisher House

http://www.militaryscholar.org/

Run by the commissaries. A minimum of one $2,000 scholarship is awarded through every commissary location, although more might be possible depending on funding. Award may be used for payment of tuition, books, lab fees, or other education-related expenses. Scholarship is open to children of active duty, retired, or reserve service members. Applicant must have a minimum 3.0 GPA on a 4.0 scale.

The Joanne Holbrook Patton Military Spouse Scholarships

https://militaryfamily.scholarships.ngwebsolutions.com/CMXAdmin/
Cmx_Content.aspx?cpId=561

For spouses of active duty, retired, and reserve service members. Award may be used for tuition, fees, or school room and board. The scholarship offers assistance for GED or ESL, vocational training or certification, undergraduate or graduate degrees, licensure fees, and clinical hours for mental health licensure. Applicants can attend face-to-face schooling or online.

American Legion

http://www.legion.org/scholarships

Samsung American Legion Scholarship

For high school juniors who complete a Boys State or Girls State program. Applicant must also be a direct descendant of an eligible wartime veteran (see website for more information). Scholarship is for undergraduate study only and is based on financial need. It can be used for tuition, books, fees, or room and board. Applicants must have completed a Boys State or Girls State program, be direct descendants or legally adopted children of wartime veterans (must be eligible for American Legion membership), and be in their junior year of high school. Award is up to $20,000 for an undergraduate course of study. Winners are selected based upon academic record, financial need, and participation in community activities. Application requires several mini-essays.

Legacy Scholarship

http://www.legion.org/scholarships/legacy

Eligible applicants are children or adopted children of military members who died while on active duty on or after September 11, 2001; are high school seniors or already graduated; and are pursuing an undergraduate degree.

The Baseball Scholarship

http://www.legion.org/scholarships/baseball
baseball@legion.org

Applicant must have graduated high school, be on a team affiliated with an American Legion post, and be on a current roster filed with the National Headquarters. High school transcripts, three letters of testimony, and a completed application must be filed.

National High School Oratorical Contest Scholarship

http://www.legion.org/scholarships/oratorical
oratorical@legion.org

Scholarship money (up to $18,000 for first place) can be used at any college or university within the United States. Scholarship has hundreds of small rewards involved at local levels.

Department of Michigan — American Legion Auxiliary

http://michalaux.org/scholarships/

Medical Career Scholarship

Applicants should be daughters, granddaughters, great-granddaughters, sons, grandsons, or great-grandsons of honorably discharged or deceased veterans of specific conflicts (World War I, World War II, Korea, Vietnam, Persian Gulf, etc.) and be living in Michigan. Award is $500 for tuition, room and board fees, books, and so on. Scholarship must be used at a school in Michigan, and applicants must be in their senior year of high school (top quarter of their class) and preparing to enter college. This is a need-based scholarship.

Scholarship for Nontraditional Students

One two-year scholarship of $500 per year will be awarded. Applicant must be the descendant of a veteran, over the age of twenty-two, and attending college or trade school for the first time or attending college after a significantly long break. The award may be used toward tuition and books at a school in the state of Michigan. Entries are due by March 15. Application includes short essays.

National American Legion Auxiliary — Children of Warriors Scholarship National Presidents' Scholarship

https://www.alaforveterans.org/Scholarships/Children-of-Warriors-National-Presidents--Scholarship/

Applicants must be daughters or sons, stepdaughters or stepsons, grandsons or granddaughters, step grandsons or step granddaughters, or step great-grandsons or step great-granddaughters of eligible American Legion members. Applicants should be in their senior year of high school and complete fifty hours of volunteer service. Completed applications and all documentation (includes an essay) are due to the local American Legion Auxiliary Unit by March 1, and winners are announced on March 15.

Spirit of Youth Scholarship

https://www.alaforveterans.org/Scholarships/Spirit-of-Youth-
Scholarship-Fund/

Five awards at $5,000 each for this scholarship. Applicants must be seniors
in high school and junior members of the American Legion Auxiliary for the
past three years, hold current membership, and continue membership
throughout awarding years. A 3.0 GPA is mandatory for individuals applying
for this scholarship. Applications are due by March 1; winners are announced
March 15. ACT or SAT scores, high school transcripts, four letters of recommendation, a completed FAFSA application, and essays are required.

OTHER EXTREMELY NOTEWORTHY OPTIONS

The American Military Retirees Scholarships:

http://amra1973.org/Scholarship/

Federal Sites for Scholarship Searches

http://www.careerinfonet.org/scholarshipsearch/ScholarshipCategory.
asp?searchtype=category&nodeid=22
http://studentaid.ed.gov/

Searches

https://scholars.horatioalger.org/
http://www.collegescholarships.org/scholarships/army.htm
http://www.finaid.org/military/veterans.phtml
http://www.scholarships.com
http://www.collegeboard.org
http://www.scholarships4students.com/council_of_college_and_
military_educators_scholarship.htm
http://scholarshipamerica.org/
http://www.careeronestop.org
http://www.collegedata.com
http://www.finaid.org/scholarships/
http://fedmoney.org/
http://www.militaryonesource.com

TEXTBOOK-BUYING OPTIONS

Who knew books could be so expensive? Welcome to college! The cost of books can often get out of control. If you are using transferred Post-9/11 GI Bill benefits, the books and supplies stipend maxes out at $1,000 per academic year, and often that does not begin to cover the bill.

College books are notoriously expensive. Unlike high school, a year of college requires an incredible number of books. Professors have to find supplemental materials to feed your brain and back up the information with proof. Books are still the most common, easiest way of accomplishing this task.

Now you know why you need them, but not why college books are so expensive. A few reasons come to mind—for example, copyrighted material, specialized material, and online supplements. College books can hold an incredible amount of copyrighted material. Publishers have to cover the copyright fees, as well as all other fees, within the cost of the book. Information within college books is usually quite specialized and often not found elsewhere. This means the books do not have another avenue for sales and this contributes to a highly competitive market, driving the cost up. Many books also have online supplements attached to them, and those fees must also be included in the cost.

Last—although I (Jillian) hate addressing this reason but feel I must— many professors have written books. Can you guess which books could be included in your reading list? Terrible, I agree . . . since professors get royalties just like other authors. Let's think more positively about the situation. Sometimes these books can be some of your most informative and easily organized reference material. Professors often write books based on the knowledge they have derived from their years in the classroom and field experience to help themselves or others teach. Many schools take pride in having such accomplished professors on staff. Speaking from personal experience, getting published is no easy feat. This practice may sometimes help a professor cut down on the book expenses for his or her students because the book follows along closely with the class's learning expectations, thereby allowing the student to purchase at least one less book than previously necessary.

Although many other reasons contribute to book costs, I'll get down to the reason you are reading this section: how to pay for them. The first trip to the bookstore can be excruciating as reality sets in. Do not stress yet; other options may exist. Since many books top the $100 range (sometimes closer to $200!), students should spend as much time as feasible trying to find books from alternate sources. I still recommend checking out the campus bookstore first. Some schools maintain significant used textbook sections. You will need to get to the store as early as possible to take advantage of this possibility; the discounted books will be the first ones to leave the shelves. Check to see whether you can sell your books back at the end of the semester as well. Most likely, the amount the store will offer you will be greatly reduced. Try to think of it as a "little cash is better than none," and you can roll that money into your textbooks for the following semester.

Next, you can try either renting or buying the books used online. Which path you choose depends on whether you want to keep the books. Personally, because books change every few years and the information in them becomes outdated at such a fast pace, I only kept my French books. The language was not going anywhere, so I figured I would hold on to them for future reference.

There are an astounding number of sites on the Internet that sell or rent used textbooks. Even some bigwigs have gotten into the game. Amazon has a used textbook section (at http://www.amazon.com/New-Used-Textbooks-Books/b?ie=UTF8&node=465600) that may suit all of your needs. It enables users to refer friends and earn $5 credits. While it may not seem like much, if you are the first in your group to start referring friends, you could end up with a stash of extra money to help cover your own textbook expenses. Amazon also allows users to sell books back to the store for Amazon gift cards. If you would prefer to rent (yes, for a full semester!), the site has that option available to users. If you are an Amazon Prime member (payment required: join as a student and receive a discount), you can receive your shipment in two days; otherwise, orders over $35 receive free shipping but will run on regular shipment time frames. Lastly, you can rent or buy Kindle Textbooks for Kindle Fire Tablets, or put the Kindle application on your iPad, Android tablet, PC, or Mac, and read it on your own device. You can rent the eTextbooks for an amount of time you specify. When you pick a book, Amazon lets you set the return date, although the price does go up the longer you keep the book.

Barnes & Noble offers the same services as Amazon (see http://www.barnesandnoble.com/u/textbooks-college-textbooks/379002366/). You can receive a check from the store and even get a quick quote by entering some easy information on the website. The eTextbooks offered through B&N can be viewed with a seven-day free trial before purchasing on your PC or Mac (not available for the actual NOOK device or mobile phones). This may come in handy if you are looking for an older version to save money. Make sure you compare the older version against a new version (find a friend!) before purchasing. The eTextbooks are viewed through NOOK Study (free app). You can highlight, tag, link, and conduct searches on textbooks downloaded with this app.

If I were currently attending school, I would ask for gift certificates to these two stores for every single holiday that came around. The generosity of family members could keep me going with school textbooks for quite some time.

You may also want to check out the publisher's website. Very often the book's publisher will sell the ebook or text version for a greatly reduced rate. Sometimes there is no telling what pricing or distribution disputes are ongoing to affect the prices of textbooks from various vendors.

Now, these are not the only possible sources to rent or purchase textbooks. Below are just a few other possible sources. Always compare prices at different sites to make sure you are getting the best deal possible before you proceed.

- Amazon Student Website: www.amazon.com/New-Used-Textbooks-Books/b?ie=UTF8&node=465600
- Barnes & Noble: http://www.barnesandnoble.com/u/textbooks-college-textbooks/379002366/
- Compare book prices:

  http://www.bookfinder4u.com
  http://www.textbookrentals.com

- Rent, sell, or buy back books:

  http://www.chegg.com
  http://www.campusbookrentals.com
  http://www.bookrenter.com
  http://www.valorebooks.com
  http://www.skyo.com

Here are my last few ideas on this subject. You may be incredibly shocked to learn that sometimes the library is a good place to start. Check out both your college's library and your community library. The book may not be available for rental for the full semester, but if you only need a section or two, copy machines will work nicely. Or you can become friends with someone who already took the class and has not returned his or her book and offer that individual a decent price. Check with the college's bookstore for class reading lists, or send a nice email to the professor to find out the reading list in advance, then double down on your mission. Don't forget to check the local library as well as the libraries aboard the base where you are stationed. Oftentimes, CLEP and DSST study guides can be found at these sites for free.

FREE SUBJECT MATTER STUDY SUPPORT—MILITARY BASED

This section will be short and sweet. It is packed full of free websites and preparatory programs that can help in your educational pursuits. Often, all it takes is a little extra help, or a different explanation of the same material in order to clear the cobwebs and make progress in a subject. The websites listed below have been found to have the best information/explanations to help promote learning.

Peterson's, a Nelnet Company

http://www.nelnetsolutions.com/dodlibrary/

Peterson's is a solid site for subject-matter proficiency exams and ASVAB test preparation. You can continue to use this site even after your spouse separates from the service. Here is a basic rundown of what you can access on the site:

- CLEP prep (see the CLEP section for more info)
- DSST prep (see the CLEP section for more info)
- ASVAB prep

This site also has options to help users conduct narrow searches for schools—for example, by undergraduate and graduate school, vocational-technical school, or Servicemembers Opportunity Colleges (SOC). Listed under the undergraduate and graduate school search tabs are helpful articles that may give you more guidance in your pursuit of an appropriate school, an appropriate program, or preparing for the admissions process, which can be very long and time consuming.

Lastly, on the home page of Peterson's is a link labeled "OASC, Online Academic Skills Course." The program is intended to boost the user's reading comprehension, vocabulary, and math abilities. The preassessment will determine the user's strengths and weaknesses and help design an appropriate learning plan. As a user progresses through OASC, learning is supported by interactive exercises and quizzes.

eKnowledge Corporation & NFL Players

SAT & ACT test preparation
http://www.eknowledge.com/military
(770) 992-0900
support@eknowledge.com

This program is a combined effort of the Department of Defense and some patriotic NFL players. eKnowledge Corporation donates SAT and ACT test preparation software to military families and veterans. The software usually runs approximately $200, but it is free for service members and their families. The programs include classroom instruction, interactive learning participation, and 120 classroom video lessons. Check with the school liaison officer aboard the base as well. Some of them have these CDs and can lend them to you for free.

NON-MILITARY SUPPORTED FREE SUBJECT MATTER HELP

Here is a list of free nonmilitary-related study websites I like to use when I need extra help. I have used all of them at some point and found each beneficial for one thing or another. Hopefully, you will find them constructive too.

Math

Khan Academy (https://www.khanacademy.org/)

The very first website that should be on anyone's list for math is Khan Academy. This is far and away the most amazing math help available without paying for one-on-one tutoring. You can register for the site through Facebook or Google, and it is incredibly easy to use (and of course *free*!). Videos guide the user through different problems, and discussion question threads allow the user to ask questions. The site offers other subjects besides math. Science and economics, humanities, computer science, and some test prep (SAT, MCAT, GMAT, etc.) help are available as well.

PurpleMath (http://www.purplemath.com)

Purple Math offers a wide array of math topics. You can find anything you might need on the site. The main page is a bit jumbled, and many of the links take you to external sites. Stick to the main Purple Math page. The examples are written step by step to show you how to proceed for each particular problem.

English

Grammar Bytes (http://www.chompchomp.com)

I (Jillian) dig this website. The layout is easy to understand without any mumbo jumbo to sort through. Each section has a print tab that organizes the material in an easily printed (no pictures or extra garbage to waste ink!), easily read manner. The subject matter is comprehensive, and the site even contains YouTube videos.

Purdue Owl (http://owl.english.purdue.edu/owl/)

As an English teacher, I love Purdue Owl. Everything I need is on this site. The site offers instructive writing help for thesis statement development, dealing with writer's block, and creating an outline to start a paper. If you are in need of American Psychological Association (APA) or Modern Language Association (MLA) formatting help, go to this site. APA and MLA are formatting structures that most higher education classes demand be used in writing papers.

Guide to Grammar Writing (http://grammar.ccc.commnet.edu/grammar/)

This is a no-nonsense website that has all of the basics organized in a user-friendly manner. The Editing and Rewriting Skills section has a checklist that is similar to the one I use when writing and grading papers. The checklist also offers the user links to some of the most common grammatical problems facing writers.

The Grammar Book (http://www.grammarbook.com)

Another good, no-nonsense English grammar website. The explanations are brief and easy to understand. The examples are to-the-point easy to follow. The Quizzes tab also has two sections of comprehensive free activities to test your aptitude.

Massive Open Online Courses (MOOCs)

MOOCs are the newest venture in college-level virtual education. Alarmed at the rising cost of tuition and declaring that education unto itself should be free, professors across a variety of prestigious universities began offering college-level courses online that were open to anyone with Internet access. Some of the more common organizations, such as www.coursera.org, www.edx.org, and www.udacity.com, offer free courses in many common classes found on college campuses. They function like many standard online courses, and if you get bored or no longer have the time to attend, just walk away. The beauty of MOOCs is that it allows you to enroll in a course and expose yourself to material that you will encounter in a class that costs real money with a real grade on the line. Nervous about taking Business Law or Statistics because it is required for your degree? Check out a class in that subject through a MOOC so you can gain confidence and a better understanding of the material before stepping into the classroom. While most of these classes are not currently worth college credit, you can often voluntarily choose to pay a small fee for a certificate if you successfully complete the class. If nothing else, this could be a bullet point on your resume. Some schools are looking at MOOCs as the wave of the future. For example, Arizona State University (http://gfa.asu.edu/) is offering its freshman year online through edX. Students can opt to pay a fee per credit hour for a much lower cost than attending the brick-and-mortar campus.

Citation formatting for APA and MLA references:

- http://www.citationmachine.net/
- http://www.calvin.edu/library/knightcite/

APA format guidance:

- American Psychological Association: http://www.apastyle.org
- Purdue Owl: https://owl.english.purdue.edu/owl/resource/560/01/

MLA format guidance:

- Cornell   University   Library: http://www.library.cornell.edu/resrch/cit manage/mla
- California State University Los Angeles: http://web.calstatela.edu/library/ guides/3mla.pdf
- Purdue Owl: https://owl.english.purdue.edu/owl/resource/747/01/

Chapter Eight

Prior Learning Credit

Prior learning credit allows students to use knowledge and the experiences that they have gained from outside the classroom to demonstrate college-level learning in order to gain college credit. This process allows students to gain credit without sitting through classes and sometimes without payment or with a reduced payment when compared to the full course cost. Gaining prior learning credit gives students the ability to fast track their educations and save money at the same time.

Many people, especially those connected with the military, know about the evaluation of military training and experience through the American Council on Education (ACE). Military spouses should be aware that the American Council on Education has also worked to evaluate civilian workforce experience to determine equivalent college credit recommendations.

Many schools award prior learning credit even though it is not widely advertised, but most demand that evidence of the learning that took place be supplied. Active-duty personnel and veterans are often awarded prior learning credit by institutions of higher learning through submission of their Joint Services Transcript, which is a compilation of their military training that has been evaluated by ACE. Military spouses fall under the civilian pathway for prior learning credit in most cases, although some schools participate with the Spouse Education and Career Opportunities (SECO) Learning Counts for prior learning credit by portfolio program.

This chapter includes information on the following topics:

- Prior Learning
- Spouse Education and Career Opportunities (SECO) Learning Counts Program
- Subject Matter Proficiency Exams (CLEP/DSST)
- Servicemembers Opportunity Colleges (SOC)

PRIOR LEARNING CREDIT

Military spouses should inquire about prior learning credit at their schools. Assessment methods for prior learning credit typically fall into three different categories: course work reflected on transcripts, such as through the College Level Examination Program (CLEP) and the DANTES Subject Standardized Tests (DSST), portfolio-based assessment, and any other credit earned without examinations used to demonstrate proficiency.

Each school will have its own policies on this type of credit, and they can vary greatly. Although prior learning credit is becoming more popular, double check with the institution (a counselor/advisor) you are interested in attending to determine whether the institution will grant you credit based on your experiences. Schools do not typically advertise their ability to offer prior learning credit, so it might not be widely detailed on their website. Also, most schools will require proof of your experiences through some type of written statement or resume. Even volunteer work may be used if you are able to sufficiently support your claim.

Why do you care whether the school you have chosen awards prior learning credit? Because it will help fast track your degree. Think about the flexibility you will gain if you attend an institution that awards prior learning credit. You might be able to save money and time while pursuing your degree, two precious commodities for military spouses. Spouses are often subject to frequent military moves and stressful deployment cycles. Starting and finishing a degree while stationed in one place is often a difficult task. Choosing an institution that enables students to gain prior learning credit might enable spouses to achieve their educational goals within a timeline that aligns to the schedule of their active-duty partners. At the very least, it allows for more realistic planning.

Should choosing a school that offers prior learning credit be the sole deciding factor? No, but consider the process as a beneficial pathway to helping you achieve your degree. Just don't pick a school based solely on this criterion. Remember, the point of going to school is to feed your brain.

The list of schools that offer prior learning credit is ever growing. Here is just a sampling of the schools.

- Empire College, State University of New York: http://www.esc.edu/degree-planning-academic-review/prior-learning-assessment/
- Boise State University: http://registrar.boisestate.edu/transfers/prior-learning-credit/
- Central Michigan University: http://global.cmich.edu/prior-learning/
- Thomas Edison State College: http://www.tesc.edu/degree-completion/earning-credit.cfm
- University of Maryland: http://umuc.edu/undergrad/creditoptions/prior learning/index.cfm

PRIOR LEARNING ASSESSMENT AND THE AMERICAN COUNCIL ON EDUCATION (ACE)

Most institutions granting PLA credit follow guidelines provided by ACE, which offers the ACE National Guide to College Credit for Workforce Training. Some military spouses are also veterans and have access to documents with their ACE recommended college credit for military experience and training. ACE works with the Department of Defense (DOD) to translate military training and experiences into potential college credit. ACE evaluates MOSs, ratings, formal courses, other course work, and even on-the-job experience to determine how they may potentially convert. The army, navy, Marine Corps, and coast guard currently document ACE credit recommendations on a document called the Joint Service Transcript (JST). The air force has the Community College of the Air Force to document an ACE credit recommendation on a formal transcript. In previous years the army used a document called the Army/American Council on Education Registry Transcript (AARTS). At one time all services documented ACE credits on a document called the DD 295, or the Application for the Evaluation of Learning Experiences during Military Service. It was a sparse document that did not provide descriptions of the training experience. Schools had to refer to the ACE Guides for evaluation. Many schools had little familiarity with the ACE Guides, possibly resulting in veterans missing out on receiving full credit.

If you are also a veteran, take full advantage of the new streamlined, highly detailed Joint Service Transcript or the Community College of the Air

Force transcript in order to have your school process it for potential credit. If you are not a veteran but have work and life experience, as mentioned earlier, many colleges and universities can award college credit on the basis of experience in the workplace or even for volunteer work. According to a 2010 study by the Council for Adult and Experiential Learning (CAEL), a study with forty-eight participating colleges and universities, Prior Learning Assessment (PLA) students "saved an average of between 2.5 and 10.1 months of time in earning their degrees, compared to non-PLA students earning degrees."[1]

CAEL has recommended standards to help colleges and universities develop, optimize, and set standard programs for evaluating and awarding college credit. Ten standards are posted on the organization's website (http://www.cael.org/pla.htm).

CAEL recommends evaluation of college credit equivalency through:

- Portfolio-Based Assessments
- American Council on Education Guides
- Advanced Placement Exams
- College Level Examination Program (CLEP)
- DSST Credit by Exam Program
- Excelsior College Exam
- UExcel Excelsior College Credit by Exam Program
- National College Credit Recommendation Service

Portfolio-Based Assessment

What are the advantages of portfolio-based assessment?

- Saves time and money.
- Can eliminate need to take a course in a subject the student already knows.
- The portfolio process can help you understand how you have acquired learning through employment and community activities.

Military OneSource and Department of Defense Spouse Education and Career Opportunities (SECO) is an initiative to assist military spouses in saving time and money earning college credit at the undergraduate level for experiential learning through life and work experience.[2] The free Learning-Counts™ @SECO program can help a military spouse earn college credit through volunteer and community service, work experience, training programs, and independent study. The program puts the military spouse in contact with a SECO Career Counselor (800-342-9647), who assists with the following:

- Determining eligibility
- Determining which portfolio development course is best
- Emailing the financial assistance form needed to register for a LearningCounts™ course

LearningCounts™ works best for those who meet the following criteria:

1. Have strong writing skills or have completed a college-level writing course
2. Have experience with online courses or have good computer skills
3. Have several years of work, volunteer, or life experience that can yield commensurate college course work learning outcomes (marketing, management, communications, etc.)[3]

MilitaryOneClick (http://militaryoneclick.com/get-credit-for-your-military-spouse-life/) and the LearningCounts™ program (http://www.learningcounts.org/) offer free services to spouses eligible for SECO. Spouses either enroll in a six-week online course or take advantage of a do-it-yourself online tool to start the process of building a learning portfolio. Enrollment is through Military OneSource. More information on LearningCounts™ can be found later in this chapter.

The following information encompasses the portfolio assessment programs offered through three different schools and will give you an idea of the various procedures used for prior learning assessment:

The University of Maryland University College (UMUC), part of the state-supported University of Maryland system, offers degree programs on many US military installations overseas and also has extensive online degree offerings. To complete an application for portfolio assessment, students must enroll in EXCL 301, Learning Analysis and Planning, a three-semester-unit course in which the student learns to prepare a portfolio of college-level learning from past experience. The course is demanding, and UMUC recommends not enrolling in more than one course during the same session. Experiential credit is awarded at both upper and lower levels, is awarded a grade of "S" for satisfactory, and will not be computed in the student's grade point

average. For more information, visit the following site: http://umuc.edu/
undergrad/creditoptions/priorlearning/index.cfm.

Central Michigan University (CMU), through the Global Campus, offers
degree programs at many military bases and sites in Michigan, Canada, metro Washington, DC, metro Atlanta, Georgia, and through online learning.
CMU's Global Campus offers the option of prior learning assessment for
credit at the undergraduate and graduate levels. No formal course on the
subject of portfolio assessment has to be completed; instead, the student
watches a PowerPoint presentation and becomes familiar with a detailed
Prior Learning Student Handbook. The Prior Learning Student Handbook
even has undergraduate and graduate sample portfolios. More information
can be found on the following websites: http://global.cmich.edu/prior-
learning/handbook.aspx and https://www.cmich.edu/global/prior-learning/
Pages/default.aspx.

Thomas Edison State College is a state-supported college established by
the state of New Jersey to assist nontraditional students in earning college
degrees. Degree programs at the associate's, bachelor's, and master's degree
levels can be completed entirely online. The school has many military students as well as many dependent military family members and accepts military credits, experiential credits, and credits earned through testing. The
school's portfolio assessment program allows students to gain experiential
college credits at the undergraduate and graduate levels. Students have to
enroll in two courses as part of the process for undergraduate experiential
credits: PLA-100, Introduction to Prior Learning Assessment, and PLA-200,
Introduction to Portfolio Assessment. For graduate-level programs, the process takes place over a twelve-week term and must be preapproved by the
dean of the school offering the graduate degree, and a mentor is assigned.

American Council on Education Guides

Most institutions granting PLA credit follow guidelines provided by the
American Council on Education, which offers the ACE National Guide to
College Credit for Workforce Training (http://www2.acenet.edu/credit/?
fuseaction=browse.main). The ACE has reviewed and provided credit recommendations for over thirty-five thousand courses, examinations, certifications, apprenticeships, and other forms of learning. Over two thousand colleges and universities are part of the ACE Credit College and University
Network. A complete list can be found at http://www2.acenet.edu/
CREDITCollegeNetwork/.

Advanced Placement Exams

Many spouses completed Advanced Placement (AP) courses and exams while in high school. Thousands of colleges and universities can offer AP college credit to students who enroll in their schools as degree-seeking candidates. There are over thirty college subjects offered through AP. Each college makes its own decision on accepting the exams. AP exam results, even those older than four years, can be requested and sent to a college or university. Visit the following websites for more information: https://apstudent. collegeboard.org/creditandplacement/how-to-earn-credit-for-your-scores and http://apcentral.collegeboard.com/apc/public/courses/index.html.

UExcel Excelsior College Credit Exam Program

UExcel credit exams are available on fifty-four subjects (http://www. excelsior.edu/exams/uexcel-home). While not as universally accepted as CLEP exams, there are hundreds of schools that accept the credits. Here are a few examples: Excelsior College, Thomas Edison State College, Ohio State University, Florida State University, State University of New York campuses, and University of Texas. Visit http://www.excelsior.edu/who-accepts-uexcel-credits for a complete list. Exams are administered by Pearson VUE centers (http://www.pearsonvue.com/uexcel/).

National College Credit Recommendation Service (NCCRS)

The National College Credit Recommendation Service (NCCRS) evaluates training and education programs offered outside the traditional college classroom setting. NCCRS accomplishes this by coordinating teams of college credit evaluators to review training programs offered by corporations, unions, religious programs, and even proprietary schools (http://www. nationalccrs.org/about/). Over 1,500 colleges and universities will consider granting college credits on the basis of NCCRS evaluations.

The following is an example of a spouse who has decided to work on a bachelor's degree in business management through Central Michigan University on a military base:

Jane Lopez has never attended college but would like to try to expedite earning college credits. She has a few options she can pursue. She completed three AP courses during high school and passed the corresponding exams. She requested a transcript be sent to CMU, and the school awarded her nine semester hours or the equivalent of three college courses. Next, Jane visited the base education center for recommendations on college credit exams (CLEP/DSST). Though not free to her, the cost of $100 (costs can vary per base) per exam, much lower in cost than completing the course, appealed to her. She contacted CMU for a list of college credit exams accepted for her degree program. The base education center provided recommendations on study preparation and recommended websites to assist her with her studies (www.petersons.com/dod). She passed eight different CLEP and DSST exams that fulfilled some of the general education requirements for CMU.

Jane had taken part in voluntary work and had on-the-job employment experience. She worked as a volunteer for the base thrift store for two years running the cash register, taking inventory, evaluating donations, and eventually keeping the books. Later she worked in a paid position as assistant manager at a major hamburger restaurant chain. Jane decided to demonstrate experiential learning through CMU's portfolio assessment option. As a result, she was awarded college credits for business and management courses. All of her efforts through testing and portfolio assessment earned her over one year of college credit, shaving significant time and money off her goal of a business management degree.

College credit earned through portfolio assessment can save time and money toward the process of finishing a degree. A word of warning is necessary about diploma mills that advertise college degrees awarded on the basis of work and life experience. According to the Federal Trade Commission, "A diploma mill is a company that offers degrees for a flat fee in a short amount of time and requires little to no course work. They offer 'degrees' for work or life experience alone. Degrees awarded through diploma mills are not legitimate, and can cost you more than just your money."[4] Employer human resource departments easily identify such so-called degrees as fake. Occasionally someone manages to get hired on the basis of a diploma mill degree but ultimately is found out and terminated for fraud and deception in the hiring process.

Recently the *New York Times* ran a story about a Pakistani diploma mill called Axact that earned millions of dollars by selling phony degrees around the world, even to Americans. Many of the schools have names similar to American universities, links to fictitious accrediting bodies, and even toll-free American contact numbers. In Washington State, the US Department of Justice prosecuted 350 federal employees who had secured promotions based on degrees purchased through Axact (http://www.nytimes.com/2015/

05/18/world/asia/fake-diplomas-real-cash-pakistani-company-axact-reaps-millions-columbiana-barkley.html).

Diploma mill scams occur in many forms time after time. Always check with your base education center to determine the legitimacy of a degree program. If it sounds too good to be true, it probably is.

Another scam to avoid is the CLEP (or DSST) study guide scam found in many military towns. The College Board advises students to look for the following red flags (https://clep.collegeboard.org/study-resources):

- Attempts to sell study guides for many exams at once with sizeable up-front payment required
- Credit agreements with a company other than the one selling the material
- Promises that you can receive college credits (or even degrees) without enrolling in a college program of study[5]

The local base education center can offer advice on how to prepare for college credit exams. Test preparation on many subjects is available free to service members and their spouses at https://www.petersons.com/dod. Additionally, guides can be checked out at the base, or local, library for free. Just be aware of the edition and date of publication.

Take advantage of these programs to help you earn college credit. While they may take some time to complete, the long-term benefit will be worth the extra effort.

SPOUSE EDUCATION AND CAREER OPPORTUNITIES (SECO) LEARNINGCOUNTS™ PROGRAM

The Spouse Education and Career Opportunities (SECO) LearningCounts™ program (http://seco.learningcounts.org/) was designed in tandem with the Department of Defense to help military spouses pursue college credit for knowledge they already possess through a learning portfolio process. The goal is to assist the population in fast tracking their educations. This is not a new concept in higher education, as many schools already offer potential college credit for community service or work or life experience, but most charge for the award. The LearningCounts™ program offered by SECO enables spouses to get the initial course, which, according to the Learning-Counts™ program, "will guide you through the process of identifying your skills and areas of expertise that may be worth college credit"[6] for free.

Participation in the program requires spouses to attend a short online course that assists students in preparing a portfolio to submit to their school. Not every school in the country participates in LearningCounts™. A list of participating institutions can be found on this website (https://learningcounts. org/seco/how-it-works).

There are four steps that students must follow in order to participate in LearningCounts™:

- Identify areas of knowledge
- Create your Learning Portfolio
- Submit the online Learning Portfolio that demonstrates knowledge learned (you will find out within three weeks if your portfolio has been approved for a credit recommendation)
- Take your LearningCounts™ credit recommendation to your college/university[7] (the school may charge a fee for awarding the credit)

After compiling the required information, participants will align their knowledge with a specific course offered through their institution of choice. For example, many spouses work with the family services departments aboard the military bases. Some work in the child-care centers or run in-home daycare centers. Most are required to attend ongoing education classes through the departments to stay current with methods of care and governing rules. So, spouses could align these experiences with an early childhood education class, for example. Students should always verify that the class will fit within their degree plans with an academic advisor before determining which pathway to develop.

To be eligible for LearningCounts™ through the Spouse Education and Career Opportunities program, spouses must be:

- Married to a service member serving in the army, navy, Marine Corps, air force, or National Guard on active duty or with a reserve command.
- Married to a service member who has been separated from active duty, National Guard, and Reserve components for less than 180 days.
- The surviving spouse of a military member who died while on active duty.

There are two different ways in which spouses can participate with the program, an online instructor-led pathway or a self-paced course. The instructor-led pathway might lead to three transferable credits, but students will need to pay a $15 fee in order to receive a transcript for their college. While there are no specific check-in times for this class, students will need to access the online program several times per week in order to maintain up-to-date knowledge pertaining to the materials and to make sure assignments are completed on time.

The self-paced course does not offer any transferable college credit, nor is there an instructor available, but it does give students the flexibility to access the course at their convenience. Students work their way through eight modules that guide them through the portfolio process and take approximately four to six hours to complete. This pathway might be a better option for students who are strong writers and have significant experience taking college-level courses already.

If time and money have created delays for you in pursuing a degree, this program may be able to help. The LearningCounts™ program that assists you in organizing your portfolio is free, but each school will have set fees in place that must be paid in order for the institution to award the credit. Some schools even charge the same amount as the actual class, just as if you took it though the school. Verify with the school first before you determine whether the cost and time are worth the effort.

Consider the time you have given to volunteer work, training programs, independent study, community service, or work and think about the knowledge you might have already gained. Then take a look at your degree plan to determine where you think that knowledge might fit. If something appears to be a match, cross-reference it with the description of the class in the school's course catalog to see whether the description of the class meets with the knowledge you gained. Remember, many degrees have a number of elective credits built in to the requirements. The elective credits can come from all different subject areas. That means that you potentially have an array of classes from which to choose to align your knowledge to a course subject matter learning parameters.

For more information on the program, visit the following sites:

- https://myseco.militaryonesource.mil/Portal/Content/View/2660
- https://learningcounts.org/seco/

SUBJECT MATTER PROFICIENCY EXAMS

Subject matter proficiency exams allow students to earn college credit by taking tests as opposed to sitting through the traditional class. The exams enable students to save money and time, prepare on their own timeline, and fast track their degrees. These reasons are incredibly important for spouses and dependent children using transferred GI Bill benefits who have to maintain a class load specified by the VA if they want to continue with full benefits.

The testing centers aboard the military bases offer the CLEP and DSST exams. The US government through the Defense Activity for Non-Traditional Education Support (DANTES) funds the exams for service members (https://clep.collegeboard.org/military), but not for spouses or dependent children. Governmental personnel at the education centers typically do not proctor the exams. The education centers on the military bases have contracted with different schools to have the tests offered aboard the bases, usually through a National Testing Center (NTC) contract. Fees for CLEPs and DSSTs offered aboard school campuses can vary as well, so always conduct reconnaissance before making a decision. The base cost for both exams is $80, but most schools take on an extra fee in order to fund the facilitation of the exams for their students. If the fees are less at your school, as opposed to the base education center, then chose that instead. Always double check the CLEP (https://clep.collegeboard.org/) and DSST (http://getcollegecredit.com/) websites prior to testing, because sometimes there are discounts available. For example, in April 2016, DSST offered a "buy two, get one free" option.

The first thing students should do prior to taking CLEP or DSST exams is to verify with their school that the institution accepts these exams, which version, and in which subjects. There is no point in taking exams for no reason. Many colleges and universities do accept subject matter proficiency exams, but they limit the amount of credit awarded through this pathway. Sometimes they limit which subjects they accept as well as the minimum score required for passing. Be aware that CLEPs are typically more widely accepted than DSSTs.

After verifying exam acceptance through your school, look at http://www.petersons.com/dod. The Peterson's website maintains free study material for all of the CLEP and DSST exams offered on the bases. Now it is time to study, study, study! After all, who wants to have to pay to test twice? Double check at the base libraries and the education centers for extra study material. While the preparation material on the Peterson's website is comprehensive, every extra bit of study assistance you can find will help you increase your chances to pass the test on the first try.

Once you have determined that you are ready to test, contact the education center on the base or your school depending upon where you have chosen to test and book an appointment. If the local center offers computerized testing, you will receive instant results for all exams except for the English essay component. The essay must be sent off to be graded.

CLEP has thirty-three tests available in six different subject areas: English composition, humanities, mathematics, natural science, social sciences, and history. The exams cover material typically learned during the first two years of college. The College Composition exam is 120 minutes, but all other exams are ninety minutes. Most exams are multiple choice, although some, including the College Composition, have essays or other varieties of questions. CLEP or the institution giving the exam scores the CLEP essays. If CLEP holds responsibility for scoring, essays are reviewed and scored by two different English composition professors. The scores are combined and then weighted with the multiple-choice section. Exams usually match college classes that are one semester in duration.

The DSST exam program has thirty-eight available tests. DSST exams cover lower- and upper-division classes. This is beneficial for students who have deep knowledge of certain subjects, as it will enable them to test further along the degree pathway. Testing further into a specific subject area may also enable a student to participate in classes that can usually only be accessed after prerequisites are completed. Two tests include optional essays, "Ethics in America" and "Technical Writing." Essays are not scored by DSST; they are forwarded to the institution that the test taker designates on his or her application and graded by the college or university. DSST exams are offered only for three-credit courses.

If you are using transferred GI Bill benefits from your spouse and you take and pass CLEP or DSST exams, it will help you extend the life of the benefits. This might mean building a buffer into your semesters, saving benefits for other classes, saving benefits for an advanced degree, or simply help you fast track your degree.

The VA demands that students using the GI Bill maintain a minimum of twelve credit hours per semester in order to rate the full housing and book stipend. If your spouse is still on active duty, you will not receive the housing stipend, but you will receive the book stipend. Twelve credits equals four classes. Maintaining four classes per semester is not a difficult course load; however, if your goal is a bachelor's degree and you have no previous college credit, you will need to take five classes (which typically equals fifteen semester hours) every semester, which is the traditional semester credit load. Most bachelor's degrees demand 120 semester hours (SH) of predetermined courses (found on your degree plan) in order to graduate. If your spouse transferred all thirty-six months of his or her Post-9/11 GI Bill to you, and you only earn twelve SHs each semester, that totals ninety-six semester credit hours at the end of four years. That is not sufficient to graduate, and you will be out of monthly benefits. If you can add some CLEP or DSST scores into each semester, you will have reduced your required course load.

Remember, if you are using your spouse's transferred GI Bill benefits, those are benefits he or she no longer has. This is a financial benefit for you but a loss for your spouse, so make the most of it. Follow the appropriate credit hour load each semester and supplement with CLEPs or DSSTs when possible. Finishing within the allotted amount of months will eliminate your risk of having to take out student loans on top of transferred GI Bill benefits.

Reaching graduation early can be a boost to many spouses, especially those with families. Spouses who have completed CLEP or DSST credit may be able to combine those exams with other types of prior learning credit and finish their degrees in less than the four years normally required. This enables students to get into the workforce faster as well as cope with any upcoming permanent change of station orders.

CLEPs and DSSTs can also be a great way for spouses to pursue college credit even if, at the time, attending college is not an option. Always check with the school that you are interested in attending before scheduling a test. If you are attending a community college to gain transfer credit before your spouse separates from the service and intend to pursue a degree at that time, contact the universities that you are interested in attending and request the list of CLEPs and DSSTs that are accepted. Cross-reference the lists and start taking the tests that all of the schools will take. This will enable you to build credit without actually attending school.

SERVICEMEMBERS OPPORTUNITY COLLEGES

SOC was created to assist active-duty service members and their spouses in their pursuit of education. SOC operates in collaboration with higher-education associations, the Department of Defense (DOD), and active and reserve components of the military. The Defense Activity for Non-Traditional Education Support (DANTES) manages the contract that is funded through the DOD. The group aims to improve higher-education opportunities for active-duty military members and their spouses. Attending SOC schools can benefit spouses. They are familiar with the difficulties of pursuing college credit while dealing with the concerns that active-duty service can create.

Service members and military spouses often face roadblocks when pursuing higher education during their active-duty time. The SOC Consortium tries to eliminate many of these roadblocks by working with educational institutions and creating higher degrees of flexibility. The point is to facilitate military degree completion as opposed to simply compiling course credits.

SOC also houses an articulation guide on its website (http://www.soc. aascu.org/socdns/GrntdTransfCrs.html). Having an articulation guide available means that you are not waiting for an institution to give you an answer as to whether you will receive credit. You will also have a better understanding of whether the school is the best bet in terms of accepting your previous credit. This allows you to compare the credits you may receive from a variety of schools without having to approach each one and obtain an answer, which might take months. The guide allows spouses to retain more decision-making control in their quest for a degree. In other words, if you are going to take classes at a community college that is listed on the articulation guide, plan on transferring to a four-year institution that is listed on the articulation guide, and the classes you pick are on the articulation guide, then all of the credits awarded at the two-year institution will count at the four-year institution. This can assist you in maximizing the amount of credit you have earned.

Let's say you took a course at Coastline Community College, ACCTC100, Introduction to Accounting, with a SOC code of AC401A. To determine which schools have prearticulated the transfer of this class, start on the main SOC website: http://www.soc.aascu.org/. Hover over the "SOC Degree Network System" tab and click on "Guaranteed Transfer Courses." Select the option for "Associate Degree Home Colleges," then select Coastline Community College from the list. Introduction to Accounting is the first course listed. To the far right, the "Course Category" list has the links for checking each particular class; in this case the SOC code is AC401A. The final list shows the eighteen schools that have prearticulated agreements for the transfer of this class. Now you know that taking this course will gain you the applicable credit at any one of the eighteen schools listed.

Chapter Nine

Vocational Pathways

Not all spouses want to pursue traditional education. Some prefer vocational training that might include an apprenticeship or on-the-job training. There are numerous training options available for those interested in career pathways that do not require traditional higher education, and some of them pay salaries straight away. New apprenticeship fields, such as those based on green technology, are on the rise. For spouses who are veterans or for those using transferred benefits, the GI Bills offer great flexibility in the different types of programs that the benefits might be applied toward. More information on how to use the GI Bill for vocational pathways can be found on the GI Bill website: http://www.benefits.va.gov/gibill/onthejob_apprenticeship. asp.

This chapter includes information on the following topics:

• OJT
• Apprenticeship programs

ON-THE-JOB TRAINING (OJT)

Some companies use on-the-job (OJT) training to tailor their workforce needs, and others use it to enhance an individual's preexisting skill set. Typically, a combination of tactics is used to train employees to operate functionally in their new or changing environment. OJT is one strategy that is used in almost all instances, for blue-collar and white-collar job positions, and is designed to help hire and train employees who might not already possess the required knowledge for the position.

If you are a veteran, think about your time in the military. You were trained to do a specific task, then sent to your duty station. Did your new duty station operate exactly like the school where you learned your new skill, or did you need to have OJT to learn how to function properly within your new unit? The same strategy is often used in the civilian workforce. For example, you might already know how to install and maintain cable systems, but if you take that skill set to a civilian company, they will want to train you to their standards. Oftentimes, in vocational fields, OJT is the form of training that will be used to accomplish this task.

Employers and employees reap numerous benefits from participating in OJT. OJT allows companies to use their preexisting environment to train new employees while instilling performance expectations at the same time. It is cost effective, increases productivity, and produces employees that are taught to company-driven standards. Employers training employees using OJT promote a good public image through their commitment to the community, help create a more skilled workforce, and see immediate return on their investment. The skills, knowledge, and competencies that are needed to perform a specific job within a specific workplace are delivered from day one, typically by another employee or mentor (mandatory for the GI Bills) who can already perform his or her duties competently. Sometimes special training rooms or equipment are used to demonstrate performance parameters. OJT is different from apprenticeship programs in length and training style. OJT typically does not require any formal classroom training and is also shorter in duration, lasting somewhere between four weeks and one year.

Employees also benefit from OJT. They begin earning wages as they learn a new skill, gain job experience, and develop a new marketable skill set, oftentimes by earning certifications or journeyman standing. Productivity is increased on both sides as training progresses, as does trust as relationships develop through teamwork.

Some potential fields of employment for OJT are bank teller, customer service representative, sales representative, patient representative, home care aide, medical transportation agent, law enforcement, welder, machinist, tool and die maker, and construction worker. If you are looking for a program that is VA approved, contact the state approving agency at http://www.nasaa-vetseducation.com/Contacts.aspx, or search participating employers on the

US Department of Veterans Affairs, GI Bill Comparison Tool website: https://www.vets.gov/gi-bill-comparison-tool.

APPRENTICESHIP PROGRAMS

The US Department of Labor (DOL) oversees registered apprenticeship programs through its Employment and Training section. According to the DOL:

> Registered Apprenticeship programs meet the skilled workforce needs of American industry, training millions of qualified individuals for lifelong careers since 1937. Registered Apprenticeship helps mobilize America's workforce with structured, on-the-job training in traditional industries such as construction and manufacturing, as well as new high-growth industries such as health care, information technology, energy, telecommunications, advanced manufacturing and more. [1]

The DOL uses this section to connect potential employees to employers by working with a variety of different companies and organizations, such as community colleges, labor organizations, and state workforce agencies. The federal program has regional contacts in almost every state, which can be found here: http://www.doleta.gov/oa/regdirlist.cfm. State-based apprenticeship searches on the DOL site can be conducted here: http://oa.doleta.gov/bat.cfm?start.

Many people believe that registered apprenticeships are only available in career fields considered to be trades, but that is far from the truth. Registered apprenticeships are available in a variety of different career fields, such as accounting technician, ambulance attendant, animal trainer, banker, biomedical equipment technician, community health worker, cosmetologist, dental ceramist, film developer, general insurance associate, health information technology specialist, pharmacy support staff, post office clerk, quality assurance inspector, solar technician, and veterinary technician. A list of apprenticeable trades can be found here: https://www.doleta.gov/oa/occupations. cfm. More information regarding apprenticeships can be found on the following sites:

- http://www.dir.ca.gov/das/apprenticeship.pdf
- http://www.mass.gov/lwd/labor-standards/das/apprenticeship-program/apprenticeable-occupations/
- https://www.oregon.gov/boli/ATD/Pages/A_AG_FAQ.aspx

- https://www.doleta.gov/oa/apprentices.cfm
- https://www.mynextmove.org/find/apprenticeship

Like OJT, the GI Bill can be used toward apprenticeship training. Programs can last anywhere from one to six years, although most are geared for two to four years, depending upon the technical field, and you work under a tradesman during that time before you earn the same status. Assessments throughout the program, mandatory testing, and work inspection conducted by a master tradesman are part of the apprenticeship process. Formal classroom training is also part of an apprenticeship. Classes typically include general education, such as math and English, and classes pertaining to technical theory and applied skills. State-mandated licensing for many fields, such as plumbing, can demand numerous study hours and formal preparation prior to testing.

Oftentimes, skilled trades require formal licensure, which is obtained partly by working under a journeyman within the field, but this is only the starting point; journeyman, then master tradesman, are the following two steps. A journeyman or master tradesman oversees apprentices, and the journeyman is ultimately responsible for your work at that time. The goal, over time and with continuing education, is to reach journeyman or master tradesman status. High-level tradesman status leads to higher pay.

Registered apprenticeship participants receive pay starting from the first day of the program. This pay will grow over time as the apprentice learns more skill. Many programs have mandatory college classes, usually at the local community college, built into the program. Typically, the employer pays for these classes. Participants in apprenticeship programs often finish without any education debt. Completing a registered apprenticeship program earns participants certification that is recognized across the country, making them highly portable career fields.

Major companies such as UPS, CVS, Simplex-Grinnell, Werner Enterprises, and CN (railways) provide apprenticeship opportunities. Green technology has a bright future for growth. Areas such as recycling in the green technology field have some of the fastest-growing apprenticeship programs. Wind turbine technicians, hydrologists, and toxic waste cleanup specialists are all in demand.

The US Department of Labor's website has a wealth of information regarding apprenticeship programs (http://www.doleta.gov/oa/). The DOL site has links to search for state apprenticeship agencies, all approved apprenticeship programs, and state-based program sponsors. Contacts can also be found on the National Association of State Approving Agencies website (http://www.nasaa-vetseducation.com/).

CareerOneStop (http://www.careeronestop.org/), covered in chapter 3, is a free resource tool that can help apprentice seekers find career-based information and training pathways. I (Jillian) often use this resource during my counseling sessions. On the main page there are six main search tabs:

- Explore Careers
- Education and Training
- Resumes and Interviews
- Salary and Benefits
- Job Search
- People and Places to Help

All six sections host valuable information for apprentice seekers, but "Education and Training" is most informative regarding the topic at hand. After selecting "Education and Training" choose the "Apprenticeships" tab. This section allows for detailed exploration of apprenticeships including work option videos, a state-based search site, information from the Department of Labor, and a local job center search. Users can even target specific states for their apprenticeship research. For more information regarding CareerOneStop, see chapter 3.

Unions and Apprenticeships

Some training for unionized trade fields, such as auto mechanic, can be completed through a local community college instead of through an apprenticeship program. Students gain the certification they need to work by completing required classes. After completing the training, students can decide to enter the local union where they can work as floaters (job-to-job contracts) or try to find employment in a full-time capacity with one company. Either way, union employees would receive the same wage.

Some union programs also make participants take classes as a condition of certification. In many cases these classes can count toward an associate's degree if the participant decides to pursue more formal education. Depending upon the type of degree the school awards in this subject field, an associate's degree of art/science or an associate's degree in applied science, will determine how many general education classes will be required in order to attain degree completion.

Other types of trade-based apprenticeship programs can often only be completed through a union-based apprenticeship, such as stonemason. While these programs are not exclusive to unions, community colleges and trade schools do not usually offer programs of this type unless they fall under a workforce development program and are offered on a noncredit awarding basis. Noncredit awarding means that students are not earning transferable college credit. For example, the College of Western Idaho offers a stone masonry apprenticeship program. Learning through this format requires the student to pay a predetermined cost, although it is often small. This particular program states that fees run about $1,200 annually. If you were to complete the same type of apprenticeship training through a union, you would begin earning wages (lower wages during student status) while at the same time completing a formalized training program for free.

The different locations for the unions are referred to as locals. These local union-based apprenticeship programs have more variations than traditional university study. In other words, academic study typically doesn't change much from institution to institution. If you study mechanical engineering in one school, the course of study at another institution will be similar in nature. This is not the same case from local to local. The course of study, or apprenticeship, can take on many different pathways depending on the needs of the local. This also means that each local might have a slightly different focus. You need to do your research to determine which local will be the best fit. Also, there will be an interview as part of the admissions pathway. Interviews for union careers are more like job interviews than college admissions interviews, so prepare accordingly. Reach out to the organization to request information, research the local's website, and see whether the local has participants that are willing to speak with you regarding their experiences with the organization in order to make your best choice.

Chapter Ten

Spousal- and Dependent Children–Based Programs/ Organizations

Many programs are available for dependents to assist in education and career development. Some of the programs are volunteer based; others are run on set schedules through institutions of higher learning. Several spouses I know (Jillian) have gone through the programs listed in this chapter, and all speak highly of their experiences.

In this chapter, we will discuss:

- Programs available for spouses and dependent children
- General advice for spouses and dependent children
- Study resources

PROGRAMS AVAILABLE TO SPOUSES AND DEPENDENT CHILDREN

Since military families move around quite frequently, it is often hard for spouses to find employment when they first arrive at a new duty station. Consider taking advantage of any employment-based skills development programs that might be available either online or in the area. Some programs, such as Syracuse University's IVMF program, have portions that can be completed online. Another option to fill in your resume during down time is volunteer work. Typically, there are numerous possibilities to volunteer right on the base where you are stationed. Volunteering is a great way for spouses to keep work experience current on their resumes, build upon their skills, and stay active while in-between jobs. Plus it can often provide purpose to our daily demands.

Some bases host skills-training programs. The available options can vary depending upon the base or area where you are stationed. Stay on the lookout for anything that gets your attention, and always check with the base education and transition departments to see whether they are aware of anything in the nearby community or any programs available on the base as well. For example, the army has created the Career Skills Program (CSP) which assists transitioning service-members in training and job placement in particular fields. If not enough service members apply, the slots are open to dependents and even civilians and contractors. Common programs are commercial driver's license (CDL), pipe-fitting, robotic machinery operation, automotive technician, and OSHA certification.

While I (Jillian) am sure many more wonderful programs are available, the following organizations and programs are just a few I have found that many of the dependents with whom I work have considered especially beneficial in the past. I have also included a few of the newer programs that are just getting started, so they are not located on every base.

Syracuse University Institute for Veterans and Military Families (IVMF)

http://vets.syr.edu/

Syracuse University, partnered with JPMorgan Chase & Company, has several programs available through the IVMF to assist transitioning post-9/11 service members' spouses with future career plans depending upon their interests and pursuits.

Many of the programs consist of free online courses that users can access from any location at any time to promote career preparedness and understanding of the civilian sector. Other courses are offered in a face-to-face format that last roughly one to two weeks, and they are now available in a couple of different locations. IVMF offers courses for veterans, active duty, active-duty spouses, and disabled veterans.

The programs currently offered by IVMF for dependents include the following:

- EBV-F: Entrepreneurship Bootcamp for Veterans' Families (caregivers and family members)
- V-WISE: Veteran Women Igniting the Spirit of Entrepreneurship for veteran women, female active duty, and female family members
- E&G: Operation Endure & Grow for guard and reserve members and family
- Operation Boots to Business: From Service to Startup (B2B)
- Veterans' Career Transition Program (VCTP)

Entrepreneurship Bootcamp (EBV-F)

http://ebv.vets.syr.edu/families/

Entrepreneurship Bootcamp for Veterans' Families is offered through Syracuse University's Whitman School of Management and the Florida State University College of Business. The cost-free (including travel and lodging) nine-day program assists family members in their pursuit to launch and maintain small businesses. The program operates in a three-step process.

1. A thirty-day online course that assists students in learning the necessary basic skills of entrepreneurship.
2. A nine-day course through a participating EBV university where students receive over eighty hours of instruction pertaining to business ownership.
3. Twelve months of follow-on assistance through the EBV Technical Assistance Program (TAP).

Eligible spouses include the following:

- A spouse, parent, sibling, or adult child who has a role supporting the veteran (health, education, work, etc.)
- A surviving spouse or adult child of a service member who died while serving after September 11, 2001
- An active-duty service member's spouse

V-Wise

http://whitman.syr.edu/vwise/

Veteran Women Igniting the Spirit of Entrepreneurship is a joint venture with the US Small Business Administration (SBA). The program helps female veterans and female spouses of active-duty personnel along the entrepreneurship and small business pathway by arming them with savvy business skills that enable them to turn business ideas into growing ventures. Business planning, marketing, accounting, operations, and human resources are covered. The three-phase approach consists of a fifteen-day online course teaching the basic skills pertaining to being an entrepreneur, a three-day conference with two tracks (for startups or those already in business), and delivery of a comprehensive listing packet that details the community-level resources available to participants.

Eligible participants include active women service members, all honorably discharged women service members, and women spouses/life partners of all honorably discharged service members or active-duty service members. Hotel rooms and taxes are covered, but other fees apply, such as travel.

Endure & Grow

http://vets.syr.edu/education/endure-grow/

Operation Endure & Grow is a free online training program open to National Guard, reservists, and their first-degree family members. The program has two tracks: one for startups and the other for those who have been in business for more than three years. The tracks are designed to assist participants in creating a new business and all related fundamentals, or to help an operating business stimulate growth.

Operation Boots to Business (B2B): From Service to Startup

http://boots2business.org/

Active-duty service members and their spouses or partners are eligible to participate in B2B during the separation process. The entire B2B program is free. Speak to your career planner about electing the Entrepreneurship Pathway during TRS.

B2B is a partnership with the Syracuse University Whitman School of Business and the SBA. The program goal is to train transitioning service members and their spouses to be business owners through three phases. Phases 1 and 2 are taken while the service member is still on active duty, preparing to transition to the civilian world and attending the Transition Readiness Seminar (TRS). The third phase is accessible if participants elect to continue and consists of an intensive instructor-led eight-week online "mini" MBA.

Veterans' Career Transition Program (VCTP)

http://vets.syr.edu/education/employment-programs/

The VCTP offers numerous classes for career training and preparation. Many of the courses lead to high-demand industry-level certifications. This free online program is available to eligible post-9/11 veterans and their spouses. The program is geared to help veterans understand corporate culture in the civilian business world. VCTP is a three-track program that includes:

- professional skills
- tech
- independent study tracks

The professional skills track aims at training veterans and military spouses in "soft" skills—mainly how to prepare for and implement job searches by conducting company research and creating cover letters and resumes. Foundations for advanced-level courses in Microsoft Office Word, Excel, PowerPoint, and Outlook can be achieved within this track. If a spouse participates in this track, he or she becomes an official Syracuse University student and receives a non-credit-based certificate upon completion.

The tech track is geared to prepare participants for careers in operations or information technology (IT). Industry-level certifications are offered at this level, and, where applicable, VCTP will cover exam fees. Participants also become Syracuse University students and receive non-credit-awarding certificates upon completion. Certificates include proficiency in subject areas such as Comp TIA (Server+, Network+, and A+), Oracle Database 11G, CCNA with CCENT certification, and Lean Six Sigma Green Belt.

The independent study track hosts a large library of online course work. Course work includes subject matter pertaining to professional and personal development, leadership, IT, and accounting and finance. Course work is determined by veterans' demands and learning needs. Students will not be considered Syracuse University students.

Onward to Opportunity (O2O)

http://onward2opportunity.com/

Onward to Opportunity is a non-fee-based program launched by Syracuse University's IVMF and the Schultz Family Foundation. While currently operating aboard the Camp Pendleton Marine Corps Base (California), Joint Base San Antonio (Texas), and Joint Base Lewis-McCord (Washington), the organizers do have plans to expand to sixteen other locations aboard bases for each of the different branches, including Tri-Base Jacksonville (Florida), Camp Lejeune (North Carolina), and Fort Gordon (Georgia). The program is open to active-duty service members within six months of their date of separation from the service, members of the Selective Reserve who have at least 180 days of service, and spouses of active-duty service members or Selective Reservists.

There are four pathways to the O2O program. All participants participate in the first pathway, Onward to Your Career. There are six modules under this pathway that are intended to introduce students to "the new concepts, cultures, and organizational structures they may face upon transition into the civilian sector, as well as teaching participants job search and negotiation tactics to prepare them for their next steps."[1] Upon completion, students move on to one of two possible follow-on pathways: Customer Excellence or Information Technology.

O2O is committed to organizing at least one interview per student through contacts with its numerous partner companies after the student successfully completes the program. O2O's partner companies can be found here: http://onward2opportunity.com/onward-opportunity-participants/inter view-matching/. Students are also given assistance in building their resumes and preparing for interviews.

American Corporate Partners (ACP)

http://www.acp-usa.org/
http://www.acp-advisornet.org

The ACP programs are open for post-9/11 veterans and spouses of those wounded or killed in action. American Corporate Partners is a New York City–based national nonprofit organization founded in 2008 to help veterans transition from active duty into the civilian workforce by enlisting the help of business professionals nationwide. Through mentoring, career counseling, and networking possibilities, ACP's goal is to build greater connections between corporate America and veterans' communities. ACP has two available programs: ACP Advisor-Net and a one-on-one mentoring program. ACP Advisor-Net is an online business community that offers eligible participants online career advice through Q&A discussions. The mentoring program connects employees from ACP's participating institutions with veterans or their spouses for mentoring options, networking assistance, and career development. More than fifty major companies are participating in ACP's mentoring program, and success stories and videos are available on ACP's website (http://www.acp-usa.org).

Hiring Our Heroes

http://www.uschamber.com/hiringourheroes

The US Chamber of Commerce Foundation launched Hiring Our Heroes in 2011 to help veterans and spouses of active-duty service members find employment. The program works with state and local chambers as well as partners in the public, private, and nonprofit sectors. Hiring Our Heroes hosts career fairs at military bases. The program offers transition assistance, personal branding, and resume workshops.

Accredited Financial Counselor (AFC®) Certification through the Investor Education Foundation (FINRA) Military Spouse Fellowship Program

https://www.saveandinvest.org/military/military-spouse-fellowship-program

Military spouses can gain the Accredited Financial Counselor certification for free through the Military Spouse Fellowship Program. This is a career-enhancing certificate that requires six steps for completion:

- Complete the education requirement.
- Pass the required exam.
- Complete the experience component, which includes one thousand hours of financial counseling.
- Submit three letters of recommendation.
- Sign the AFC Code of Ethics.
- Renew the certificate when applicable.

For a video regarding the purpose of the AFC® credential, use this link: http://www.afcpe.org/certification/curriculum/accredited-financial-counselor/.

IBM® i2® Analyst's Notebook® Training in conjunction with Corporate America Supports You (CASY) and the Military Spouses Corporate Career Network (CASY-MSCCN)

http://casy.msccn.org/Training/i2Training.html

CASY launched the IBM® i2® Analyst's Notebook® Training for military service members and spouses in 2014, and in the first cohort 90 percent of those who participated attained the credential after successful completion of the program and passing the exam and received job-placement assistance through CASY-MSCCN. While the program is grant based and only offered on a few bases, it is growing and will be hosted in many different locations during 2016 (http://casy.msccn.org/Training/i2TrainingCalendar.html). The program is geared toward service members, but there are one to two spots per class available for spouses.

The certification is geared to help individuals in the field of data analytics. According to the IBM website (http://www-03.ibm.com/software/products/en/analysts-notebook), the IBM® i2® Analyst's Notebook® training "is a visual intelligence analysis environment that can optimize the value of massive amounts of information collected by government agencies and businesses."[2]

Blue Star SPOUSE FORCE

https://bluestarfam.org/lead/spouseforce

Blue Star Families is an organization that offers military spouses "a platform where military family members can join with civilian communities and leaders to address the challenges of military life."[3] Blue Star Families offers a program designed to assist military spouses in their quest for employment: Blue Star Careers. It assists spouses in finding contract-based employment no matter where they are stationed. Examples of potential work subject areas include, but are not limited to, web development, customer service, networking and information systems, and writing and translation. Be aware that the work you do is contracted through Upwork (https://www.upwork.com/) and that Blue Star Families does earn a referral fee for any jobs that you contract. The fee is used to support the spousal career programs that Blue Star offers.

Blue Star Families has also recently begun offering another program, SPOUSE FORCE. The first cohort of SPOUSE FORCE launched in the spring of 2016 and is set to roll out in other locations soon. Together with the Clinton Health Matters Initiative and Salesforce, Blue Star Families created and launched this eight-week training program that assists students in preparing to take the Salesforce Certified Administrator exam. The program also includes sales and technology training, connections to career coaching, and job search support, and upon completion it can offer spouses a new and portable career. Check out the following article for more information: http://www.militarytimes.com/story/military/benefits/2016/01/25/free-salesforce-training-military-spouses-5000-value-could-key-lucrative-portable-career/79306808/.

GENERAL ADVICE FOR SPOUSES AND DEPENDENT CHILDREN

Unfortunately, besides MyCAA, no other direct financial assistance is available for spouses to pursue their education. If spouses are just beginning their education, willing to attend the local community college, and eligible to use the benefit, MyCAA will typically cover an associate's degree, depending upon the cost of the school. Many community colleges offer associate's degrees fully online, which may also offer spouses with children more flexibility.

Past the associate's degree, Pell Grant, scholarship options (see the "Scholarship" section in chapter 7), and, in a few cases, transferring GI Bill benefits from the active-duty spouse are the best bets. Many universities and colleges offer tuition discounts to spouses of active-duty service members, but usually not enough to fully alleviate the financial burden. Always ask your school if the institution offers any financial assistance for military spouses.

Spouses should also apply for Federal Student Aid through the Free Application for Federal Student Aid (FAFSA). More information on Federal Student Aid can be found in chapter 7, "Cost and Payment Resources." Many spouses receive all or a portion of the Pell Grant money (see the "Federal Student Aid" section in chapter 7), which does not need to be paid back.

Spouses are entitled to receive in-state tuition rates at state schools in whatever state they are stationed with their active-duty service member. The Higher Education Opportunity Act (H.R. 4137), signed into law on August 14, 2008, guarantees this benefit. This law eliminates all out-of-state tuition fees for service members and their dependents in the state where they are stationed and at least eases the financial burden of pursuing higher education. Be aware that many schools will want to see a copy of the service members' orders to verify in-state tuition.

Some states offer low-income tuition waivers to residents, usually through the state-based community colleges. Because spouses are eligible for in-state tuition (so are active duty), they may be eligible for this type of waiver as well.

For example, California offers the Board of Governor's (BOG) Fee Waiver (see http://home.cccapply.org/money/bog-fee-waiver) through the state community colleges. Many dependents stationed in California with their active-duty service family members are attending community colleges in California and receiving this waiver, and they do not pay to attend school. In fact, many service members receive this waiver as well and are not bound by the rules of tuition assistance.

Always check with the local community colleges first if you are a spouse or dependent child and are just getting started. In most cases, it is hard to beat their low tuition rates and the flexible class offerings. Community colleges typically also offer vocational programs at drastically reduced prices when compared to private institutions. They should be your number-one starting point!

The Officers' Spouses' Clubs on the different bases usually offer scholarships for dependents. If you can write an essay and watch the deadline dates, scholarships are a decent option for a funding source. As a last resort, you may want to discuss GI Bill transferability with an education counselor at your base. Just remember, if you go that route, those are benefits your active-duty spouse will not have later. For more information regarding eligibility and the process to transfer the GI Bill, see chapter 7.

Transferring the GI Bill to a spouse so that he or she can use it while the service member is on active duty is not my (Jillian) first goal in most cases. Spouses are not eligible for the housing stipend while the service member is still actively serving, but currently children are eligible. Consider the following case:

A soldier transfers his GI Bill to his spouse while still on active duty. She uses the benefit to attend California State University, San Marcos (CSUSM). Although she will receive the book stipend, she will not receive the housing allowance. Her school is paid for, and she has some extra money for books. Another soldier transfers his GI Bill to his daughter. His daughter attends the same institution and receives the book stipend as well as the housing stipend, which is currently $2,341 per month. At the end of a nine-month school year, the monthly stipend totals $21,069. That is the amount of money the spouse did *not* get while using the benefit. Now consider the same monthly amount (even though it receives cost-of-living adjustments) over a four-year bachelor's degree: $84,276.

For this reason, only in very few circumstances do I recommend spouses using transferred GI Bill benefits while the service member is still on active duty. Obviously, this does not take into account different variables. For example, maybe the couple does not plan to have children, maybe the service member has attained the maximum level of education he or she is interested in pursuing, or maybe the children are very young and the spouse has no other resources. Or perhaps the family unit finds itself in the right circumstances for the spouse to spend time obtaining a credential to eventually contribute more financially to the needs to the family in the long run. In the end, the decision is personal, and all outlets should be pursued.

Dependent children in many states have another option: dual enrollment or dual credit. Dual enrollment occurs when high school students enroll in college courses while they are still in high school but only earn college credit from these courses. Dual-credit classes allow students to earn credit for high school classes and college courses simultaneously. Did I mention that these programs are often free or offered at a low cost? Some, like the Move on When Ready program in Georgia and the program available through the University of Florida, also offer free books. This is a great way for dependent children to cut down on their future college costs and gain their degrees at a faster pace. Since the program requirements vary greatly by state, always check with a counselor at your high school to determine whether your school is participating in the program and in which grade the system allows students to begin. For example, some schools permit dual enrollment from freshman year, while others do not allow it until the student enters his or her junior year of high school.

Students gain other benefits besides saving money and graduating early through dual enrollment courses. For example:

- Many students gain time management and study skills that will benefit them in college.
- Dual enrollment may improve a student's chance at getting into college.
- Students can gain a better understanding of the subject in which they would like to major and/or their future career paths.
- Some students might now have the opportunity to double major.
- Students gain the ability to delve deeper into subjects that interest them when they have access to college-level course work.

Dual-enrollment classes can be taken during the day, in the evening, or online. Some schools offer classes on the weekends, and sometimes the classes are offered right on the high school campus. Make sure to determine which manner of learning is best for you. Some high school–aged students are already adept at online learning, and others might feel more confident in a face-to-face environment. If you are unsure of your ability to be an online learner, take the DANTES Distance Learning Readiness Assessment (https://dlrsa.dodmou.com/). The results will help you to better understand your strengths and weaknesses, which will allow you to plan accordingly.

Dual enrollment students won't necessarily get a taste of college life through this pathway as oftentimes the face-to-face college classes may still be taught by high school teachers; however, they may also be taught by community college or university professors.

Some participating schools and school systems include but are not limited to the following:

- Alabama Community College System: https://www.accs.cc/index.cfm/workforce-development/career-technical-education/dual-enrollment/
- Austin Community College District: http://www.austincc.edu/high-school-to-college
- Central Arizona College: http://www.centralaz.edu/Home/Admissions/High_School_Outreach_Programs/Dual_Enrollment.htm
- Central New Mexico Community College: https://www.cnm.edu/depts/outreach/dual-credit/high-school-and-dual-credit-programs
- City College of Chicago: http://www.ccc.edu/departments/Pages/Early-College.aspx
- The City University of New York (CUNY): http://collegenow.cuny.edu/faqs/

- College of DuPage (Illinois): http://www.cod.edu/academics/ohsp/dualcrediths.aspx
- Eastern Kentucky University: http://dualcredit.eku.edu/
- Edmonds Community College (Washington): http://www.edcc.edu/highschool/chs/default.html
- Florida Department of Education: http://www.fldoe.org/core/fileparse.php/5423/urlt/DualEnrollmentFAQ.pdf
- Louisiana Department of Education: https://www.louisianabelieves.com/courses/dual-enrollment
- Metropolitan State University of Denver: https://www.msudenver.edu/admissions/apply/concurrentlyenrolled/
- Minnesota Department of Education's Postsecondary Enrollment Options (PSEO): http://education.state.mn.us/MDE/StuSuc/CollReadi/PSEO/
- Move on When Ready (Georgia): https://apps.gsfc.org/Main/publishing/pdf/common/MOWR%20Student%20Parent%20FAQs.pdf
- Northern Virginia Community College: http://www.nvcc.edu/dual-enrollment/
- Ohio Department of Education: http://education.ohio.gov/Topics/Quality-School-Choice/College-Credit-Plus
- Oklahoma Department of Education: https://secure.okcollegestart.org/College_Planning/Prepare_for_College/_default.aspx
- Public Schools of North Carolina: http://www.dpi.state.nc.us/ccp/
- Saddleback Community College (California): http://www.saddleback.edu/outreach/high-school-partnership-program
- South Dakota Department of Education: http://doe.sd.gov/octe/dualcredit.aspx
- Southwestern Illinois College: http://www.swic.edu/high-school-programs/
- University of California: http://www.uconline.edu/audiences/high-school-students/
- University of Florida: http://www.cpet.ufl.edu/students/dce/faqs/
- University of Idaho: http://dualcredit.uidaho.edu/students/
- University of Missouri–Kansas City: http://cas.umkc.edu/hscp/
- Wyoming Department of Education: http://edu.wyoming.gov/beyond-the-classroom/college-career/dual-enrollment/

If you are interested in learning more information regarding the benefits of a dual enrollment or dual credit program, take a look at the following articles:

- American College Testing (ACT.org): https://www.act.org/content/dam/ act/unsecured/documents/UsingDualEnrollment_2015.pdf
- *Education Week*: http://www.edweek.org/ew/articles/2014/12/10/colleges -vary-on-credit-for-ap-ib.html
- *Inside Higher Ed*: https://www.insidehighered.com/news/2015/11/02/feds -encourage-dual-enrollment-through-experimental-access-pell-grants
- *U.S. News & World Report*: http://www.usnews.com/education/online- education/articles/2013/07/16/consider-online-college-courses-in-high- school, http://www.usnews.com/education/best-colleges/articles/2012/03/ 09/some-teens-start-college-work-early-via-dual-enrollment

Many universities and nonprofit organizations offer summer college pro- grams for high-schoolers and sometimes even middle school students. The programs vary greatly in content, cost, and eligibility parameters based upon the school or the organization that offers them. Tuition can run from free to a few hundred dollars to several thousand dollars. Some offer financial aid or a reduction in tuition for low-income students or minority students. There are even study abroad options for those so inclined. If you dig deep enough, you can find free programs such as the College Camp program in Illinois or the free/low cost Governor's School programs (http://ncogs.org/index.php/faqs/ governor-s-school-faqs) available in certain states.

Students can use these different summer programs to help enhance their college admission's applications. But think long and hard before you send your high-school-aged child away to a summer academic camp. According to *U.S. News and World Report*, "Pre-college summer programs often give teens a taste of the most attractive aspects of college life: dorm housing, challenging classes and a parent-free environment."[4]

Students do typically stay in the school dormitories for the residential programs and do not have the same level of monitoring that they would receive at home. If they are day-based programs, then students remain at home and attend the camp during daytime work hours. The programs can be beneficial for high school students in that they get a taste of what college life can be like. The camps might even help your high-school-age student decide that attending school on a big college campus is the goal or that it isn't to their liking and he or she may prefer a smaller setting in which to pursue their degree.

Some summer camps are geared toward learning about specific sub- jects—for example, the engineering-based summer internship program offered through the Saturday Academy's ASE program in Oregon (https://www.saturdayacademy.org/internships) or the University of Pennsylvania's Summer Academies program (http://www.sas.upenn.edu/summer/programs/high-school/academies), in which students can focus on subjects such as chemistry or biomedical research, among others.

One program that many military children take advantage of is the American Legion's Girls State and Boys State. The Girls State and Boys State (http://www.boysandgirlsstate.org/girls.html) programs teach students how their state and local governments work. According to the Girls State website, "Participants learn how to participate in the functioning of their state's government in preparation for their future roles as responsible adult citizens."[5] And according to the Boys State website, "Activities include legislative sessions, court proceedings, law enforcement presentations, assemblies, bands, chorus and recreational programs."[6] Students must have completed their junior year of high school to be eligible. Girls and Boys State students may be eligible to apply for the American Legion Samsung Scholarship (http://www.legion.org/scholarships/samsung).

A more obscure program is the US Department of State–sponsored National Security Language Initiative for Youth (NSLI-Y) program (http://www.nsliforyouth.org/). Interested in foreign languages and studying abroad? Then this program is the gold standard! There are two types of programs with seven languages: Arabic, Mandarin Chinese, Korean, Hindi, Persian, Russian, and Turkish. Almost all of the costs associated with the programs are covered. The costs not covered include obtaining a passport, required medical exams/immunizations, baggage fees, and pocket money. Students can opt for a six-to eight-week summertime program or a more intensive academic-year-based program. Students live with a host family and are immersed in the language and culture of their host countries. As someone (Jillian) who learned a foreign language later in life, I believe that living in a foreign country is the only way to gain working knowledge of the intricacies of that language. Learning from a book is just not the same as listening to daily conversations. What foreign language can I speak? Turkish, which is one of the selections! To see videos about the program, visit the following site: http://nsliy-interactive.org/category/turkish.

Other summer programs are more generic in nature and are geared toward academic preparation for college-level learning or standardized test taking (ACT and SAT), such as Georgetown University's College Preparatory Program (http://scs.georgetown.edu/departments/21/summer-programs-for-high

-school-students/format/college-prep) or the Summerfuel program that is offered through partnerships with schools such as the University of California, Berkeley (http://www.summerfuel.com/cap/uc_berkeley). The Summerfuel program also offers study abroad options (http://www.summerfuel.com/compare#tab-lci).

The following programs are just a small demonstration of the summer programs that are available for high school students. Don't be surprised by some of the costs. The programs available at many of the Ivy League institutions run in the range of several thousand dollars. Check out the costs through some of the nonprofit organizations or the state universities to get a more thorough understanding of what is available and also cost effective.

- Camp College (Illinois) area of emphasis: precollege planning (free program for those who qualify) (https://www.iacac.org/camp/)
- University of Chicago area of emphasis: Biotechnology for the 21st Century, Contagion: Infectious Agents and Emerging Diseases, and Explorations in Neuroscience (http://summer.uchicago.edu/high-school/ribs)
- Tufts University area of emphasis: adventures in veterinary medicine (http://www.collegexpress.com/summer-programs/tufts-university-adventures-in-veterinary-medicine/2672/)
- Columbia University area of emphasis: journalism workshop (http://cspa.columbia.edu/conventions-and-workshops/summer-journalism-workshop)
- Florida State University area of emphasis: music (http://www.music.fsu.edu/Quicklinks/Summer-Music-Camps)
- Massachusetts Institute of Technology area of emphasis: minority students pursuing engineering and science. This program is free but only open to students from backgrounds traditionally underrepresented in science, engineering, and technology (http://www.collegexpress.com/summer-programs/massachusetts-institute-of-technology-minority-introduction-to-engineering-and-science/2642/; other MIT-based summer programs located at http://mitadmissions.org/apply/prepare/summer)
- Missouri University area of emphasis: minority students pursuing technology and engineering (http://futurestudents.mst.edu/summercamps/mite/)
- Rochester Institute of Technology area of emphasis: bioscience exploration for middle and high school students (http://www.rit.edu/healthsciences/cbet/camps.php)

- Scripps College Academy area of emphasis: this program is a free year-round college-readiness program for high-achieving young women in the Los Angeles area (http://www.scrippscollege.edu/academy/about)
- University of California Academic Connections area of emphasis: multiple subjects available in different locations, including environmental leadership and ecosystems and climate zones of the Hawaiian Islands (http://academicconnections.ucsd.edu/)
- Virginia State University area of emphasis: agriculture and hospitality and tourism (http://agriculture.vsu.edu/special-programs/summer-high-school-programs.php)
- California State University, Northridge, Summer Academic Enrichment Program area of emphasis: general college preparation (http://www.csun.edu/eisner-education/summer-academic-enrichment-program)
- Texas State University area of emphasis: mathematics (http://www.txstate.edu/mathworks/camps/hsmc.html)
- Morgan State University area of emphasis: mathematics and science (http://www.morgan.edu/school_of_computer_mathematical_and_natural_sciences/high_school_outreach.html)
- Iowa State University CY-TAG area of emphasis: varies (http://www.opptag.iastate.edu/cytag/index.php)
- Tennessee State University area of emphasis: engineering (http://www.tnstate.edu/engineering/precollege.aspx)
- University of Michigan area of emphasis: varies (http://www.ceo.umich.edu/summer.html)
- University of Wisconsin–Madison area of emphasis: engineering. This is a six-week free program for selected students (http://www.engr.wisc.edu/current/coe-dao-engineering-summer-program-esp.html)
- The National High Magnetic Field Laboratory and WFSU/NPR (Florida) area of emphasis: science for middle school girls (https://nationalmaglab.org/education/k12-students/summer-camps/scigirls-summer-camp)
- Governor's School at Radford University (free!) areas of emphasis: humanities and visual and performing arts (http://www.radford.edu/content/gov-school/home.html)
- Governor's School of New Jersey (free!) area of emphasis: science, technology, engineering, mathematics (STEM) (http://www.nj.gov/govschool)
- Indiana University, Kelley School of Business, Young Women's Institute (free!) area of emphasis: business/career (http://kelley.iu.edu/Ugrad/PreCollege/YWI/page39078.html)

- California Youth Think Tank at the University of Southern California, emphasis on middle school and high school-age students (reduced fees available for those students who participate in free and reduced lunch program) (http://www.theyoungcenter.com/CYTT.html)

For more information regarding summer precollege camps, research the information found on the following sites:

- https://www.petersons.com/college-search/college-prep-summer-opportunities.aspx
- https://bigfuture.collegeboard.org/get-started/inside-the-classroom/summer-learning-programs-what-why-and-how

STUDY RESOURCES

The below-listed websites are those that I (Jillian) find helpful to the population I counsel. All of the listed sites are free except for the ACT, SAT, and Law School Admission Test (LSAT) study material. The SAT and ACT materials are free, but the delivery method is not. The materials can be sent in CD ROM format or accessed through the iCloud at a cost of around $20. The LSAT (for admission to law school) materials are offered at a greatly reduced price, currently the cost is $125. The Graduate Record Examination (GRE) and Graduate Management Admission Test (GMAT) websites have limited free test preparation as well. The information is located here: (GRE) www.ets.org/gre/revised_general/prepare/?WT.ac=grehome_greprepare_b_150213; (GMAT) www.mba.com/us/the-gmat-exam/prepare-for-the-gmat-exam/test-prep-materials/free-gmat-prep-software.aspx. Before paying for expensive test preparation, try the following sites.

- CLEP and DSST exam study guides: http://www.nelnetsolutions.com/dodlibrary/
- Online Academic Skills Course (OASC), remedial math, and English subject-matter assistance: http://www.nelnetsolutions.com/dodlibrary/
- College Placement Skills Training (CPST), remedial math, and English subject-matter assistance that is designed to help students place better on the community college assessment exams: http://www.nelnetsolutions.com/DantesNet/

- SAT and ACT study material (materials are free but delivery method is not): http://www.eknowledge.com/Affiliate_Welcome.asp?coupon=3A8E9CEFCE
- LSAT (law school) study material, offered at a discounted price: http://www.eknowledge.com/Affiliate_Welcome.asp?coupon=3A8E9CEFCE
- Math help:

  - Khan Academy (includes SAT and GMAT math help): https://www.khanacademy.org/
  - The World of Math: https://www.purplemath.com/
  - Discovery Education: http://www.webmath.com/

- English help:

  - Purdue Owl: https://owl.english.purdue.edu/owl/
  - Guide to Grammar and Writing: http://grammar.ccc.commnet.edu/grammar/
  - Grammar Bytes: http://www.chompchomp.com/menu.htm

- APA format:

  - American Psychological Association: http://www.apastyle.org/
  - Purdue Owl: https://owl.english.purdue.edu/owl/section/2/10/

- MLA format:

  - Purdue Owl: https://owl.english.purdue.edu/owl/resource/747/01/
  - California State University Los Angeles: http://web.calstatela.edu/library/guides/3mla.pdf

- Citation assistance:

  - Cite This for Me: https://www.citethisforme.com/
  - Citation Machine: http://www.citationmachine.net/
  - Citefast: http://www.citefast.com/

- Tutor.com for certain eligible dependents of service members. Cite offers free, live tutors for numerous different subjects, including math, English, foreign language, social studies, and ACT/SAT test preparation assistance: http://military.tutor.com/home.

Appendix A

Commonly Used Acronyms

AA: Associate of Arts

AAS: Associate of Applied Science

ACE: American Council on Education

ACT: American College Testing

AS: Associate of Science

ASSIST: Articulation System Stimulating Interinstitutional Student Transfer

BA: Bachelor of Arts

BOG Waiver: Board of Governors Waiver

BS: Bachelor of Science

CAAHEP: Commission on Accreditation of Allied Health Education Programs

CC: Community College

CDA: Child Development Associate

CEU: Continuing Education Unit

CHEA: Council for Higher Education Accreditation

CLEP: College-Level Examination Program

COA: Cost of Attendance

COE: Certificate of Eligibility

CPST: College Placement Skills Testing

DANTES: Defense Activity for Non-Traditional Education Support

DAV: Disabled American Veterans

DEA: Dependents' Educational Assistance Program
DNS: Degree Network System
DoD: Department of Defense
DoEd: Department of Education
DOL: Department of Labor
DSST: DANTES Subject Standardized Test
ECE: Early Childhood Education
EFC: Expected Family Contribution
FAFSA: Free Application for Federal Student Aid
FSA: Federal Student Aid
FY: Fiscal Year
GER: General Education Requirements
GMAT: Graduate Management Admission Test
GPA: Grade Point Average
GRE: Graduate Record Exam
HLC: Higher Learning Commission
LCPC: Licensed Clinical Professional Counselor
LPC: Licensed Professional Counselor
LPCC: Licensed Professional Clinical Counselor
LPN: Licensed Practical Nurse
LSAT: Law School Admission Test
LVN: Licensed Vocational Nurse
MA: Master of Arts
MAEd: Master of Arts in Education
MD: Doctor of Medicine
MHA: Monthly Housing Allowance
MS: Master of Science
MSCHE: Middle States Commission on Higher Education
MSEP: Midwest Student Exchange Program
MSW: Master of Social Work
MyCAA: Military Spouse Career Advancement Accounts
NAEYC: National Association of the Education of Young Children
NBCC: National Board for Certified Counselors
NCB: National Certification Board
NCCRS: National College Credit Recommendation Service
NCE: National Counselor Examination for Licensure and Certification
NCMHCE: National Clinical Mental Health Counseling Examination

NEASC-CIHE: New England Association of Schools and Colleges Commission on Institutions of Higher Education

NWCCU: Northwest Commission on Colleges and Universities

OASC: Online Academic Skills Course

OJT: On-the-Job-Training

PCS: Permanent Change of Station

PDU: Professional Development Units

PhD: Doctor of Philosophy

PLA: Prior Learning Assessment

RN: Registered Nurse

SACSCOC: Southern Association of Colleges and Schools Commission on Colleges

SAT: Scholastic Aptitude Test

SECO: Spouse Education and Career Opportunities

SOC: Servicemembers Opportunity Colleges

VA: US Department of Veterans Affairs

Vet Reps: Veterans Representatives

VFW: Veterans of Foreign Wars

Voc Rehab: Vocational Rehabilitation

VONAPP: Veterans Online Application

VOTECH: Vocational Technical

WASC: Western Association of Schools and Colleges

YRP: Yellow Ribbon Program

Appendix B

Resources

REGIONAL ACCREDITING BODIES

- Higher Learning Commission: http://www.ncahlc.org/
- Middle States Association of Colleges and Schools: http://www.msche.org/
- New England Association of School and Colleges: http://cihe.neasc.org/
- Northwest Commission on Colleges and Universities: http://www.nwccu.org
- Southern Association of Colleges and Schools: http://www.sacscoc.org/
- Western Association of Schools and Colleges, Accrediting Commission for Community and Junior Colleges: http://www.accjc.org
- Western Association of Schools and Colleges, Accrediting Commission for Senior Colleges and Universities: http://www.wascweb.org/

NOTABLE NATIONALLY ACCREDITING BODIES

- Accrediting Commission of Career Schools and Colleges: http://www.accsc.org
- Council on Occupational and Education: http://www.council.org
- Distance Education Accrediting Commission: http://www.deac.org

RESOURCE WEBSITES

- Accredited Financial Counselor (AFC®) Certification: https://www.saveandinvest.org/military/military-spouse-fellowship-program
- American College Testing (ACT): http://www.act.org
- American Corporate Partners (ACP): http://www.acp-usa.org/; www.acpadvisornet.org
- American Council on Education: http://www.acenet.edu
- American Psychological Association (APA): http://www.apa.org
- ASSIST: http://www.assist.org/web-assist/welcome.html
- Blue Star Spouse Force: https://bluestarfam.org/lead/spouseforce
- Bureau of Labor Statistics Occupational Outlook Handbook: http://www.bls.gov/ooh/
- California Board of Governors (BOG) Waiver: http://home.cccapply.org/money/bog-fee-waiver
- California CareerZone: https://www.cacareerzone.org/
- CareerOneStop: http://www.careeronestop.org/credentialing/CredentialingHomeReadMore.asp
- CareerScope®: http://benefits.va.gov/gibill/careerscope.asp
- Cash for College: http://www.calgrants.org/index.cfm?navid=16
- College Board College Search: https://bigfuture.collegeboard.org/college-search
- College-Level Examination Preparation: https://clep.collegeboard.org/
- College Navigator: http://nces.ed.gov/collegenavigator/
- Council for Higher Education Accreditation (CHEA): http://www.chea.org/search/default.asp
- DANTES Kuder: http://www.dantes.kuder.com/
- Defense Activity for Non-Traditional Education Support: http://getcollegecredit.com/
- Department of Labor: http://www.dol.gov/
- eKnowledge Corporation & NFL Players: http://www.eknowledge.com/military
- Federal Student Aid: http://www.fafsa.ed.gov/
- Federal Student ID Site: https://fsaid.ed.gov/npas/index.htm
- GI Bill Apprenticeship and OJT: http://www.benefits.va.gov/gibill/onthejob_apprenticeship.asp
- GI Bill Comparison Tool: http://www.benefits.va.gov/gibill/comparison
- GI Bill Information: http://www.benefits.va.gov/gibill/

- GI Bill Tutorial Assistance: http://www.benefits.va.gov/gibill/tutorial_assistance.asp
- Google for Veterans and Families: http://www.googleforveterans.com/
- Graduate Management Admission Test (GMAT): http://www.mba.com/us/the-gmat-exam.aspx
- Graduate Record Examination (GRE): http://www.ets.org/gre
- Grammar Book: http://www.grammarbook.com
- Grammar Bytes: http://www.chompchomp.com
- Guide to Grammar Writing: http://grammar.ccc.commnet.edu/grammar/
- Hiring Our Heroes: http://www.uschamber.com/hiringourheroes
- IBM® i2® Analyst's Notebook® Training in conjunction with Corporate America Supports You (CASY) and the Military Spouses Corporate Career Network (CASY-MSCCN): http://casy.msccn.org/Training/i2Training.html
- Institutional Accreditation Search: http://ope.ed.gov/accreditation/, http://www.chea.org/search/default.asp, http://nces.ed.gov/collegenavigator/
- Khan Academy: http://www.khanacademy.org
- Midwest Student Exchange Program: http://msep.mhec.org/
- Military One Source: http://www.militaryonesource.mil/
- Military Spouse Career Advancement Accounts (MyCAA): https://aiportal.acc.af.mil/mycaa/Default.aspx
- National Association of Credential Evaluation Services: http://www.naces.org/
- National Association of State Approving Agencies: http://www.nasaa-vetseducation.com/Contacts.aspx
- National Student Loan Data System: https://www.nslds.ed.gov
- Oklahoma Tuition Assistance Grant (OTAG): https://www.okhighered.org/admin-fac/FinAidResources/otag.shtml
- O*NET OnLine: http://www.onetonline.org/
- Onward to Opportunity: http://onward2opportunity.com/
- Peterson's: http://www.petersons.com/dantes
- Purdue Owl: http://owl.english.purdue.edu/owl/
- Purple Math: http://www.purplemath.com
- Scholastic Aptitude Test (SAT): http://www.collegeboard.org
- Servicemembers Opportunity Colleges (SOC): http://www.soc.aascu.org/
- Spouse Education and Career Opportunities (SECO) LearningCounts™: http://seco.learningcounts.org
- State workforce agencies: http://www.servicelocator.org/OWSLinks.asp

- Syracuse University Institute for Veterans and Military Families (IVMF): http://vets.syr.edu/
- University of San Diego's Veterans' Legal Clinic: http://www.sandiego.edu/veteransclinic/
- US Department of Education—national accrediting agencies: http://ope.ed.gov/accreditation/
- US Department of Education College Affordability and Transparency Center: http://collegecost.ed.gov/
- US Department of Education College Scorecard: https://collegescorecard.ed.gov/
- US Department of Labor Apprenticeship Information: http://www.doleta.gov/oa/
- US Department of Labor's Career Search Tool: http://www.mynextmove.org/
- US Department of Labor Unemployment Information: http://workforcesecurity.doleta.gov/unemploy/uifactsheet.asp
- US Department of Veterans Affairs (VA): http://www.va.gov
- VA Regional Centers: http://www.va.gov/directory/guide/map_flsh.asp
- VA Vet Centers: http://www.vetcenter.va.gov/index.asp
- VA Yellow Ribbon Program: http://www.benefits.va.gov/gibill/yellow_ribbon.asp
- Vet Net on Google+: http://www.vetnethq.com/
- Veterans On-Line Application (VONAPP): http://vabenefits.vba.va.gov/vonapp/

APA FORMAT GUIDANCE

- American Psychological Association: http://www.apastyle.org
- Purdue Owl: https://owl.english.purdue.edu/owl/resource/560/01/

CITATION FORMATTING

- Citation Machine: http://citationmachine.net/index2.php
- KnightCite: https://www.calvin.edu/library/knightcite/

MLA FORMAT GUIDANCE

- California State University, Los Angeles: http://web.calstatela.edu/library/ guides/3mla.pdf
- Cornell University Library: http://www.library.cornell.edu/resrch/ citmanage/mla
- Purdue Owl: https://owl.english.purdue.edu/owl/resource/747/01/

STATES CURRENTLY WITH STATE-BASED EDUCATION BENEFITS FOR SPOUSES/DEPENDENT CHILDREN

Alabama: http://www.va.state.al.us/gi_dep_scholarship.aspx, http://www. va.state.al.us/otherbenefits.aspx

California: https://www.calvet.ca.gov/VetServices/Pages/College-Fee-Waiver.aspx

Illinois: https://secure.osfa.illinois.edu/scholarship-database/detail.aspx? id=1522

Indiana: http://www.in.gov/dva/2378.htm

Maryland: http://www.mdva.state.md.us/state/scholarships.html

New York: http://www.hesc.ny.gov/pay-for-college/financial-aid/types-of-financial-aid/nys-grants-scholarships-awards/msrs-scholarship. html

North Carolina: http://www.doa.state.nc.us/vets/scholarshipclasses.aspx

South Carolina: http://va.sc.gov/benefits.html

Texas: http://veterans.portal.texas.gov/en/Pages/education.aspx

Wisconsin: http://dva.state.wi.us/Pages/educationEmployment/Education .aspx

Wyoming: http://www.communitycolleges.wy.edu/Data/Sites/1/commis sionFiles/Programs/Veteran/_doc/statue-19-14-106.pdf

STATE-BASED EDUCATION BENEFITS BASED ON SEVERE LEVELS OF DISABILITY OR DEATH

Alabama: http://www.va.state.al.us/gi_dep_scholarship.aspx

Alaska: http://veterans.alaska.gov/education-benefits.html

Arkansas: http://www.veterans.arkansas.gov/benefits/state-benefits

California: https://www.calvet.ca.gov/VetServices/Pages/College-Fee-Waiver.aspx

Appendix B

Delaware: http://veteransaffairs.delaware.gov/veterans_benefits.shtml

Florida: http://floridavets.org/?page_id=60

Idaho: https://boardofed.idaho.gov/scholarship/pub_safety.asp

Iowa: http://www.in.gov/dva/2378.htm

Kentucky: http://veterans.ky.gov/Benefits/Documents/KDVAInfoBook letIssueAugust2010.pdf

Louisiana: http://www.vetaffairs.la.gov/

Maine: http://www.maine.gov/dvem/bvs/VDEB_2.pdf

Maryland: http://veterans.maryland.gov/wp-content/uploads/sites/2/2013/ 10/MDBenefitsGuide.pdf

Massachusetts: www.mass.gov/veterans/education/for-family/mslf.html

Michigan: http://www.michigan.gov/documents/mistudentaid/CVTGFact Sheet_271497_7.pdf

Minnesota: http://www.mdva.state.mn.us/education/SurvivingSpouse DependentInformationSheet.pdf

Missouri: http://mvc.dps.mo.gov/docs/veterans-benefits-guide.pdf

Montana: http://montanadma.org/state-montana-veterans-benefits

Nebraska: http://www.vets.state.ne.us/waiver.html

New Hampshire: http://www.nh.gov/nhveterans/benefits/education.htm

New Jersey: http://www.state.nj.us/military/veterans/programs.html

New Mexico: http://www.dvs.state.nm.us/benefits.html

New York: http://www.veterans.ny.gov/

North Carolina: http://www.doa.nc.gov/vets/benefitslist.aspx?pid= scholarships

North Dakota: http://www.nd.gov/veterans/benefits/nd-dependent-tuition-waiver

Ohio: https://www.ohiohighered.org/ohio-war-orphans

Oregon: http://www.oregon.gov/ODVA/Pages/index.aspx

Pennsylvania: http://www.pheaa.org/funding-opportunities/other-educa tional-aid/postsecondary-educational-gratuity.shtml

South Carolina: http://va.sc.gov/benefits.html

South Dakota: http://vetaffairs.sd.gov/benefits/State/State%20Education %20Programs.aspx

Tennessee: http://www.state.tn.us/veteran/state_benifits/dep_tuition.html

Texas: http://www.tvc.texas.gov/Hazlewood-Act.aspx

Utah: http://veterans.utah.gov/state-benefits/

Virginia: http://www.dvs.virginia.gov/veterans-benefits.shtml

Washington: http://www.dva.wa.gov/benefits/education-and-training

Wisconsin:	http://dva.state.wi.us/Pages/educationEmployment/Education.aspx

West Virginia: http://www.veterans.wv.gov/programs/Pages/default.aspx

Wyoming: http://www.frabr245.org/Vet%20State%20Benefits%20&%20Discounts%20-%20WY%202014.pdf

Notes

1. MILITARY SPOUSE EDUCATION CONCERNS

1. Bureau of Labor Statistics Occupational Outlook Handbook, "Frequently Asked Questions," http://www.bls.gov/ooh/about/ooh-faqs.htm#growth1, accessed April 2, 2016.
2. Bureau of Labor Statistics Occupational Outlook Handbook, "Frequently Asked Questions."
3. Bureau of Labor Statistics Occupational Outlook Handbook, "High School Teachers," http://www.bls.gov/ooh/education-training-and-library/high-school-teachers.htm, accessed April 2, 2016.
4. Bureau of Labor Statistics Occupational Outlook Handbook, "Diagnostic Medical Sonographers and Cardiovascular Technologists and Technicians, Including Vascular Technologists," http://www.bls.gov/ooh/healthcare/diagnostic-medical-sonographers.htm, accessed April 2, 2016.
5. US Employment and Training Administration's "Projections Central," http://www.projectionscentral.com/Projections/LongTerm, accessed January 17, 2016.
6. Federal Reserve Bank of Dallas, "Growth Rates Versus Levels," http://www.dallasfed.org/research/basics/growth.cfm, accessed December 12, 2015.
7. O*NET OnLine, "Summary Report for: Medical Assistants," http://www.onetonline.org/link/summary/31-9092.00, accessed April 26, 2016.

2. EDUCATIONAL CONCERNS FOR SPOUSES OF ACTIVE-DUTY PERSONNEL, RESERVISTS, AND VETERANS

1. Kimberly Griffin and Claire Gilbert, Center for American Progress, "Easing the Transition from Combat to Classroom," last modified April 2012, http://www.americanprogress.org/wp-content/uploads/issues/2012/04/pdf/student_veterans.pdf, accessed June 2, 2013.

3. ACADEMIC AND CAREER-BASED
RESEARCH TOOLS

1. Military OneSource, "Career & Education," http://www.militaryonesource.mil/MOS/f? p=MOSNEWS:ARTICLE:0::::MONTH,YEAR,COHE,PAGE:June,2013,271731,4,   accessed April 1, 2016.

2. California Career Zone, "Assess Yourself," https://www.cacareerzone.org/assessments, accessed April 1, 2016.

4. DEGREE TYPES AND DIFFERENCES

1. Bureau of Labor Statistics, "STEM 101: Intro to Tomorrow's Jobs," http://www.bls.gov/careeroutlook/2014/spring/art01.pdf, accessed December 2, 2015.

2. U.S. Department of Education, "Science, Technology, Engineering and Math: Education for Global Leadership," http://www.ed.gov/stem, accessed December 2, 2015.

3. Melissa Korn, "Liberal Arts Salaries Are a Marathon, Not a Sprint," *Wall Street Journal*, January 29, 2014, http://blogs.wsj.com/atwork/2014/01/22/liberal-arts-salaries-are-a-marathon-not-a-sprint/, accessed December 6, 2015.

4. *The Motley Fool*, "Liberal Arts Degrees Can Net Big Salaries—If You Wait Long Enough," http://www.fool.com/investing/general/2014/10/12/liberal-arts-degrees-can-net-big-salaries-if-you-w.aspx, accessed December 6, 2015.

5. Bureau of Labor Statistics Occupational Outlook Handbook, "Mental Health Counselors and Marriage and Family Therapists," http://www.bls.gov/ooh/community-and-social-service/mental-health-counselors-and-marriage-and-family-therapists.htm#tab-4, accessed January 19, 2016.

6. *The Economist*, "Doctoral Degrees: The Disposable Academic," http://www.economist.com/node/17723223, December 16, 2010, accessed February 10, 2016.

7. The University of California at Berkeley, "Career Destinations Survey Class of 2015," https://career.berkeley.edu/Survey/2015Emp, accessed February 14, 2016.

8. The National Center for Education Statistics, "Fast Facts," https://nces.ed.gov/fastfacts/display.asp?id=37, accessed April 15, 2016.

9. Jack Linshi, "10 CEOs Who Prove Your Liberal Arts Degree Is Not Worthless," *Time*, July 23, 2015, http://time.com/3964415/ceo-degree-liberal-arts/, accessed February 9, 2016.

10. George Anders, "That 'Useless' Liberal Arts Degree Has Become Tech's Hottest Ticket," *Forbes*/Tech, August 17, 2015, http://www.forbes.com/sites/georgeanders/2015/07/29/liberal-arts-degree-tech/#49fbbffe5a75, accessed February 9, 2016.

5. LICENSING AND CERTIFICATION

1. National Environmental Health Association, "Difference Between Credentials and Certifications," http://www.neha.org/professional-development/education-and-training/differences-between-credentials-certifications, accessed April 11, 2016.

6. WHAT SHOULD I LOOK FOR IN A SCHOOL?

1. College Board, "Trends in Higher Education," http://trends.collegeboard.org/college-pricing/figures-tables/average-published-undergraduate-charges-sector-2015-16, accessed April 8, 2016.

2. Sandy Baum and Jennifer Ma, "Trends in Higher Education 2014," College Board, https://secure-media.collegeboard.org/digitalServices/misc/trends/2014-trends-college-pricing-report-final.pdf, accessed October 21, 2014.

3. National Association of Independent Colleges and Universities, "Independent Colleges and Universities: A National Profile," https://www.naicu.edu/docLib/20110308_NAICU_profiles.pdf, accessed April 8, 2016.

4. Judith Eaton, "An Overview of U.S. Accreditation," Council for Higher Education Accreditation, http://www.chea.org/pdf/Overview%20of%20US%20Accreditation%202012.pdf, last modified August 2012.

5. Barbara Brittingham, Mary Jane Harris, Michael Lambert, Frank Murray, George Peterson, Jerry Trapnell, Peter Vlasses, Belle Wheelan, Ralph Wolff, Susan Zlotlow, and Judith Eaton, "The Value of Accreditation," Council for Higher Education Accreditation, June 1, 2010, http://www.chea.org/pdf/Value of US Accreditation 06.29.2010_buttons.pdf.

7. COST AND PAYMENT RESOURCES

1. Federal Student Aid, "Things to Consider," https://studentaid.ed.gov/sa/prepare-for-college/choosing-schools/consider, accessed April 28, 2016.

2. Federal Student Aid, "How Aid Is Calculated," https://studentaid.ed.gov/fafsa/next-steps/how-calculated, accessed April 28, 2016.

3. Federal Student Aid, "How Aid Is Calculated."

4. State of Alaska, "Alaska Performance Scholarship," http://acpe.alaska.gov/FINANCIAL_AID/Grants_Scholarships/Alaska_Performance_Scholarship, accessed April 28, 2016.

5. Oklahoma State Regents for Higher Education, "Oklahoma Grants Based on Need," https://secure.okcollegestart.org/financial_aid_planning/oklahoma_grants/oklahoma_tuition_aid_grant.aspx, accessed May 1, 2016.

8. PRIOR LEARNING CREDIT

1. The Council for Adult and Experiential Learning, "Fueling the Race to Postsecondary Success: A 48-Institution Study of Prior Learning Assessment and Adult Student Outcomes," http://www.cael.org/pdfs/pla_fueling-the-race, March 2010.

2. Military OneSource, "LearningCounts @SECO," https://myseco.militaryonesource.mil/Portal/Content/View/2660, accessed February 10, 2016.

3. Military OneSource, "LearningCounts @SECO."

4. Federal Trade Commission, "College Degree Scams," https://www.consumer.ftc.gov/articles/0206-college-degree-scams, accessed March 19, 2016.

5. CLEP, "Study Guides," https://clep.collegeboard.org/study-resources, accessed March 20, 2016.

6. LearningCounts™, "Earn College Credit for Knowledge You Already Have!" https://learningcounts.org/seco/how-it-works, accessed April 13, 2016.

7. LearningCounts™, "Earn College Credit for Knowledge You Already Have!"

9. VOCATIONAL PATHWAYS

1. "Registered Apprenticeship," United States Department of Labor Employment and Training Administration, January 7, 2010, http://www.doleta.gov/oa/aboutus.cfm#admin.

10. SPOUSAL- AND DEPENDENT CHILDREN–BASED PROGRAMS/ORGANIZATIONS

1. Onward to Opportunity, "Onward to Your Career," http://onward2opportunity.com/onward-opportunity-participants/learning-pathways/onward-to-your-career/, accessed January 5, 2016.

2. IBM, "i2 Analyst's Notebook," http://www-03.ibm.com/software/products/en/analysts-notebook, accessed February 22, 2016.

3. Blue Star Families, "Strengthening America's Military Families," https://bluestarfam.org/, accessed April 13, 2016.

4. *US News and World Report*, "Prepare Teens for Summer College Prep Programs," http://www.usnews.com/education/high-schools/articles/2013/04/23/prepare-teens-for-summer-college-prep-programs, accessed March 20, 2016.

5. American Legion Auxiliary, "Girls State," http://www.boysandgirlsstate.org/girls.html, accessed March 21, 2016.

6. American Legion Auxiliary, "Boys State," http://www.boysandgirlsstate.org/boys.html, accessed March 21, 2016.

Bibliography

Accredited Financial Counselor. Association for Financial Counseling Planning Counseling. http://www.afcpe.org/certification/curriculum/accredited-financial-counselor/.

ACE Credit College and University Network. American Council on Education. http://www2.acenet.edu/CREDITCollegeNetwork/.

ACT. www.act.org.

ACT. Products and Services. http://www.act.org/content/act/en/products-and-services.html.

ACT. Test for Students. http://www.act.org/content/act/en/products-and-services/the-act/taking-the-test.html.

ACT. Using Dual Enrollment to Improve Educational Outcomes of High School Students. https://www.act.org/content/dam/act/unsecured/documents/UsingDualEnrollment_2015.pdf.

Adams, Caralee. "Colleges Vary on Credit for AP, IB, Dual Classes." *Education Week*, December 9, 2014. http://www.edweek.org/ew/articles/2014/12/10/colleges-vary-on-credit-for-ap-ib.html.

AdvisorNet. http://www.acp-advisornet.org.

Alabama Community College System. https://www.accs.cc/index.cfm/workforce-development/career-technical-education/dual-enrollment/.

American Corporate Partners. http://www.acp-usa.org/.

American Legion Auxiliary Boys State. http://www.boysandgirlsstate.org/boys.html.

American Legion Auxiliary Girls State. http://www.boysandgirlsstate.org/girls.html.

AP Central. College Board. http://apcentral.collegeboard.com/apc/public/courses/index.html.

AP Students. How to Earn Credit for Your Scores, College Board. https://apstudent.collegeboard.org/creditandplacement/how-to-earn-credit-for-your-scores.

Arizona State University Transfer Students. https://transfer.asu.edu/credits.

Austin Community College District. High School to College. http://www.austincc.edu/high-school-to-college.

Baum, Sandy, and Jennifer Ma. College Board. "Trends in Higher Education 2012." https://secure-media.collegeboard.org/digitalServices/misc/trends/2014-trends-college-pricing-report-final.pdf.

"Best Practices for GMAT Preparation." YouTube Video, 39:13. Posted by "Georgetown University Alumni Career Services," March 7, 2013. http://www.youtube.com/watch?v=xFyqJSucqSo.

Big Future by the College Board. https://bigfuture.collegeboard.org/get-started/inside-the-classroom/summer-learning-programs-what-why-and-how.

Blue Star SPOUSE FORCE. https://bluestarfam.org/lead/spouseforce.

Boise State University Credit for Prior Learning. http://registrar.boisestate.edu/transfers/prior-learning-credit/.

Brittingham, Barbara, Mary Jane Harris, Michael Lambert, Frank Murray, George Peterson, Jerry Trapnell, Peter Vlasses, Belle Wheelan, Ralph Wolff, Susan Zlotlow, and Judith Eaton. "The Value of Accreditation." Council for Higher Education Accreditation, June 1, 2010. http://www.chea.org/pdf/Value of US Accreditation 06.29.2010_buttons.pdf.

Bureau of Labor Statistics Occupational Outlook Handbook. "Diagnostic Medical Sonographers and Cardiovascular Technologists and Technicians, Including Vascular Technologists." http://www.bls.gov/ooh/healthcare/diagnostic-medical-sonographers.htm.

Bureau of Labor Statistics Occupational Outlook Handbook. "Frequently Asked Questions." http://www.bls.gov/ooh/about/ooh-faqs.htm#growth1.

Bureau of Labor Statistics Occupational Outlook Handbook. "High School Teachers." http://www.bls.gov/ooh/education-training-and-library/high-school-teachers.htm.

CAEL Prior Learning Assessment. http://www.cael.org/pla.htm.

California Board of Governors Fee Waiver. http://home.cccapply.org/money/bog-fee-waiver.

California Board of Vocational Nursing and Psychiatric Technicians. http://www.bvnpt.ca.gov/licensees/index.shtml.

California CareerZone. https://www.cacareerzone.org/.

California State University, Northridge, Summer Academic Enrichment Program. http://www.csun.edu/eisner-education/summer-academic-enrichment-program.

California State University, San Marcos, LVN to BSN. https://www.csusm.edu/nursing/prospective/programs/pro_lvnbsn/.

CareerOneStop. http://www.careeronestop.org/.

CareerScope. http://www.gibill.va.gov/studenttools/careerscope/index.htmlhttp://www.gibill.va.gov/studenttools/careerscope/index.html.

Central Arizona College Dual Enrollment for High School Students. http://www.centralaz.edu/Home/Admissions/High_School_Outreach_Programs/Dual_Enrollment.htm.

Central Michigan University Prior Learning Credit. http://global.cmich.edu/prior-learning/.

Central New Mexico Community College High School and Dual Credit Programs. https://www.cnm.edu/depts/outreach/dual-credit/high-school-and-dual-credit-programs.

City College of Chicago Early College Programs for High School Students. http://www.ccc.edu/departments/Pages/Early-College.aspx.

City University of New York. http://collegenow.cuny.edu/faqs/.

CLEP. "Study Guides." https://clep.collegeboard.org/study-resources.

CLEP. "Study Resources." https://clep.collegeboard.org/study-resources.

CLEP for Military. https://clep.collegeboard.org/military.

College Board. www.collegeboard.org.

College Board. Fees. https://collegereadiness.collegeboard.org/sat/register/fees#.

College Board. Getting Scores. https://collegereadiness.collegeboard.org/sat/scores/getting-scores.

College Board. Trends in Higher Education. http://trends.collegeboard.org/college-pricing/figures-tables/average-published-undergraduate-charges-sector-2015-16.

College Credit for What You Already Know. Learning Counts. http://www.learningcounts.org.

College of DuPage Dual Credit for High Schools. http://www.cod.edu/academics/ohsp/dualcrediths.aspx.

Columbia University Summer Journalism Workshop. http://cspa.columbia.edu/conventions-and-workshops/summer-journalism-workshop.

Commission on Teaching Credentialing. http://www.ctc.ca.gov/.

Council for Adult and Experiential Learning. "Fueling the Race to Postsecondary Success: A 48-Institution Study of Prior Learning Assessment and Adult Student Outcomes." http://www.cael.org/pdfs/pla_fueling-the-race.

Council for Higher Education Accreditation. http://www.chea.org/Directories/special.asp.

DANTES Distance Learning Readiness Assessment. https://dlrsa.dodmou.com/.

DANTES Self-Evaluation for Students Considering Taking Distance Learning Courses. https://dlrsa.dodmou.com/.

DSST. Get College Credit.com. http://getcollegecredit.com/.

Eastern Kentucky University Dual Credit. http://dualcredit.eku.edu/.

Eaton, Judith. "An Overview of U.S. Accreditation." Council for Higher Education Accreditation. http://www.chea.org/pdf/Overview%20of%20US%20Accreditation%202012.pdf.

Edmonds Community College High School Dual Enrollment Programs. http://www.edcc.edu/highschool/chs/default.html.

Fain, Paul, "Pell Grants in High School." *Inside Higher Education*, November 2, 2015. https://www.insidehighered.com/news/2015/11/02/feds-encourage-dual-enrollment-through-experimental-access-pell-grants.

Federal Reserve Bank of Dallas. "Growth Rates Versus Levels." http://www.dallasfed.org/research/basics/growth.cfm.

Federal Student Aid. https://studentaid.ed.gov/sa/fafsa/filling-out/dependency.

Federal Trade Commission. "College Degree Scams." https://www.consumer.ftc.gov/articles/0206-college-degree-scams.

Florida Department of Education Dual Enrollment. http://www.fldoe.org/schools/higher-ed/fl-college-system/academic-student-affairs/dual-enrollment.stml.

Florida State University Summer Music Camps. http://www.music.fsu.edu/Quicklinks/Summer-Music-Camps.

Free GMAT Prep Software. http://www.mba.com/us/the-gmat-exam/prepare-for-the-gmat-exam/test-prep-materials/free-gmat-prep-software.aspx.

Free SAT/ACT PowerPrep. http://www.eknowledge.com/Affiliate_Welcome.asp?coupon=3A8E9CEFCE.

Georgetown University College Preparatory Program. http://scs.georgetown.edu/departments/21/summer-programs-for-high-school-students/format/college-prep.

Georgia Student Finance Committee Move on When Ready. https://apps.gsfc.org/Main/publishing/pdf/common/MOWR%20Student%20Parent%20FAQs.pdf.

Get Credit for Your Military Spouse Life. MilitaryOneClick. http://militaryoneclick.com/get-credit-for-your-military-spouse-life/.

GI Bill Comparison Tool. https://www.vets.gov/gi-bill-comparison-tool.

GMAT. http://www.mba.com/us/the-gmat-exam/prepare-for-the-gmatexam/test-prep-materials/free-gmat-prep-software.

Governor's School at Radford University. http://www.radford.edu/content/gov-school/home.html.

GRE Practice Test. https://www.ets.org/s/gre/pdf/practice_book_GRE_pb_revised_general_test.pdf.

Griffin, Kimberly, and Gilbert Claire. Center for American Progress. "Easing the Transition from Combat to Classroom." http://www.americanprogress.org/wp-content/uploads/issues/2012/04/pdf/student_veterans.pdf.

Haynie, Devon. "Consider Online College Courses in High School." *U.S. News and World Report*, July 16, 2013. http://www.usnews.com/education/online-education/articles/2013/07/16/consider-online-college-courses-in-high-school.

Higher Learning Commission. https://www.hlcommission.org/.

Hiring Our Heroes. US Chamber of Commerce Foundation. http://www.uschamber.com/hiringourheroes.

IBM® i2® Analyst's Notebook® Training, Corporate America Supports You (CASY) and the Military Spouses Corporate Career Network (CASY-MSCCN). http://casy.msccn.org/Training/i2Training.html.

Illinois Associate for College Admission Counseling. https://www.iacac.org/camp/.

Illinois Department of Veterans Affairs. https://www.illinois.gov/veterans/programs/Pages/StateLicensesMilitaryTraining.aspx.

Indiana University. Kelley School of Business, Young Women's Institute. http://kelley.iu.edu/Ugrad/PreCollege/YWI/page39078.html.

International Sports Science Association. http://www.issaonline.edu/certification/personal-trainer-certification/issa.cfm.

Iowa State University High School Outreach. http://www.opptag.iastate.edu/cytag/index.php.

Jacobs, Joanne. "Some Teens Start College Work Early Via Dual Enrollment." *U.S. News and World Report*, March 9, 2012. http://www.usnews.com/education/best-colleges/articles/2012/03/09/some-teens-start-college-work-early-via-dual-enrollment.

Jowers, Karen. "Free Salesforce Training for Military Spouses—$5,000 Value, Could Be the Key to a Lucrative, Portable Career." *Military Times*, February 2, 2016. http://www.militarytimes.com/story/military/benefits/2016/01/25/free-salesforce-training-military-spouses-5000-value-could-key-lucrative-portable-career/79306808/.

Khan Academy. http://www.khanacademy.org.

Kuder® Journey™. http://www.dantes.kuder.com/.

LaGuardia Community College LPN to RN. https://www.laguardia.edu/LPNtoRNPathway/.

LearningCounts™. "Earn College Credit for Knowledge You Already Have!" https://learningcounts.org/seco/how-it-works.

Louisiana Department of Education Dual Enrollment. https://www.louisianabelieves.com/courses/dual-enrollment.

Marine Corps Community Services Camp Pendleton Joint Education Center. www.mccscp.com/jec.

Massachusetts Institute of Technology Minority Introduction to Engineering and Science. www.collegeexpress.com/summer-programs/massachusetts-institute-of-technology-minority-introduction-to-engineering-and-science/2642/.

Massachusetts Institute of Technology Summer Programs. http://mitadmissions.org/apply/prepare/summer.

MBA Programs Accepting the GRE. http://www.princetonreview.com/uploadedFiles/Sitemap/Home_Page/Business_Hub/Opinions_and_Advice/MBAAcceptingGRE.pdf.

Mercy School of Nursing. http://www.carolinashealthcare.org/cmc-mercy-school-of-nursing-curriculum-description.

Metropolitan State University of Denver Concurrently Enrolled High School Students. https://www.msudenver.edu/admissions/apply/concurrentlyenrolled/.

Middle States Association of Colleges and Schools. http://www.msche.org/.

Midwest Student Exchange Program. http://msep.mhec.org.

Military OneSource. "Career & Education." http://www.militaryonesource.mil/MOS/f?p=
MOSNEWS:ARTICLE:0::::MONTH,YEAR,COHE,PAGE:June,2013,271731,4.

Military OneSource. "LearningCounts @SECO." https://myseco.militaryonesource.mil/Portal/
Content/View/2660.

Military Spouse Fellowship Program. SaveandInvest.org. https://www.saveandinvest.org/
military/military-spouse-fellowship-program.

Minnesota Department of Education Postsecondary Enrollment Options. http://education.state.
mn.us/MDE/StuSuc/CollReadi/PSEO/.

Missouri University of Science and Technology Minority Introduction to Technology and
Engineering. http://futurestudents.mst.edu/summercamps/mite/.

Morgan State University High School Outreach. http://www.morgan.edu/school_of_computer_
mathematical_and_natural_sciences/high_school_outreach.html.

My Career Advancement Account. https://aiportal.acc.af.mil/mycaa.

My Next Move for Veterans. http://www.mynextmove.org/vets/.

My Spouse Education and Career Opportunities. https://myseco.militaryonesource.mil/Portal/
Content/View/2813.

National Association of Credential Evaluation Services. http://www.naces.org/.

National Association of Independent Colleges and Universities. "Independent Colleges and
Universities: A National Profile." https://www.naicu.edu/docLib/20110308_NAICU_
profiles.pdf.

National Board for Certified Counselors. http://www.nbcc.org/Exam/StateLicensure
ExamRegistration.

National Center for Education Statistics College Navigator. http://nces.ed.gov/
collegenavigator/.

National College Credit Recommendation Service. The State University of New York. http://
www.nationalccrs.org/about/.

National Conference of Governor's Schools. http://www.ncogs.org/.

National Environmental Health Association. "Difference Between Credentials and Certifications." http://www.neha.org/professional-development/education-and-training/differences-
between-credentials-certifications.

National Guide to College Credit for Workforce Training. American Council on Education.
http://www2.acenet.edu/credit/?fuseaction=browse.main.

National High Magnetic Field Laboratory and WFSU/NPR (Florida). https://nationalmaglab.
org/education/k12-students/summer-camps/scigirls-summer-camp.

New England Association of Schools and Colleges. https://www.neasc.org/.

Northern Virginia Community College High School Dual Enrollment. http://www.nvcc.edu/
dual-enrollment/.

Northern Virginia Community College Licensed Practical Nurse to Registered Nurse Transition Track. https://www.nvcc.edu/medical/divisions/nursing/lpn-rn-program.html.

Northwest Commission on Colleges and Universities. http://www.nwccu.org/.

Ohio Department of Education College Credit Plus. http://education.ohio.gov/Topics/Quality-
School-Choice/College-Credit-Plus.

Oklahoma Department of Education Prepare for College. https://secure.okcollegestart.org/
College_Planning/Prepare_for_College/_default.aspx.

O*NET Online. http://www.onetonline.org/.

Onward to Opportunity. http://onward2opportunity.com/.

Operation Boots to Business. http://boots2business.org/.

Pearson Vue. http://www.pearsonvue.com/uexcel/.

Penn Summer Scholars Program. http://www.sas.upenn.edu/summer/programs/highschool/summerscholars.

Peterson's DOD MWR Libraries. http://www.petersons.com/DOD.

Peterson's Pre-College Summer Programs for High School Students. https://www.petersons.com/college-search/college-prep-summer-opportunities.aspx.

Prairie View A&M University LVN to BSN. https://www.pvamu.edu/nursing/academics/undergraduate-degree-programs/lvn-bsn-program/.

Public Schools of North Carolina Career and College Promise. http://www.dpi.state.nc.us/ccp/.

Regent University. http://www.regent.edu/military/education_benefits/dependent_spouse.cfm.

Rochester Institute of Technology Bioscience Exploration for Middle and High School Students. http://www.rit.edu/healthsciences/cbet/camps.php.

Saddleback College (California) High School Partnership Program. http://www.saddleback.edu/outreach/high-school-partnership-program.

Samsung American Legion Scholarship. http://www.legion.org/scholarships/samsung.

Saturday Academy Apprenticeships in Science and Engineering (ASE) Program. http://www.saturdayacademy.org/ase.

Scripps College Academy. http://www.scrippscollege.edu/academy/.

(SECO) LearningCounts™ Program. http://seco.learningcounts.org/.

Senate Health, Education, Labor, and Pensions Committee. "For Profit Higher Education: The Failure to Safeguard the Federal Investment and Ensure Student Success. Majority Committee Staff Report and Accompanying Minority Committee Staff Views." 112th Congress. http://www.help.senate.gov/imo/media/for_profit_report/PartI.pdf.

Servicemembers Opportunity Colleges. http://www.soc.aascu.org/.

Smith-Barrow, Delece. "Prepare Teens for Summer College Prep Programs." *U.S. News and World Report*, April 23, 2013. http://www.usnews.com/education/high-schools/articles/2013/04/23/prepare-teens-for-summer-college-prep-programs.

SOC DNS Guaranteed-Transfer Courses, Service Members Opportunity Colleges. http://www.soc.aascu.org/socdns/GrntdTransfCrs.html.

South Dakota Department of Education Dual Credit. http://doe.sd.gov/octe/dualcredit.aspx.

Southern Association of Colleges and Schools. http://www.sacscoc.org/.

Southwestern Illinois College High School Partnership Programs. http://www.swic.edu/high-school-programs/.

"Strengthening America's Military Families." Blue Star Families. https://bluestarfam.org/about.

SUNY Empire State College, Degree Planning and Academic Review. http://www.esc.edu/degree-planning-academic-review/prior-learning-assessment/.

Syracuse University Endure and Grow. http://vets.syr.edu/education/endure-grow/.

Syracuse University Entrepreneurship Bootcamp (EBV-F). http://ebv.vets.syr.edu/families/.

Syracuse University Institute for Veterans and Military Families (IVMF). http://vets.syr.edu/.

Syracuse University Veterans Career Transition Program. http://vets.syr.edu/education/employment-programs/.

Syracuse University VWise. http://whitman.syr.edu/vwise/.

Tennessee State University College of Engineering. http://www.tnstate.edu/engineering/precollege.aspx.

Texas Board of Nursing. https://www.bon.texas.gov/military.asp.

Texas State University. Summer Math Program for High School Students: Honors Summer Math Camp. http://www.txstate.edu/mathworks/camps/hsmc.html.

Thomas Edison State College. Getting Credit for What You Already Know. http://www.tesc.edu/degree-completion/earning-credit.cfm.

Tufts University Adventures in Veterinary Medicine. http://www.collegexpress.com/summer-programs/tufts-university-adventures-in-veterinary-medicine/2672/.

UExcel® Exams. Excelsior College. http://www.excelsior.edu/exams/uexcel-home.

University of California Academic Connections. http://academicconnections.ucsd.edu/.

University of California, Berkeley, Summer Abroad. http://www.summerfuel.com/compare#tab-lci.

University of California, Berkeley, Summerfuel. http://www.summerfuel.com/cap/uc_berkeley.

University of California Information for High School Students. http://www.uconline.edu/audiences/high-school-students/.

University of Chicago Summer Session. https://summer.uchicago.edu/.

University of Florida Center for Precollegiate Education and Training. http://www.cpet.ufl.edu/students/dce/faqs/.

University of Idaho Dual Credit. http://dualcredit.uidaho.edu/students/.

University of Maryland University College Prior Learning. http://umuc.edu/undergrad/creditoptions/priorlearning/index.cfm.

University of Michigan Summer Programs. http://www.ceo.umich.edu/summer.html.

University of Missouri High School/College Dual Credit Partnership. http://cas.umkc.edu/hscp.

University of Southern California, California Youth Think Tank. http://www.theyoungcenter.com/CYTT.html.

University of Wisconsin–Madison Diversity Affairs Office. http://www.engr.wisc.edu/current/coe-dao-engineering-summer-program-esp.html.

Upword. https://www.upwork.com/.

US Department of Education. The Database of Accredited Postsecondary Institutions and Programs. http://ope.ed.gov/accreditation/.

US Department of Labor. https://www.dol.gov/featured/apprenticeship.

US Department of State National Security Language Initiative for Youth (NSLI-Y) Program. http://www.nsliforyouth.org/.

US Department of State National Security Language Initiative for Youth—Turkish. http://nsliy-interactive.org/category/turkish/.

US Employment and Training Administration's "Projections Central." http://www.projectionscentral.com/Projections/LongTerm.

Veterans Legal Clinic. http://www.sandiego.edu/veterans-clinic/.

Virginia State University Summer High School Programs. http://agriculture.vsu.edu/special-programs/summer-high-school-programs.php.

Vocational Rehabilitation and Counseling. http://www.benefits.va.gov/vocrehab/edu_voc_counseling.asp.

Vocational Rehabilitation and Employment (VR&E). http://www.vba.va.gov/pubs/forms/VBA-28-8832-ARE.pdf.

Walsh, Declan. "Fake Diplomas, Real Cash: Pakistani Company Axact Reaps Millions." *New York Times*, May 17, 2015. http://www.nytimes.com/2015/05/18/world/asia/fake-diplomas-real-cash-pakistani-company-axact-reaps-millions-columbiana-barkley.html.

Welcome to Assist. http://www.assist.org.

Western Association of Schools and Colleges Four Year Schools. http://www.wascweb.org/.

Western Association of Schools and Colleges Two Year Schools. http://www.accjc.org/.

Who Accepts UExcel® Credits? Excelsior College. http://www.excelsior.edu/who-accepts-uexcel-credits.

Wyoming Department of Education Dual and Concurrent Enrollment. https://edu.wyoming.gov/beyond-the-classroom/college-career/dual-enrollment/.

Index